FOOTBALL'S
GREATEST
Characters

FOOTBALL'S
GREATEST
Characters

Amazing Stories of
Hard Men, Hellraisers
and Crowd-Pleasers

GEOFF TIBBALLS

BOOKS

First published in Great Britain in 2008 by
JR Books, 10 Greenland Street,
London NW1 0ND
www.jrbooks.com

A catalogue record for this book is available from the British Library.

ISBN 978-1-906217-29-7

1 3 5 7 9 10 8 6 4 2

Printed by MPG Books, Bodmin, Cornwall

CONTENTS

INTRODUCTION

When I was a boy supporting Millwall in the 1960s, Harry Cripps was the crowd favourite, the darling of the Den. A left-back of the sturdy variety, he certainly wasn't the most skilful player in the side but he was the biggest character, one who compensated for his artistic shortcomings with sheer sweat and endeavour. The fans loved him and, in return, he loved the fans. After a match no autograph request was ever refused, while a friendly wave from Harry at the end of a long away day at somewhere like Burnley made it all seem worthwhile, even in defeat. Few supporters outside south-east London knew much about the late Harry Cripps, but to all those who saw him play he qualifies as one of football's greatest characters.

If you were to ask a thousand people to name the 70 greatest characters in the history of the game, you would get a thousand different answers, partly because not everyone's definition of a character is the same. Characters can be good or bad – they can be genuine entertainers like Frank Worthington, Tosh Chamberlain or Jimmy Johnstone, or fearsome psychopaths like the Aston Villa and Manchester United star of the 1920s, Frank Barson. They can have led troubled lives like George Best, Garrincha or Jim Baxter, or be charismatic managers like Brian Clough, Ian Holloway or Bill Shankly. Many of their stories are well known, so I have also delved deep into the lower divisions to unearth unsung heroes such as Robin Friday, 'Vodka Vic' Kasule, Chic Charnley, Alec Stock and, of course, Harry Cripps. Although Best, Diego Maradona, Jimmy Greaves and a few others are obvious exceptions, the greatest characters are not necessarily the greatest players, which is why there is no place in this book for the likes of Bobby Charlton, Bobby Moore or Pele. And it is one place where Vinnie Jones does no more than rub shoulders with Paul Gascoigne.

It is generally accepted that there are fewer characters in football these days. With the vast sums of money at stake, no Premiership manager would tolerate Len Shackleton sitting on the ball during play, Stan Bowles reading the racing page while waiting for a corner to be taken, or goalkeeper Sam Bartram dribbling to the opposition penalty area for a shot on goal. So what better excuse for remembering some of the amazing personalities – the eccentrics, the bone-crushers, the dictators, the comedians – who, over the past hundred years and more, have helped to make football the people's game?

Compiling this book has been very much a labour of love and I am grateful to Nottinghamshire Library Services for their research facilities and to Jeremy Robson for his continued support and enthusiasm.

Geoff Tibballs

CRAZY KEEPERS

Fabien Barthez
A Modern Entertainer

The sanity of goalkeepers has long been called into question and in terms of eccentricity, Fabien Barthez was right up there with the best of them. Whether it was with Manchester United or in his native France, Barthez – a dead ringer for actor Donald Pleasence – was the supreme entertainer, taunting opposing forwards by dribbling the ball past them, or dummying them by means of elaborate step-overs. The crowds loved it; his managers held their breath…and prayed. Usually he got away with these forays from goal, but occasionally he was left with egg on his face. For all the brilliant, acrobatic saves he made, he could do undo the good work with a moment's madness, a blunder of epic proportions. Of all the adjectives that could be applied to Barthez, 'safe' is not one of them.

The son of a professional rugby player, Barthez was born in Lavelanet on 28 June 1971 and made his senior debut for Toulouse at the age of 20. In 1992 he joined Olympique Marseille, helping his new club to both the French title and the European Cup in his first season there. In the process he became the youngest goalkeeper to earn a European Cup winners' medal. However, the success was tainted when Marseille were stripped of their domestic title following an infamous match-fixing scandal. Throughout his time at Marseille, during which they were also forcibly relegated to the Second Division, Barthez demonstrated his unconventional agility and he was rewarded in 2004 with the first of his 87 French caps, keeping a clean sheet in victory over Australia.

In 1995 he signed for AS Monaco with whom he went on to win two French League titles, in 1997 and 2000, the only blot on his copybook being a four-month ban in 1996 for the use of recreational drugs. The highspot of this period was undoubtedly the 1998 World Cup. Barthez was in magnificent form throughout the tournament, conceding only two goals in the finals as France triumphed on home soil. Moreover, he established himself as a true character, with television viewers warming to the bizarre ritual whereby French captain Laurent Blanc kissed Barthez's bald head before each game, supposedly for good luck. Two years later he helped France win Euro 2000, but by then he had joined Manchester United for £7.8 million – a then British record for a goalkeeper – following a major bust-up with the Monaco coach after a match against Marseille.

Sir Alex Ferguson had struggled to find a replacement for Peter Schmeichel but Barthez quickly proved himself a worthy successor to the Great Dane, making crucial saves and entertaining the fans with his tricks and sorties as United picked up their third Premier League title in a row. Barthez even persuaded Ferguson to play him on the wing in a pre-season friendly in Singapore in July 2001, and he came on as substitute in an 8-1 victory. Ferguson might have been tempted to leave him in an outfield position, judging by his form in the first half of the 2001–02 season. Time after time his eccentricity became a liability, notably when making two costly errors in the Champions League tie with Deportivo La Coruña and the following month when he gifted Thierry Henry two goals at Highbury, first miscuing a simple clearance to the feet of his fellow Frenchman and then spilling a long through ball. To Barthez's credit, he answered his critics with vastly more assured performances from Christmas onwards, and then in 2002–03 he helped United create the best defensive record in the Premiership en route to another title. He may have had a reputation as something of a clown but events took a more serious turn in September 2002 when he was questioned by police for allegedly throwing or kicking a plastic bottle, which hit a disabled Leeds fan in the face at Elland Road. Barthez was subsequently cleared of any wrongdoing. However, he did not escape the wrath of his manager in April 2003 after allowing Real Madrid's Ronaldo to beat him at the near post in a Champions League quarter-final at Old Trafford – a result that sent United crashing out of the competition. It was to be his last game for United and the following year he rejoined Marseille.

In February 2005, during a friendly with Moroccan team Raja Casablanca, a mass brawl broke out following the dismissal of a Marseille player. Barthez was reported for spitting at the referee and was suspended for six months. Controversy now seemed to follow him everywhere; he was accused of making obscene gestures at away fans and it was even alleged that he had urinated on the pitch in front of 60,000 people during Marseille's UEFA Cup tie with Inter Milan.

He left Marseille in the summer of 2006 and announced his retirement after the World Cup, only to return to the game in December of that year with Nantes. However, he quit the club in March 2007 following a violent post-match run-in with a group of disgruntled Nantes supporters. Barracked throughout a home defeat to Rennes, Barthez was accosted in the stadium car park after the game. Angry fans insulted him, attacked his car and tried to drag him from the driver's seat.

It was the final straw for the charismatic goalkeeper whose hobbies have been listed as swimming with dolphins and smoking. But football was always his real passion. He once explained: 'Unconsciously, I fell in love with the small, round sphere with its amusing and capricious rebounds which sometimes play with me.' Sometimes the ball did more than just play with him; it tormented him mercilessly. But that was the joy of Fabien Barthez. He was predictable only in his unpredictability.

Sam Bartram
The Supreme Showman

For 22 years goalkeeper Sam Bartram was the darling of Charlton Athletic as he became the first player to make 500 League appearances for a single club. His wavy red hair was indicative of a flamboyant nature and regulars at The Valley grew accustomed to a bravery that bordered on the reckless, an agility that was second to none and showmanship that would not have been out of place in a circus. Yet that was Bartram's problem, the reason why he was never capped at senior level and was destined to go down in history as the finest goalkeeper never to play for England. He was simply too sensational and was regularly criticised for playing to the gallery. Sam never took the easy option. If there was a routine catch to make, he preferred to launch himself into a spectacular dive, clutching the ball in mid-air for what seemed like five seconds, the last three for the photographers.

Bartram was not blind to his faults. Guesting for York City in a wartime Cup semi-final against Sheffield Wednesday, he dribbled the ball out of his own area and right up into Wednesday's box, where he promptly lost possession. He recalled: 'Tony Masserella, Wednesday outside-right, got possession and set off for our open goal. Me after him. Unfortunately, it was like a carthorse trying to catch a Lincoln winner – and I was the carthorse. Tony left me yards behind. But then Tony shot. And his shooting wasn't half as good as his running. He put the ball yards wide! Was I relieved!' Nobody doubted Bartram's ability, but with escapades such as these (and they were by no means confined to friendlies or wartime matches), he was not deemed a reliable successor to his great idol, Harry Hibbs, who was England's keeper in the early 1930s. One national newspaper summed up Bartram perfectly: 'Many of his saves would make classic Harry Hibbs shudder. Yet he gets there. He invents saves.' It was just that the selectors always preferred somebody safer, like Frank Swift or Ted Ditchburn. In many respects, Sam was his own worst enemy.

Given Bartram's fondness for venturing out of goal, it should come as no surprise to learn that he started his career as an outfield player. The young Durham miner began as a centre-forward before switching to wing-half for his local team, Boldon Villa. A trial with Reading came to nothing and when Boldon's regular keeper was injured, Bartram volunteered to play in goal one afternoon. It so happened that the match was being watched by a Charlton scout, Anthony Seed, who was so impressed by Bartram that he recommended him to his brother Jimmy, the Charlton manager. The year was 1934 and Jimmy Seed needed a new goalkeeper because Alec Wright had recently been killed in a bathing accident. Acting on his brother's advice, Jimmy Seed gave the 20-year-old Bartram a trial, but it was scarcely an unqualified success as he conceded eight goals in two reserve games. Yet Seed persevered and by December Bartram was the first choice, keeping his place until his retirement in 1956!

That Bartram was a larger-than-life character was underlined by two events in 1937. In September he got married on a Saturday morning, helped Charlton to a 1-0 victory over Middlesbrough in the afternoon (having run on to the pitch to the sound of the band playing 'The Wedding March'), and half an hour after the final whistle he was back at the reception. Three months later, on Christmas Day, he was involved in an even more bizarre scenario, at Stamford Bridge.

He recounted the incident in his autobiography. 'Soon after the kick-off [fog] began to thicken rapidly at the far end, travelling past Vic Woodley in the Chelsea goal and rolling steadily towards me. The referee stopped the game, and then, as visibility became clearer, restarted it. We were on top at this time, and I saw fewer and fewer figures as we attacked steadily.' Bartram continued pacing up and down his goal-line, content that Chelsea were being pinned in their own half, but the game went unusually silent. 'Time passed, and I made several advances towards the edge of the penalty area, peering through the murk which was getting thicker every minute. Still I could see nothing. The Chelsea defence was clearly being run off its feet. After a long time a figure loomed out of the curtain of fog in front of me. It was a policeman, and he gaped at me incredulously. "What on earth are you doing here?" he gasped. "The game was stopped a quarter of an hour ago. The field's completely empty." And when I groped my way to the dressing room the rest of the Charlton team, already out of the bath, were convulsed with laughter.'

Bartram was at the centre of a more sinister drama the following year when Charlton played at Portsmouth. Shortly after he had saved a penalty, tempers became frayed and two players were sent off. Irate Pompey fans set Bartram's goal net on fire and one threw half a house brick at him, hitting him on the head and felling him as he was about to take a goal-kick. He gained his revenge on the Portsmouth supporters while he was guesting there in a wartime game for West Ham. He was beaten by a penalty but the ball flew through a large hole in the net and ended up among the crowd behind the goal. To the fury of the home support, he retrieved the ball, calmly put it down for a goal-kick and proceeded with the game, the referee being none the wiser.

Bartram's arrival at The Valley had brought about an immediate upturn in Charlton's fortunes and he helped them from the old Third Division (South) to the First Division in successive seasons and very nearly to the League title itself, missing out by three points to Manchester City in 1937. After the war, he took them to successive Cup finals, the second, in 1947, ending in a single-goal victory over Burnley. It was to be Bartram's only major honour. He was recognised at 'B' international level and went on an FA tour to South Africa from which he was just happy to return home in one piece. The party were staying in a rural hotel but were kept awake at night by a noise outside, prompting one of the squad to ask the hotel manager, 'Can't you keep your dogs quiet?' 'Dogs!' exclaimed the manager. 'They're not dogs, they're lions. They'll keep this up till dawn. Nothing to worry about.' Bartram recalled: 'Eighteen intrepid English footballers, eighteen usually brave forwards and defenders – not to mention the goalkeeper – determined that they too would await the dawn wide awake just in case! And the hotel manager gave us the comfort of a gun in our bedroom, also just in case.'

He may have been continually overlooked at international level but he could do no wrong in the eyes of Charlton fans. He excelled at saving penalties, would give sweets to the kids behind the goal and used to rush from his area, whip off his cap and head the ball clear from an onrushing forward. The fans loved every minute. They roared in anticipation during a match in 1946 when, with Charlton leading Birmingham City 1-0 four minutes from time, Bartram ran upfield to take a penalty. However, his kick hit the bar and ballooned up in the air, leaving him with a frantic dash back the length of the pitch to protect his goal. The crowd roared with laughter then, and even saw the funny side when he made a costly excursion from goal against Chelsea. With nobody closing him down, Bartram decided to dribble all the way into the Chelsea half, hoping to have a shot on goal, which he had done in the past. But this time he lost the ball to the opposition centre-forward who raced away and put the ball in the empty net. The Charlton fans just shrugged their shoulders – it was all part of life with Sam. His team-mates and manager were probably less impressed, but weighed against the points he saved the club season after season, he could be forgiven the odd aberration.

Ever the showman, he and his opposite number at Manchester City, Frank Swift, enjoyed a personal duel in one game. They arranged between themselves to kick the ball from one end to the other, much to the dismay of the referee who had to keep sprinting back and forth in order to keep up with play. When it happened for a fourth time, the crowd started laughing and the referee was forced to call a halt to their ruse.

Bartram may have liked a joke but this should not disguise the fact that he was a fierce competitor. Playing for York City in a wartime friendly at Barnsley, he was so angry at being sent the wrong way with a cheeky penalty that he petulantly booted the ball over the stand and into the street, necessitating a lengthy search. Even at the age of 38, he had plenty to say for himself. Reporting in the *Daily Express* on a match at Portsmouth, Desmond Hackett wrote: 'Bartram had a running commentary duel with the crowd, a personal battle with Portsmouth centre-forward Albert Mundy, and in between blasted high-powered criticism at his own defence when he thought their tackling was too timid.' John Arlott was equally intrigued by Bartram's demeanour. 'Cast an eye in his direction sometimes when he is not in action,' wrote Arlott. 'With the ball forty yards away you will see Sam on tiptoe, arms lifted and gloved hands palms downward, looking somewhat like Toscanini about to call the NBC orchestra into action.'

After 623 appearances for Charlton, Bartram made his final appearance on 10 March 1956. The 42-year-old was made captain for the day and helped Charlton to a 2-0 victory over Arsenal. He became a manager at first York and then Luton but found more satisfaction as a sports reporter with the *Sunday People*.

He died in 1981 but Charlton fans never forgot him and in 2005 a 9-foot statue of Bartram was erected outside The Valley to celebrate the club's centenary. They had much to be grateful for: he had brought them their greatest years and had kept them entertained for nearly a quarter of a century...blunders and all. As John Arlott put it: 'Sam Bartram makes mistakes; but he has a gloriously human way of retrieving them.'

John Burridge
A Serial Obsessive

Dedication is an overused word in sport, but nobody could ever question the devotion to his craft of goalkeeper John Burridge, a man who made a total of 771 League appearances between 1970 and 1996 and turned out for a record 20 English and Scottish League clubs. Indeed, Burridge's determination to stay fit and focused throughout his career became an obsession, night and day, creating a larger-than-life figure still fondly remembered today by fans at every club he played for.

Burridge never switched off between games and consequently neither did his wife, Janet. A quiet evening watching television would see Janet handed a bag of oranges with instructions to throw an orange across his line of vision without warning in order to keep his reflexes sharp. One second he would be watching *Coronation Street*, the next he would be diving full length to pluck an orange out of the air before it hit the carpet. There was not even respite when they went to bed. On the night before a game, he would sometimes dream he was making a save and suddenly dive across the bed. He would also conduct imaginary 10-minute interviews with reporter Gerald Sinstadt in his sleep or shout warnings to defenders before waking up with a start. Burridge liked to dress the part, too, and was known to wear his goalkeeper's jersey, gloves and occasionally even his boots in bed. Sometimes he took a ball to bed as well! He also liked to wear his full goalkeeping kit to watch *Match of the Day*. It is by no means unusual for doctors to be on duty 24 hours a day, but this is the only recorded case of a goalkeeper.

There was more. On the way to games, Burridge would listen to motivational tapes designed to build up his confidence – and it was rumoured that when in the role of spectator he took his kit along to England matches, just in case any of the selected keepers were injured. The fanaticism extended to his diet; he used to eat baby food because it was high in protein and he thought it would help him bulk up. Burridge modelled himself on Peter Shilton to the extent that he had his hair cut in the style of his hero. It almost goes without saying that his car registration number was A5AVE. When supporters sang, 'There's only one John Burridge', no one could possibly argue with the statement.

His pre-match warm-up consisted of doing handstands and somersaults on the pitch, much to the delight of fans who would turn up early just to witness the ritual. In his eternal quest for peak fitness, perhaps he should have been mindful of the tale of Mick O'Brien who kept goal for the Irish club Athlone Town in the 1970s. Playing in an FAI semi-final against Finn Harps, O'Brien succeeded in snapping the crossbar not once, but twice. O'Brien, who also liked to perform somersaults in the goalmouth, broke the bar once while swinging on it to see the ball to safety, and the second time while climbing on it to make sure it did not collapse again. His mistake was forgetting that the neutral venue for the semi had a wooden bar and not a metal one as he was used to at Athlone. His manager called him 'very dedicated and a bit headstrong' while O'Brien himself admitted: 'I think I might be over-fit.' The description could just as easily have applied to Burridge who, almost inevitably, enjoyed his own peculiar crossbar experience. In Burridge's case, he once spent part of a match sitting on top of the crossbar while play was concentrated at the other end. A similar story claims that Burridge once jumped into the Newcastle crowd during a boring passage of play and sat in the stand behind the goal – but this is likely to be apocryphal since it is hard to imagine such a conscientious individual deserting his post even for a moment.

Born in December 1951, 'Budgie' Burridge started out in League football with his hometown club, Workington. In one of his first games, Workington were leading Southend 6-0 when Burridge, thinking he had heard the final whistle, caught the ball and joyously booted it into the back of his net. However, it turned out that the whistler was someone in the crowd and, to Burridge's horror, the referee awarded a goal. That rush of blood did nothing to hinder his climb up the soccer ladder and in 1971 he joined Blackpool, where he spent four seasons and picked up his first trophy, the Anglo-Italian Cup. The only other club with whom he made a century of appearances was Sheffield United, between 1984 and 1987. His full list of League clubs reads: Workington, Blackpool, Aston Villa, Southend United, Crystal Palace, Queens Park Rangers, Wolves, Derby County, Sheffield United, Southampton, Newcastle United, Hibernian, Scarborough, Lincoln City, Aberdeen, Dumbarton, Falkirk, Manchester City, Darlington and Queen of the South.

Age proved no barrier and between 1993 and 1997 he turned out for no fewer than 14 League and non-League clubs in a bid to postpone his retirement, often travelling the length of the country for the occasional game. Although based in the north-east at the time, he signed for Enfield in 1994 and when the team were drawn away to Bishop Auckland in the FA Trophy, he insisted on travelling down south to catch the team coach going up to the north-east because he said it was good for team spirit. Before Enfield signed him, their chairman expressed doubts about having a goalkeeper older than he was, whereupon Burridge proved his fitness by diving over the boardroom table three times. When he stood in goal for Manchester City in 1995 at the age of 43, Burridge became the oldest player to appear in the Premiership. He finally retired in 1997 at the age of 45 after a spell as player-manager of Blyth Spartans. He has subsequently become a goalkeeping coach and TV pundit in Dubai.

Burridge himself used to play down the idea that he was eccentric. 'I'm the most boring person you'll ever meet. I come home and I'm quite content just to sit watching television. All I want to do in life is make great saves.' With oranges...

A journalist who interviewed him a few years ago remembers that Burridge was still as football crazy as ever. 'We were in his mother-in-law's living room and he pulled out a footstool, put two peppermints on it, and used them to demonstrate the way Steve Coppell and Kenny Sansom used to play. His wife just shook her head.'

José Luis Chilavert
Free-kick Specialist

From the very birth of football, the widely held belief has been that the role of the goalkeeper is to stop goals rather than score them. Try telling that to the extrovert Paraguayan José Luis Chilavert who, with a career total of 62 goals (including eight in internationals), boasts a record that some strikers can only dream of.

For 20 years Chilavert was the most famous face in Paraguayan football, immortalised by the snarling bulldog image that he wore on his goalkeeper's jersey. Bulldog T-shirts sold in their thousands and the Paraguayan FA even staged a competition among Asunción pet owners to find the dog that most resembled the one on Chilavert's shirt. The snarling expression was fitting because Chilavert himself was hot-headed and fearless and enjoyed nothing more than taunting rival goalkeepers, particularly if they happened to be Argentinian. But it was his goalscoring exploits that really made him a national hero; if there was a vital free-kick or penalty to be taken, Chilavert was the man.

He was born in 1965 in the Paraguayan district of Luque. As a boy, he first put his hands to use by milking the family's cows. At 15, he joined the Paraguayan Second Division side Sportivo Luqueño and made such an impact that by 1984 he had signed for San Lorenzo, who played in the top flight of Argentine football. It was there that he practised his shooting by aiming at Coca-Cola bottles. In 1989 he earned his first international cap and marked the occasion in style by venturing upfield to score the 88th-minute penalty that gave Paraguay a 2-1 victory over Colombia in a crucial World Cup qualifier. The man he beat was René Higuita, an eccentric South American goalkeeper in his own right, forever remembered for the remarkable 'scorpion save' he made at Wembley in 1995.

By now Chilavert was plying his trade in Spain with Real Zaragoza and, having developed a taste for goals, scored his first at club level in 1990 in the victory over Real Sociedad. In 1991 he returned to Argentina to sign for Vélez Sarsfield, with whom he would stay for nine seasons and enjoy the best days of his career. The goals came thick and fast. In 1996 alone, he scored eight goals for his club plus one for his country. In a League match against River Plate, he netted a spectacular 60-yard free-kick, taken quickly after he spotted his opposite number, German Burgos, off his line. The two men met again for an Argentina-Paraguay World Cup qualifier in Buenos Aires. Even though he played his club football in Argentina, where the fans can turn ugly if provoked, Chilavert did not believe in exercising tact and diplomacy during the build-up to the big match. Instead, proclaiming himself to be the finest goalkeeper in the world, he ridiculed Burgos and boasted that he would score again. So when Paraguay were awarded a free-kick 25 yards out, nobody was going to prevent Chilavert trying his luck. Photographers gathered behind the goal said that Burgos was visibly trembling as Chilavert lined up his left-footed strike, and although Burgos managed to get both hands on the ball, he allowed it to slip from his grasp and over the line. Chilavert's celebrations showed no hint of restraint.

Already voted World Goalkeeper of the Year in 1995, 1997 and 1998, Chilavert's cult status scaled new heights in 1999 when, playing for Vélez against Ferro Carril Oeste, he became the first goalkeeper in the history of football to score a hat-trick. He went on to spearhead Paraguay's qualification for the 2002 World Cup by scoring four goals, including two stunning free-kicks in the 5-1 victory over Bolivia. However, he blotted his copybook by having a penalty saved against Chile and by receiving a three-match ban for spitting on Brazil's Roberto Carlos, which forced him to sit out the first two games of the finals.

He finally retired in 2004 but did not stay out of the news for long, because the following year he was sentenced to six months in jail over the use of false documents connected with his two years at Racing Club of Strasbourg at the start of the century.

Chilavert was a man of contrasts. He frequently fell out with team-mates and coaches, and he could be fiery and temperamental, but he also gave generously to the poor, remembering his own modest start in life. Above all, he had an ego the size of South America. He thought he was the best, that his records would never be broken. And he was right...until in 2006 Brazilian Rogério Ceni became the world's highest-scoring goalkeeper. The bulldog was almost certainly snarling that night.

William 'Fatty' Foulke
Larger Than Life

William Henry Foulke, known for reasons that will become obvious as 'Fatty', was the heaviest player in the history of professional football. Although estimates of his size vary, it is generally accepted that by the end of his career he weighed in at a colossal 25 stone, roughly the equivalent of two and a half Michael Owens. He stood 6 feet 2½ inches tall, wore size 12 boots and shirts with 24-inch collars. When in 1907 he was playing for Bradford City against Accrington Stanley, his red goalkeeping jersey clashed with the Accrington shirts. Since nobody could find a white shirt large enough to fit him, it is said that he played the game wrapped in a sheet, borrowed from a nearby house. Bradford went on to win 1-0 and since Foulke was not required to dive during the match, he achieved the distinction of keeping a clean sheet both meta-phorically and literally.

Make no mistake, Foulke was more than just a freak show. He was remarkably agile for his size and could even get down to low shots, although sometimes he needed a couple of minutes' notice. His massive bulk filled the goal, giving forwards precious little to aim at, and in an era when it was permissible to shoulder-charge goalkeepers into the net, Foulke had a distinct advantage. *Athletic News* described one optimistic forward's attempt to barge Fouke over the line as being 'like a fly trying to knock an elephant over'. Commanding in the air, he could punch a ball to the halfway line and kick the ball from one end of the pitch to the other with a minimum of effort. These qualities meant that he was good enough to play for the best clubs in the land and earned him an England cap against Wales in 1897. He also played four first-class matches for Derbyshire County Cricket Club in 1900.

Anyone who teased him about his girth was liable to be sat on…or worse. For although he was usually equable, he did possess a fearsome temper when roused. Playing for Sheffield United against Liverpool, he once picked up the opposing centre-forward, George Allan, turned him upside down and stood him on his head in the penalty-area mud. The resultant penalty changed the course of the game and afterwards Foulke felt obliged to apologise to his team-mates for his momentary loss of control, before adding mischievously: 'I made a right toffee-apple out of him, didn't I?'

It is worth noting that on the rare occasions Foulke was injured in action, it needed at least six men to carry him from the field as no stretcher yet invented could bear his weight.

Foulke was born in Dawley, Shropshire, on 12 April 1874. He was spotted by Sheffield United playing for village side Blackwell in a Derbyshire Cup tie at Ilkeston Town. In attempting to punch the ball away, he missed and knocked out an Ilkeston forward's front row of teeth. When the scout explained what had happened, the United manager replied: ''E'll do for me!' Foulke made his United debut in 1894, inspiring the first use of the chant 'Who ate all the pies?', directed at him by his own fans to the tune of 'Knees Up Mother Brown'. He led the team to three FA Cup finals (winning two) and a League Championship. The 1902 final at Crystal Palace finished in a 1-1 draw and at the end Foulke was still protesting that Southampton's equaliser should not have been allowed. He stormed back to the dressing room, tore off his clothes and, stark naked, set off in pursuit of referee Tom Kirkham. Fearful of the outcome should Foulke catch him, Mr Kirkham sought refuge in a broom cupboard – but even then it was only the timely intervention of a group of FA officials that prevented the raging bull from wrenching the cupboard door from its hinges so that he could get at the referee. Foulke's mood may have improved after United won the replay 2-1.

After making 352 appearances for United, Foulke joined Chelsea in 1905 for a fee of £50. Worshipped by the Chelsea supporters, he was made captain but failed to lead by example in a fixture at Burslem Port Vale where, in a fit of temper, he grabbed a home forward by the waist and hurled him into the back of the net. The referee, T.J. Howcroft, had no choice but to award a penalty. Later he said of Foulke: 'I was not fool enough or brave enough to send Bill off. I had been a linesman in the 1902 FA Cup final and knew what he was like when he was riled. When I awarded a penalty he came looking for my scalp, but the Chelsea captain, J.T. Robertson, ordered him back to the goal-line. He did not try to save the shot but stood glaring at me. I kept a reasonable distance until the close of the game, and then made my way quicker than usual to the dressing room. If Foulke had put one of those large hands on me, I might have been short of some part of my anatomy. But you could not hold a grudge against him. He was such a cheerful, likeable fellow once his temper was under control.'

Foulke used to say: 'I don't mind what they call me, as long as they don't call me late for lunch.' To emphasise the point, he would often deliberately arrive early for the team's breakfast or dinner, see the food laid out for the whole team, and proceed to scoff the lot before the others turned up! The day after one such binge, he was keeping goal for Chelsea against Burton Albion and saved two penalties. The player who missed the penalties complained afterwards: 'Where else could I have placed the kicks? There was nowhere else to aim!'

He played 35 games in his year at Chelsea before moving to his last club, Bradford City. By this time he was so heavy that in one game he snapped the crossbar in trying to make a save, while at Stockport he landed on a home forward and broke the poor man's leg. On an occasion when Bradford played in London, Foulke attended the theatre in the evening and afterwards he slipped in front of a horse-drawn cab while attempting to cross the busy Strand. No doubt treating the fallen Foulke as an early roundabout, the horse managed to sidestep him neatly, but the newspapers made great play of the incident, one headline reading: 'CAB HORSE IN PERIL – NEARLY COLLIDES WITH FOULKE'.

His final game was on 9 February 1907. He let in four goals in the first 20 minutes as City crashed 4-1 at Gainsborough Trinity. It was time to call it a day. When his career was over, some sources state that he set up a penalty-kick business on Blackpool beach, charging a penny a shot and offering threepence back for each goal scored against him. What is certain is that this outsize character died in Sheffield on 1 May 1916, aged just 42, from cirrhosis.

Bruce Grobbelaar
Spaghetti Legs

Bruce Grobbelaar's reputation as the clown prince of 1980s football was cemented in Rome's Olympic Stadium in 1984. The European Cup final between Roma and Liverpool had gone to penalties and Liverpool manager Joe Fagan was telling his keeper: 'Look, Bruce, don't worry about how it is going to go. No one is going to blame you if they score all five. If they can't hit the target from 12 yards, they shouldn't be out here, so just give it your best shot.' Then as an afterthought he added: 'Tell you what, lad, just try and put them off. You'll think of something.'

Grobbelaar decided to focus on two of the Roma penalty takers, Bruno Conti and Francesco Graziani, as they were both seasoned internationals and he did not think it would be fair to try and distract the others on such a big occasion. Grobbelaar remembers: 'So when Conti walked up to take Roma's second kick, I started doing a Sixties disco dance, where you put your hands on your knees and keep crossing them over. Don't ask me why. I always did like doing things differently, and, as I had to keep my feet still on the line, there weren't many options. It worked anyway. He blazed the ball over.

'When it came to Graziani's turn, I turned round to the photographers behind the goal and started biting the net. I remember thinking, "This is like spaghetti. I know, I'll do a spaghetti legs on him! So I just let my legs go all limp, as if they were strands of spaghetti.'" Suitably unnerved, Graziani missed, too, and the Cup was Liverpool's. Grobbelaar rejected accusations of gamesmanship although he was sorry to learn that Graziani had been so distressed by the miss that he subsequently booked himself into a mental hospital.

Grobbelaar's antics that night in Italy made him an instant legend in the eyes of the Kop. They forgave the numerous soft shots he let in and the chaos he caused by those madcap rushes from his line; instead they came to love him for his eccentricity to the point that a recent website vote among Liverpool supporters rated him at number 17 of 100 Players Who Shook the Kop. And for all the pulling faces at the crowd and the handstands in the goalmouth, it should be remembered that in his time at Anfield he won six Championship medals, three FA Cup winners' medals, three League Cup winners' medals and, of course, that European Cup winners' medal. Not bad for someone who, shortly after his Liverpool debut, was considered so erratic that an Everton fan presented him with a jester's hat.

Born in Durban, South Africa, in 1957, Grobbelaar developed into a promising cricketer and footballer but his sporting activities were postponed when he was called up for two years' active National Service with the Rhodesian National Guard. This, curiously, formed the basis for his clowning on the football pitch. He reasoned that having fought in a bloody civil war, he could appreciate that a game of football was not as serious a matter as some people would have us believe. In 1979 he was signed by Vancouver Whitecaps after attending their scouting camp in South Africa, and at the end of the year was sent out on loan to England with Fourth Division Crewe Alexandra. Although Crewe endured a miserable season, the theatrical Grobbelaar endeared himself to the fans by chatting to them during the match and making crazy dribbling runs out of his box. He also kept eight clean sheets and rounded off his short stay by scoring a penalty in a 2-0 victory over York City on the final day of the season. Meanwhile, Liverpool had been monitoring his progress and in March 1981 Bob Paisley paid £250,000 to bring him to Merseyside as back-up to the long-serving Ray Clemence. However, when Clemence left for Spurs that summer, Grobbelaar was thrown in at the deep end.

Grobbelaar's early days at Anfield were marred by some dreadful howlers. Although his agility and reflexes were not in question, he frequently appeared to be an accident waiting to happen. However, his strength of character and ability to pull off breathtaking saves won over the Liverpool faithful, and even though he was still prone to the occasional blunder, he gradually settled into the role. There was never a dull moment with Grobbelaar, whether it was bawling out team-mate Jim Beglin during the 1986 FA Cup final or running out at Anfield one Christmas wearing a cap with a plastic duck on it.

After making 627 appearances for Liverpool, in 1994 he was given a free transfer to Southampton and from there he moved to Plymouth Argyle, but this period of his life was overshadowed by allegations of match-fixing. He was eventually cleared and awarded damages of £85,000 against the *Sun* for libel. However, when the newspaper appealed, his damages were slashed to £1 and he was ordered to pay the *Sun*'s legal costs, estimated at £500,000. Unable to pay the money, he was later declared bankrupt.

Currently coaching in South Africa, he reflects: 'The Britons bankrupted me. I came to their country with £10 in my pocket and they gave me £1 back. But in between I had one hell of a ride!'

Albert Iremonger
Mad, Bad and Dangerous to Know

Off the field Albert Iremonger was quiet and unassuming; but on it he was a veritable firebrand who thought nothing of rushing from his goal to remonstrate with the match officials in the middle of the pitch...sometimes while play was still continuing. On one occasion he chased Harry Hampton, the Aston Villa centre-forward, half the length of the field, aimed a mighty kick at his backside and then ran off. With Iremonger standing 6 feet 5½ inches tall, it must have looked like Basil Fawlty in pursuit of Manuel.

Iremonger, who made 564 appearances for Notts County between 1905 and 1926, was the tallest player in the League at that time. He has been described as having hands as large as dinner plates and he could throw the ball further than most men could kick it. He always wore woollen gloves and the longest, loosest jersey, which served to accentuate his height. Derby and England forward Steve Bloomer said that 'Albert's head reached up to the crossbar and his arms reached up to heaven'. Like 'Fatty' Foulke, he must have presented an intimidating sight to opposing forwards.

Iremonger was born in Wilford, Nottingham, on 15 June 1884. He signed for Notts County from local club Notts Jardines and made his debut against Sheffield Wednesday on 1 April 1905. In view of some of his subsequent antics, the date might be viewed as prophetic. It was not long before he was stamping his mark on the team, venturing from goal at every opportunity, even to take throw-ins. Naturally this alarmed his team-mates who preferred to see him back in his natural habitat between the posts, but it seems that Albert was a born wanderer. After one of his sorties to the halfway line to argue with the referee, his captain gave him 10 seconds to get back in goal. His behaviour caused anxiety at board level, too. The minute-book entry for 9 November reads: 'Iremonger appeared and was spoken to with regard to his gallery play at Trent Bridge and Bury.' It clearly had little effect, as another board minute, this time from 1923, instructed: 'Secretary to inform Iremonger not to leave his goal to argue with Referee or Linesmen.'

His favourite form of protest was to sit on the ball and refuse to return it after any decision that had not gone his way. He once wrapped his long arms around an opposing forward who had just scored and said he was holding him hostage until the end of the game because 'I'm not having you knocking any more goals past me'. When a referee was about to send off one of his team-mates for a bad tackle, Iremonger ran from his goal-line to the opposing penalty area to debate the decision. Eventually he begged: 'For goodness' sake don't send *him* off, ref. There'll be nothing left in our pockets when we get back to the dressing room!'

His most spectacular expedition has passed into County folklore. Apparently, in a match against Blackburn, he volunteered to take a penalty, only for his ferociously struck kick to smack against the bar and rebound into play, over his head and towards the vacant Notts County goal. In a manner to be replicated by Bartram years later, Iremonger turned on his heels and hared back towards goal but whereas the gods smiled on Sam, they clearly had it in for Albert. It developed into a mad race between Iremonger and the Blackburn winger and it seemed that Albert had averted the crisis of his own causing when, by means of a desperate lunge, he managed to boot the ball away from the forward. Alas, he merely succeeded in slicing the ball into his own net.

His build and temperament made him a natural target for opposing supporters. At Villa Park he was pelted with oranges, which he quietly collected and placed in the back of his net. When a helpful policeman tried to remove them, Iremonger told him: 'You leave them alone – they're mine.' And at a promotion-decider at West Ham in 1923, another running feud with a referee prompted a woman spectator to run on to the pitch and hit Iremonger over the head with an umbrella. 'That'll teach you to get on with the game,' she yelled.

In spite of his appetite for destruction, Iremonger was a consistent performer and notched up 222 consecutive appearances for County before, almost inevitably, the run was halted by suspension. He also earned a Football League cap in 1912 and many observers believe him unfortunate never to have played for his country. Like his older brother James (who played cricket for England), Albert was a fine cricketer and played for Nottinghamshire between 1906 and 1910 as a right-handed bat and medium pace bowler. At the age of 42 he finally left Notts to join Lincoln City on a short-term deal, playing 35 games for them. He later became landlord of a Nottingham pub.

Albert Iremonger died on 9 March 1958 but his memory lives on at Notts County, with a road behind the Meadow Lane ground named after him. It is a suitable tribute to a man described by writer Ivan Sharpe as 'seventy-six inches of elasticity, electricity and eccentricity'.

Leigh Richmond Roose
The First Playboy Footballer

More than 60 years before George Best was staggering out of his first nightclub, Leigh Richmond Roose could lay claim to being the first playboy footballer. The imposing Welsh international goalkeeper was a popular figure with the ladies and enjoyed close relationships with several women, including the celebrated music hall star Marie Lloyd. In 1905, the *Daily Mail* named him as one of London's most eligible bachelors – second only to cricketer Jack Hobbs – and at that time Roose's face was considered to be among the 10 most recognisable in the entire capital. He led a glamorous life, keeping an apartment in the centre of London even though he played chiefly for provincial teams, and buying expensive suits from Savile Row. He dined at the smartest restaurants, often in full morning dress and top hat, and was a real man about town. He would travel to matches by train and when a carriage picked him up from the station to take him to the game, excited schoolboys would run after it, eager to catch a glimpse of one of the most charismatic sporting heroes of the Edwardian period.

At a time when most players were professional, Roose was a wealthy amateur, a doctor of bacteriology. As an amateur, he filled in a weekly expenses form, leaving no item unclaimed, and because he suffered from the odd bout of pre-match jitters, his submission often began: 'Use of toilet twice…two pence.' He liked to catch as late a train as possible to the match, timing it so that he arrived at the ground only a short while before kick-off. As he entered the changing room, his team-mates would breathe a collective sigh of relief that one of them would not be forced to deputise in goal. When he was with Stoke City, he once cut his travel arrangements too fine and ended up missing the London to Birmingham train prior to a match at Aston Villa. In those days, railway companies kept private trains ready at a platform for hire by wealthy travellers, and so Roose hired one such train and had it take him, in solitary splendour, all the way to Birmingham at a cost of five shillings per mile plus the ordinary fare. Upon arrival, he arranged for the bill – a whopping £31 – to be forwarded to the club.

It was possibly best that Roose travelled alone from time to time as his eccentric behaviour might have embarrassed any companion. He was a renowned practical joker and indulged in a particular routine to pass the time before his frequent train journeys. He would position himself in a carriage at the front of the train and ask the station porter to feed his dog, which, he said, was in the guard's van. The obedient porter would then walk the length of the train, armed with a selection of dog biscuits, only to find, on reaching the guard's van, that there was no dog. The poor man would then retrace his steps to relay the news…only to find that there was no Roose either. He had sneaked off elsewhere in search of fresh entertainment. He was quite a card was Dr Roose.

The son of a Presbyterian minister, he was born near Wrexham on 27 November 1877 and went on to study at the University of Wales in Aberystwyth and then at King's College Hospital. At 6 feet 1 inch tall and weighing 13 stone, he was ideally suited to the physical demands of goalkeeping and began his career as a 17-year-old with Aberystwyth Town. His finest hour with Aberystwyth was in the 1900 Welsh Cup final when he was carried shoulder-high from the pitch following a match-winning performance in the team's 3-0 victory over Druids. In the same year, he won the first of 24 caps for Wales, marking the occasion by sprinting from his area and shoulder-charging an Irish winger on the touchline, bundling him out of play and knocking him unconscious.

In 1901 Roose joined Stoke, for whom he would go on to make 144 League appearances, none more memorable than the fixture at Anfield on 4 January 1902. The fish that Roose and his team-mates had eaten for lunch that day was bad and by kick-off many were feeling decidedly ill. After conceding an early goal, Roose dashed from the pitch in search of a toilet, and with a pulse rate of 148, did not return to the action. At the start of the second half only seven of the Stoke players were in any fit state to continue, the dressing room resembling 'the cabin of a cross-channel steamer in bad weather'. Not surprisingly, Liverpool ran out the 7-0 winners.

For all his dapper appearance off the pitch, on it Roose looked and smelt like a vagrant who had fallen on particularly hard times. This was on account of his lucky shirt – an old black and green Aberystwyth top – that he always wore under his goalkeeping jersey. He never allowed it to be washed for fear that it would bring him bad luck, so it remained dirty throughout his career. If nothing else, it guaranteed that no opponent wanted to stand too near him at corners. In March 1904 *Cricket and Football Field* wrote: 'Roose is one of the cleanest custodians we have, but he apparently is a trifle superstitious about his football garments, for he seldom seems to trouble the charwoman with them. Considerable amusement was created at Stoke on Saturday and again at Liverpool on Monday, when it was noticed that Roose alone failed to turn out in spic and span garments. His pants, we should say, carried about them the marks of many a thrilling contest.'

Towards the end of 1904 Roose signed for Everton, helping them to reach the semi-finals of the FA Cup, and following another spell with Stoke, he joined Sunderland in 1907, making 92 appearances for the Wearsiders over three seasons. When his Sunderland career was terminated by a broken wrist (the second of his career), he turned out for Port Vale, Celtic, Huddersfield Town, Aston Villa and Woolwich Arsenal, finally retiring in 1912.

Roose was an athletic if unorthodox shot-stopper with unbounded bravery and a knack of saving penalties. His physique endowed him with a prodigious kick and he was not a man to mess with in the heat of battle. He possessed a quick temper (he once attacked a Sunderland director with such ferocity that the FA banned him for 14 days) and, as one biographer noted, 'enjoyed taunting experienced international forwards, some of whom felt the full force of his fist in goalmouth melees.' Above all, he loved to be in the thick of the action. If play were at the other end of the pitch he would sit down next to the goalposts and chat to the crowd or entertain them by putting on gymnastic displays from his crossbar. At a time when other goalkeepers walked on to the pitch, Roose used to run on, acknowledging the applause of the crowd, and when a penalty was awarded, he would wave to spectators both before and after completing a save. Here was a man who loved his job. He once wrote: 'To a goalkeeper alone is the true delight of goalkeeping known. He must be an instinctive lover of the game, otherwise goalkeeping will take it out of a man if he is not devoted to it.'

His idiosyncratic nature never deserted him. In March 1909 he arrived for an international against Ireland in Belfast with one hand heavily bandaged. He said that he had broken two fingers but was sure he was fit enough to play. The press seized on the story and, with news of Roose's injury spreading throughout the city, a huge crowd turned up in the hope of witnessing an Irish victory. However, Roose's team-mate Billy Meredith was not convinced by the story and, peering through the keyhole of the goalkeeper's hotel room, saw Roose remove the bandage and wiggle his fingers with no sign of discomfort. Sure enough, as soon as the whistle sounded for the start of the match, Roose discarded the bandage to reveal a perfectly healthy set of fingers. The charade appears to have been another of his elaborate practical jokes, but the Welsh forgave him as he played superbly in his side's 3-2 victory.

In another international Roose actually played in two positions after the Welsh full-back went off with an injury, reducing the team to 10 men. In such circumstances a forward would usually move back into defence, but to avoid disrupting the team pattern, Roose insisted on playing in goal and at full-back simultaneously, one moment making a flying save, the next a determined tackle!

Roose's individuality made him a popular figure even at visiting grounds, but there was one match when his performance sparked a riot. In April 1910 he guested for Port Vale against Stoke Reserves in a match that would decide the winner of the North Staffordshire and District League. Roose not only angered the 7,000 fans by insisting on playing against his former club while wearing his old Stoke City shirt, but he also produced a match-winning display. At the end the furious Stoke supporters swarmed on to the pitch with, according to a contemporary report, 'only the brave intervention of the local constabulary saving him from a ducking in the River Trent.' In the course of the fracas the Stoke City chairman, Reverend A.E. Hurst, ran on to the pitch to appeal for calm, only to be knocked out by one of his own forwards. When the dust eventually settled Stoke's ground was ordered to be closed for the first two weeks of the 1910–11 season, but they did appeal successfully against the inclusion of Roose in the Vale goal and the League title was declared void. Roose said afterwards that he had thought the game was merely a friendly.

Although well above the age of the average recruit, Roose joined the British Army as a private in 1916 and served in the First World War on the Western Front, where his goalkeeping skills made him a sought-after grenade thrower. Happily he did not try to catch them, too. Promoted to the rank of lance corporal, he was killed on 7 October of that year, aged 38, in the Battle of the Somme, although his body was never recovered – a sad end for one of the great characters of the early 20th century.

Frank Swift

THE FANS' FAVOURITE

The young Frank Swift made his name through a heart-warming moment of fallibility yet went on to win 19 England caps by being virtually infallible. He may have been England's number one but he was also an inveterate crowd-pleaser who saw it as his duty to give value for money, stating: 'I threw in a bit of showmanship to please the crowd. Football's only a game, after all.' He used to crack jokes with supporters and it is said that he once left his goal during a lull in play to go into the crowd and share a bar of chocolate with a spectator. If opponents tried to shoulder-charge him, he would playfully pick them up; as opposing forwards ran through on goal, he sometimes went down on one knee and pretended to shoot them; and if a decision went against him, he would kneel pleading in front of the referee.

For their part, match officials played along with his clowning. When an opposing forward cheekily threw mud in Swift's face, the goalkeeper was still wiping it out of his eyes as the ball hit the back of the net.

'But ref,' protested Swift, 'I couldn't see.'

'Well, you'd better open your eyes, then,' smiled the referee. 'And wash your face before you speak to me again!'

Swift was a big man in every respect. Standing 6 feet 2 inches tall and weighing 14 stone, his hands were described as being 'like frying pans' and were so large that, with a finger span of nearly 12 inches, he could comfortably hold the ball in one hand. England team-mate Raich Carter said that Swift looked so big in goal that as a forward it often seemed as though trying to score against him was like attempting to put the ball into a matchbox.

He was born in Blackpool on Boxing Day 1913 and on leaving school landed a job as a coke-keeper at Blackpool Gasworks, also turning out for their works side. He then joined Fleetwood as an amateur after making an impression in a trial in which he wore a pair of boots borrowed from brother Fred, who kept goal for Oldham (in summer months the brothers later ran a pleasure boat together in Blackpool). In 1932 Frank signed for Manchester City as an amateur but soon turned professional for the princely sum of 10 shillings a week. To make ends meet, he kept his job at the gasworks but was able to give it up when City realised how good he was and doubled his weekly wage to £1. He had his first taste of Wembley at the 1933 FA Cup final when, as City's third-choice keeper, he travelled down by motorcycle with a friend to watch, Swift somehow squeezing his huge frame into the sidecar. City lost 3-0 to Everton that day, making the journey home even less pleasant.

Swift finally made his first-team debut at Derby on Christmas Day 1933 – one day short of his 20th birthday – but it was scarcely an occasion to remember as he conceded four goals and was knocked unconscious by the home centre-forward. The trainer brought him round by accidentally spilling half a bottle of smelling salts down his throat! In spite of this inauspicious beginning, Swift retained his place for the rest of the season, which culminated in City's second successive trip to Wembley and the incident that elevated him to a position of national treasure.

On the night before that 1934 Cup final against Portsmouth, Swift had intended to have an early night but he was sharing a room with captain Sam Cowan who sat bathing a poisoned big toe in a bowl of hot water and kept Swift talking until three o'clock in the morning. This was a calculated ploy by Cowan, who reasoned that consequently the youngster would sleep later the next morning and have less time for pre-match nerves. All went according to plan until shortly before kick-off when Swift noticed a senior team-mate so jittery that he was unable to tie his boot laces. The nerves immediately transmitted themselves to Swift, who was promptly hauled off to the washroom by the trainer, slapped around the face and given a tot of whisky. Despite being given a settling first touch of the ball by City's right-half Matt Busby, Swift felt nervous throughout the match and when the final whistle blew to acclaim City the 2-1 winners, Swift bent down to retrieve his cap from the back of the net, and fainted. He was quickly revived with sponge and water but his misfortune had touched the hearts of the nation. He had to be helped up the steps to receive his winners' medal from King George V, who was so concerned that he sent a telegram the following week, enquiring after the young man's health.

'Big Swifty' recovered so well that between 1934 and the outbreak of war he missed only one game for City, helping them to the League Championship in 1937. Fearless and agile, he dominated his area and was the man who, with his ability to hurl the ball half the length of the pitch, pioneered the throw as an alternative method of distribution. Unlike some other crowd-pleasing keepers, he had no desire to score goals. He took only one penalty in his senior career and that was in a wartime match, when City were already winning 5-0. He recalled: 'The skipper invited me to take it. A team-mate placed the ball on the spot and I started the run-up from the edge of my own penalty area. I hit the ball with all my might and it smashed into the goal with such force that it ripped a hole in the net. The ball banged into the face of an old boy standing on the terraces behind the goal and when I went to apologise he showed me that I had broken his false teeth. I never had the appetite to take another penalty after that experience.'

At the start of the war, Swift became a special constable in charge of traffic control, but he quit after just one day and returned to football, making more than 150 unofficial appearances for City and guesting for England in wartime internationals. Surprisingly, he was overlooked for full international honours until 1947 when he won the first of 19 caps. The following year he became the first goalkeeper since 1873 to captain England when he led the team out against Italy in Turin, a decision that provoked considerable criticism as it was generally felt that a goalkeeper was too remote from the play to be able to encourage his players. Swift made the critics eat their words and was outstanding as England romped to a 4-0 victory. The closest the Italians came was when the ball hit the bar and bounced down just in front of the line. The crowd screamed for a goal but when play moved to the other end, Swift beckoned a photographer from behind the goal to step on to the pitch and take a photo of the spot where the ball had landed.

When England suddenly dropped Swift in 1949, the decision hit him hard and he stunned City by announcing that he was retiring from football altogether, having played 338 League games for the Maine Road club. He worked briefly as a sales rep for a Manchester confectioner before turning to journalism. It was in his capacity as football correspondent for the *News of the World* that he agreed to travel with Manchester United for their European Cup tie in Belgrade in February 1958, even though he hated flying. Tragically, Swift was killed in the Munich air crash, fate at least choosing to spare the former team-mate who had shown him such consideration 24 years earlier, Matt Busby.

HARD MEN

Tommy Banks
The Bolton Butcher

Back in the 1950s a trip to Bolton Wanderers was not for the faint-hearted. As well as being a very good side, they had some physically intimidating players, none more so than the full-back pairing of Roy Hartle and Tommy Banks. Jimmy Greaves used to say that Burnden Park was the only ground in the country where the front row of both stands wore shinpads. If Tom Finney was the Preston Plumber, Banks was surely the Bolton Butcher.

A formidable left-back, Banks was fond of warning opposing wingers in his broad Lancashire accent: 'Tha'd better not try to get past me unless tha wants gravel rash.' He was the human equivalent of a pit-bull – relatively short (5 feet 8 inches), sturdy (weighing around 12 stone), barrel-chested and quick. Once he had got hold of a leg, he was not easy to shake off. Bolton's midfield players relied on Banks and Hartle to cover any opposing runs. Derek Hennin would tell them: 'If my inside-forward happens to come through, chip him back to me.' He was only half joking.

Tommy Banks was born in Farnworth in 1929 and was an outstanding schoolboy player who attracted interest from a number of clubs, including Wolves and Manchester United. Wolves were extremely keen, but Banks decided against leaving home and instead joined his local club, Bolton, for a £10 signing-on fee while still working as a miner. He made his first-team debut a year later in 1948 but did not establish himself until 1953, mainly because of the presence of his brother, Ralph, who was the first-choice full-back. It was Ralph who was given the runaround by Blackpool's Stanley Matthews in the unforgettable 1953 FA Cup final, which Bolton lost 4-3. Matthews would enjoy just as many battles with Ralph's younger brother...and probably carried the scars until his dying day.

A popular rumour doing the rounds at the time – and one that Matthews eventually got to hear about – was that the wing maestro often chose not to play at Burnden because he did not relish being kicked into the stands by Banks. However, Banks dismisses it as 'a load of piffle and poppycock', adding, 'Stanley Matthews was never scared of playing against me.' Having said that, Banks admits he did prefer to play against Matthews rather than Tom Finney, because Matthews would keep to the touchline, allowing Banks to tackle with his stronger foot, whereas Finney could beat a full-back on either side.

Banks' strength and tenacity, allied to no shortage of skill, ensured that he kept his place in the Bolton team for eight seasons and 255 games. He used to cycle a round trip of 6 miles a day from Farnworth to Bolton for training sessions, in which he built up his already formidable physique by playing rugby. His outstanding year was 1958 when Bolton reached the Cup final to meet the Munich-ravaged Manchester United. Pitted against Banks on United's right-wing that day was 18-year-old Alex Dawson. Banks took one look at him and said: 'You can't put that little baby in to play against me!' Although few people outside Bolton wanted anything other than a United victory, Banks gave a typically solid and robust performance to help Wanderers to a 2-0 win, thereby succeeding where his brother had failed five years previously. Also in 1958, Banks's club displays earned him six England caps and he played in all four matches in the World Cup finals in Sweden, including the goalless draw with Brazil. A young forward named Pele did not make his bow until Brazil's next game, one theory being that the Brazilians did not want him coming face to studs with Bolton's finest, Tommy Banks.

Injuries brought an end to Banks's top-flight career in 1961 and he joined first Altrincham and then Bangor City, for whom he starred in the 1964 Welsh Cup final, in the process becoming one of the few players to appear in both the English and Welsh finals. After retiring from football, he earned a living as a bricklayer, noting that 'I earned more carrying bricks and mortar up a ladder than I did as a player.' It is somehow apt that the man who would run through brick walls for his team ended up building them.

Frank Barson
Hardest of the Hard

Comparing players of different eras in terms of ability is always dangerous as there are so many factors to consider – fitness levels, the pace of the game, the quality of the opposition and so on. However, when disregarding skill and dealing instead with soccer's hard men, comparisons are perhaps more justifiable, and the general consensus of opinion is that Vinnie Jones wouldn't have lasted two minutes in a ring with Frank Barson.

At 6 feet tall and weighing slightly under 13 stone, the Aston Villa, Manchester United and England half-back of the 1920s was built like a brick outhouse and possessed a fiery temper that brought him into countless scrapes with fans and officials and which had opponents running scared. He was sent off at least a dozen times in an era when banishment was rare, while the very thought of lining up against Barson prompted opposing players to claim they were injured. It was scarcely any safer being on Barson's side: the story goes that he once pulled a gun on one of his managers.

Barson was born in Grimesthorpe, near Sheffield, in April 1891. After starring at schoolboy level, he began his career as an amateur at Albion FC. In 1909 he signed for local team Cammell Laird while working as a blacksmith, and two years later entered the professional game with Barnsley. Before he could even make his first-team debut for Barnsley, he had to serve a two-month suspension following an ugly brawl in a pre-season friendly against Birmingham City. In January 1915 Barson had to be smuggled out of Goodison Park to avoid a large crowd that had gathered outside the ground to remonstrate with him over his behaviour in an FA Cup tie with Everton, during which he had been sent off. Further sendings-off brought further suspensions but it was a clash with the Barnsley directors over travelling expenses that eventually saw Barson sold to Villa for £2,850 in October 1919.

His rugged tackling and dominance in the air made an instant impact on a Villa side that had been struggling after the First World War. In March 1920 he won his solitary England cap – against Wales at Highbury – and a month later he helped Villa lift the FA Cup at the expense of Huddersfield. Barson must be the only player to be warned about his behaviour by a referee *before* a match. Prior to the 1920 final, referee Jack Howcroft entered the Villa dressing room and said sternly: 'The first wrong move you make, Barson, off you go.' For once fiery Frank did not step out of line, encouraging Howcroft to repeat the threat the next time he officiated a Villa match.

Wherever there was trouble, Barson was rarely far away. If any of his team-mates were on the receiving end of a bad tackle, Barson saw it is as his mission in life to impose a form of natural justice. Particularly at away games, opposing crowds howled for Barson's blood, the hatred becoming so vehement that he felt obliged to defend himself publicly on the grounds that he had been 'brought up to play hard and saw nothing wrong with an honest to goodness shoulder charge.' Whether these same fans would still have voiced their disapproval if facing Barson one-to-one is a matter for speculation.

Off the field, too, Barson was frequently in hot water, mainly due to his refusal to move from Sheffield, where he still had business interests. Villa demanded that he move to Birmingham but he flatly refused. He was not a man to argue with. Once, he and goalkeeper Sam Hardy, who lived in Chesterfield, missed their rail connection and were forced to walk 7 miles to Old Trafford in appalling weather. Naturally, iron-man Barson was the best player on the pitch that afternoon. His living arrangements caused further problems on the opening day of the 1920–21 season when he and Clem Stephenson missed a defeat at Bolton. The Villa board suspended the pair for 14 days but Barson still refused to move. Bizarrely, he was later appointed captain and marked the occasion on Boxing Day 1921 by heading a goal from 30 yards against Sheffield United. A corner was cleared to him way outside the box and as he ran in to meet the ball, he realised he was not going to be able to reach it with his feet. Instead he hurled himself forward and headed it, the ball flashing knee-high like a bullet past astonished defenders and into the net.

Barson's habit of keeping dubious company did not endear him to his employers either. He was proud to number among his friends the Fowler brothers, who were eventually hanged for murder. Indeed, while languishing in the condemned cell, they sent Barson a good luck letter before a game against Spurs.

Barson's lack of respect for authority (he even taught his pet parrot to swear) eventually brought a premature end to his Villa career. Following a match against Liverpool, he invited a friend to wait in the dressing room while he got changed. The transgression was brought to the attention of the Villa chairman who issued a stern rebuke. Characteristically, Barson refused to apologise and was handed a seven-day suspension. He responded with a transfer request and declared that he would never play for the club again. It was during this bitter stand-off that Barson is said to have pulled a gun on the manager – although some sources state that the incident took place later in his career as a novel means of negotiating a pay rise!

Despite Villa's attempts to persuade him to stay, in August 1922 Barson joined Manchester United for a cut-price £5,000. United were happy for him to live and train in Sheffield and, in what must surely be a unique clause in a player's contract, also promised him his own pub if the club won promotion within three years. They did, but when Barson, who by no stretch of the imagination could be described as a teetotaller, opened the doors of his new hostelry, he was swamped in the rush of United fans wanting to meet their hero. He was so horrified that he quickly handed the business over to his head barman. Despite the fact that he invariably stood out on the pitch for one reason or another, Barson was never comfortable with attention – even adulation – off it.

Barson's stay at Old Trafford was blighted by injury and in six years with United he made only 152 appearances, scoring four goals. When he did play he proved an inspirational captain, although the fact that he turned up for one game with a mysteriously acquired black eye suggests that not everything was rosy in the United camp. If Barson ended up with a black eye, one can only assume that his opponent ended up in casualty. The Football Association continued to take a keen interest in his behaviour and suspended him for two months for flattening a Manchester City player in the 1926 Cup semi-final, even though the referee did not see fit to send Barson off. After breaking his nose for the umpteenth time, in a freak collision with one of his team-mates at Portsmouth, Barson was considered surplus to requirements and in May 1928 he signed for Watford. But age had done nothing to mellow him and he was banned for seven months after being sent off and then brawling with police officers.

Although by now he had lost some of his speed and skill, he remained fiercely competitive. In a match at Millwall he became involved in a series of personal feuds and just before half-time he was injured in a clash of heads. Covered in mud and blood he staggered to the dressing room for treatment, booed every step of the way by The Den fans. During the break he changed strip and had a bandage wrapped around his head to protect the wound. As he emerged for the second half, a Millwall supporter yelled: 'The disguise hasn't worked, Barson. We can still recognise yer!'

In 1929 he accepted the post of player-coach at Hartlepool United but within five months he had signed for Wigan Borough. As the club's highest-paid player, the veteran Barson was expected to set an example, only for his temperament to get the better of him yet again. His last appearance for the club was against Accrington Stanley on Boxing Day 1930. Fittingly, he was sent off and received a three-month suspension along with a £5 fine. This turned out to be Wigan Borough's last season as a Football League club and that summer, in an ultimately unsuccessful attempt to stabilise the club's precarious financial position, they offloaded Barson to Rhyl Athletic. In 1932 he became player-manager of Rhyl (where inevitably he managed to get himself sent off again) and remained in North Wales until his contract was terminated in 1935. Three months later he was appointed manager of Stourbridge, but the chance to rejoin Aston Villa (where there was a new regime) as youth coach proved impossible to resist and he went on to become senior coach and head trainer at Villa Park until the outbreak of the Second World War. He served as trainer at Swansea Town from 1947 to 1954 and, after a two-year stint as trainer at Lye Town, Frank Barson retired from the game in 1956. He died 12 years later in Birmingham, aged 77.

Throughout his career Barson not only dished out the rough stuff, he took it as well. He claimed: 'I shirked no collision, and I got up with more respect for the man who had put me down.' What he failed to add was that the 'respect' would be quickly followed by retribution. After being brutally chopped down by one opponent, Barson limped towards the referee and begged: 'Don't send him off ref, I'll kick him off in the second half.'

Despite his fearsome reputation, Barson was a fine player who would surely have won more England caps if, as journalist Ivan Sharpe wrote with commendable understatement, 'he had been cooler in action'. An indication of his ability is that he is reputed to have bounced the ball on his forehead half the length of the field during one game. It sounds an incredibly impressive display of showmanship and skill but it may be, of course, that, being Frank Barson, nobody dared take the ball off him.

Billy Bremner
Tartan Terrier

Two memorable images of Billy Bremner sum up his career. The first from 1966 shows a furious Dave Mackay grabbing him by the front of his shirt as if about to throttle him. The second from 1974 is of Bremner and Kevin Keegan ripping off their shirts and trudging bare-chested from the Wembley pitch after being sent off for fighting in the Charity Shield. Those pictures said everything about Bremner. He was a born winner, even if it meant kicking the leg that a Scottish team-mate had twice recently broken or getting involved in a brawl in a meaningless pre-season friendly.

Once described by the *Sunday Times* as 'ten stone of barbed wire', Bremner was one of football's most combative characters, a demon tackler, a red-haired terrier forever snapping at opposition heels. He may have stood only 5 feet 5 inches tall but he thought nothing of clattering into much bigger men in the cause of Leeds United and Scotland. Bremner's view of the game was simple. 'Football is not all about the skill factor,' he said. 'It is about whether you are determined enough and have a greater desire to win games than the opposition.'

That determination to win governed his life, making him the ultimate competitive dad. His wife said: 'He was a terrible loser. If his team lost, even in a game that did not mean very much, he took it very personally. He just hated to lose. Even when he played games with the children, he would never let them win, unless it was on merit. That was partly to give them an edge, but it was also because he just did not like to lose at anything.'

Billy Bremner was born in Stirling in 1942 and after being rejected by Arsenal and Chelsea for being too small, signed for Leeds the day after his 17th birthday. He made his first-team debut in 1960 as a right-winger before being converted into a midfielder, in which role he became a permanent fixture in the side over the next 16 years, the driving force of the Don Revie revolution. Inheriting the captaincy from Bobby Collins in 1966, Bremner carried out manager Revie's instructions to the letter. A volcano looking for somewhere to explode, he never shirked a challenge and formed a formidable partnership with Johnny Giles, who was every bit as hard as the Scot but managed to camouflage it with his ball skills and creative passing. When one considers that behind them were the likes of Norman 'Bites Yer Legs' Hunter and Jack Charlton, it is not difficult to see why Leeds were, physically at least, the most feared team in the land. They did more than just bend the rules, they broke them in half, and happily resorted to intimidating tactics, both physically and verbally. During a game with Manchester United, Bremner called to Hunter, 'You flick him up and I'll volley him,' making sure that their target, George Best, overheard.

Bremner's value to Leeds was immeasurable. Revie said: 'No manager could wish for a greater leader or a greater player. If I was in the trenches at the front line, the man I would want on my right side is Billy Bremner.' Revie went on to recall a UEFA Cup tie at Hibernian in 1973 when Bremner demonstrated his amazing confidence and coolness under pressure. 'When Billy stopped the ball on the goal-line and stood with his foot on it and his hands on his hips, the crowd froze. Two on-rushing Hibernian forwards slithered to a halt in amazement. It was the cheekiest thing I have ever seen in football.'

Quite apart from a seemingly endless supply of stamina that would have made the Duracell bunny appear lethargic, Bremner had a knack of scoring vital goals, including winners in four major semi-finals. The little man revelled in the big occasion, finishing with an impressive total of 90 goals in his 586 League games with Leeds, and was named Footballer of the Year in 1970. As captain of the greatest team in the club's history, he lifted the League Championship twice, the FA Cup, the Inter Cities Fairs Cup (forerunner of the UEFA Cup) twice, and the Football League Cup. In addition, there were numerous near misses, Leeds being regarded as very much the bridesmaids of the day, difficult though it may be to picture Norman Hunter as a bridesmaid.

If anything, Bremner was even more committed to the Scottish cause. He won the first of his 54 caps in 1965 and captained his country at the 1974 World Cup finals. Before a Scotland-England game, Revie as England manager warned Norman Hunter not to bruise any of his Elland Road team-mates, but Hunter accidentally kicked Bremner who spent the next 20 minutes hell-bent on revenge. Bremner's international career ended on a low note when, after a 1975 game against Denmark in Copenhagen, he and four other Scottish players were thrown out of a nightclub following an altercation. Back at the team hotel, a Scottish FA official was distinctly unamused to find Bremner and another player turning a bed upside down in a drunken prank. Bremner was banned for life from international football and although the suspension was lifted the following year, he never played again for his country.

Bremner left Leeds in 1976 and went on to play 61 times for Hull City. He returned to Leeds as manager in 1985 (sandwiched between two spells in charge of Doncaster Rovers) but was unable to lead the club back to the Promised Land. He died of a heart attack in December 1997 two days before his 55th birthday. In the *Mirror* Mike Walters wrote: 'His death did more damage than leaving grown men crying in the streets of Yorkshire. It was as if the lights had been turned out on a famous chapter of soccer history.'

Fittingly, Billy Bremner's ashes were scattered at Elland Road, where a statue of him has since been erected, depicting him in familiar celebratory pose, arms aloft, fists clenched, ever the winner.

Harry Cripps
The Lionheart

If a player was ever destined to spend the majority of his career with a particular club, it was surely Harry Cripps at Millwall. Throughout the Sixties and early Seventies, the two were inexorably linked, the player's indefatigable spirit and battling qualities embodying everything that is best about the club. A dating agency would have paired them together instantly. Over a period of 13 years and more than 400 games, Cripps's fearless approach and inspirational leadership made him a true hero to Millwall fans, at the same helping to make The Den a place that visiting teams came to dread. He was a key figure in the team that went a record 59 home League games unbeaten in the mid 1960s, a feat all the more remarkable because twice the Lions had to adjust to life in a higher division, rising as they did from the Fourth to the Second.

There have been more skilful left-backs in the history of world football, but few to match the determination and charisma of Harry Cripps. He could lift an otherwise dull game just by setting off on one of his marauding runs down the wing. The whole crowd in the main stand would rise to him, even if the adventure rarely achieved more than a throw-in. Then 'Arry Boy would race back to position, like a rumbling hippopotamus, cheers ringing in his ears. Solidly built, almost square, with broad shoulders and sturdy legs, Cripps was neither particularly quick nor athletic but he made the most of his ability. Occasionally Benny Fenton, manager for the majority of Cripps's time at Millwall, would sign a replacement. Harry never complained; he simply got on with the job of winning back his place, which, inevitably and to the delight of the fans, he always did.

Cripps used positional sense to offset his lack of pace, with the result that not many wingers got the better of him. And if that failed he resorted to good old-fashioned intimidation. When a young Francis Lee, playing for Bolton Wanderers, heard the roar that greeted Cripps's introduction as substitute, he supposedly told Harry, 'I'll be keeping out of your way,' before trotting over to a safer part of the pitch. The late Keith Weller, one of Cripps's more illustrious team-mates, called him 'a nice cheat', adding: 'It was weird, he wasn't quick but he didn't get beaten often.' Not that there was anything malicious about Cripps; his tackles may sometimes have been late (although he would point out that he got there as soon as he could) but they were never designed to injure an opponent. Indeed, he was rarely cautioned, knowing full well that a friendly arm around the referee and that big beaming smile would be enough to defuse any situation. Besides, no referee would have dared send him off at The Den, for fear of ending up at New Cross Hospital for a rectal examination to remove a whistle.

In his classic book *Only a Game?*, Eamon Dunphy, another Millwall contemporary of Cripps, described him as 'the life and soul of the club...and a comical character. Jolly and heavy and a bit cumbersome. But he is very shrewd.' Dunphy went on to relate how Cripps would sell his team-mates supposedly bargain LPs, even though they could be bought cheaper in the shops. 'But the thing about him is that you can't dislike him. He is the lovable con man.'

Dunphy also discerned the essence of Harry Cripps, the desire to win every game, to give of his best. Even before a meaningless end-of-season encounter, Cripps would go around his team-mates individually in the dressing room beforehand, fists clenched, declaring: 'This is the one.' Every match mattered to him, and nobody wore the shirt or the captain's armband with greater pride. During a mid-season, mid-table game with Norwich, Cripps, as the club's designated penalty taker, stepped up to take a spot-kick but put it wide. The referee took pity on him and gave him a second chance, ruling that the Norwich keeper had moved. Cripps stepped up again...and put it wide again. But there was no hint of self-pity; instead he turned on his heels and sprinted back to position in readiness to defend the goal-kick. And when Millwall needed an equaliser later in the game, who should pop up to score but Cripps? Nobody could keep him down for long.

Despite being so closely associated with south-east London, Henry Richard Cripps was born in East Dereham, Norfolk, in 1941. Equally surprising, in view of Cripps's own persona, is that Bobby Moore should play a major role at the start and end of his career. As a youngster Cripps played for West Ham and was a team-mate of Moore in the side that reached the final of the FA Youth Cup in 1958–59. Released by West Ham, Cripps joined Millwall in 1961 and soon became a firm favourite. He played with a smile on his face and loved to pinch a few yards at free-kicks while the referee's back was turned. The crowd loved his enthusiasm. During a crucial Third Division match against Swansea in 1966, he was carried to the touchline by the trainer and the referee after taking a bad knock, but as soon as he saw the substitute about to step on to the field, he pushed aside his two helpers and sprinted back to position, leaving a bemused sub to return to the bench.

He was actually one of those players who improved with age. Playing at a higher level never fazed him and although he usually kept things simple, he could occasionally wrong-foot the opposition with a clever, disguised pass. He also proved one of the club's best finishers, regularly going forward for set pieces and sneaking in unnoticed to score. In 1970–71 he finished the season with 11 goals, reaching double figures because the vociferous Millwall crowd simply demanded that he take a penalty in an end-of-season game against Hull City even though he had been relieved of duties following one or two misses from the spot. The following season he came very close to helping Millwall into the top flight for the first time in their history, but they were cruelly pipped at the death by Birmingham City.

In 1974 after 444 games and 40 goals for Millwall, he made the short journey to Charlton where, playing in midfield, he helped them to promotion from the Third Division. He later became assistant manager at Charlton and filled the same post at Southend United as number two to his old pal Bobby Moore.

He remained a regular visitor to The Den and on his first reappearance after a health scare, the much-maligned Millwall fans stepped aside to form a spontaneous guard of honour, applauding him all the way to the ground. When he died of a heart attack on 29 December 1995 – tragically young like Bremner – the club lost someone who was more than a mere player. They don't make them like Harry Cripps anymore, and the football world is a poorer place for it.

Charlie Hurley
The King of Wearside

Even today, nearly 40 years after his last game for the club, the football-mad Sunderland supporters still speak in hushed, reverential tones of Charlie Hurley, the man they called 'The King'. An imposing figure both on and off the field, Hurley's popularity remains such that in 2000 he was voted the Black Cats' Player of the Century, and when it came to renaming an executive suite at the Stadium of Light, there was only one person in contention: it would be known henceforth as the Charlie Hurley Suite. Club chairman Niall Quinn says: 'Charlie is still a big influence on this football club; it's incredible, it gets stronger as he gets older.'

Hurley was a genial giant, a man of the people. He adored the fans and the feeling was reciprocated. Strong and forceful in the tackle and commanding in the air, as centre-halves had to be in those days, he was, however, more than just a hard man. His skill on the ground earned him 40 caps for the Republic of Ireland and when he captained Sunderland to promotion from the Second Division in 1964, he was runner-up in the Football Writers' Player of the Year poll to Bobby Moore. Among those who used to worship him from the Roker Park terraces were a young Martin O'Neill and athlete Steve Cram. Both men named Charlie Hurley as their boyhood hero. What helped establish Hurley as such a Sunderland legend was the number of goals he scored (or nearly scored) when going forward for set pieces. He was one of the first centre-halves to pose a genuine threat to the opposition goal, using his aerial strength to maximum effect. Author Graham Brack wrote of him: 'Carved from the finest mahogany, gifted on the ground and supreme in the air, his presence paralysed the opposition before he touched the ball.' With the crowd chanting 'Charlie, Charlie', he would stroll forward, raise his hand to indicate where the ball should be placed and then, when the chance arose, thump a towering header into the net. He scored 26 times in 401 appearances for Sunderland – no mean feat for a central defender, particularly as it took him 124 games to get off the mark.

Hurley was born in Cork in 1936 but his family moved to Rainham, Essex, when he was seven months old. In 1953 he joined Millwall from Rainham Youth Club for the standard £10 signing-on fee, making his Lions debut at Torquay and quickly becoming the linchpin of the defence with more than a century of appearances to his name. Much to his relief, the Millwall fans took to him. He admitted in 2007: 'The fans were fantastic. They used to scare the shite out of the opposition. Mind you, they scared the shite out of me as well!' He missed the first three months of the 1955–56 season to complete his National Service, in the course of which he picked up an injury playing football with his fellow squaddies that would deny him his first Eire cap. When he did return to club action at Shrewsbury in February 1956, he was carried off after five minutes with a torn cartilage that kept him out for the rest of the season. The 20-year-old finally made his international debut against England in a World Cup qualifier in Dublin in May 1957, giving an assured performance against a team that had thrashed the Irish 5-1 just 11 days earlier. Indeed, it needed a last-gasp equaliser from John Atyeo to deny the Irish a memorable triumph. England centre-forward Tommy Taylor had led the Irish defence a merry dance in the first game but Hurley ensured that he hardly had a kick in the return encounter. Hurley went on to win 40 caps for his country and captained the side with customary pride and passion.

Struggling in Third Division (South), cash-strapped Millwall were happy to do business when Sunderland manager Alan Brown, who had been alerted to Hurley's potential by former Millwall boss Charlie Hewitt, offered £20,000 for the new Irish international. After initial reluctance, Hurley moved north in September 1957, but made the worst possible start to his Sunderland career. His first game ended in a 7-0 rout at the hands of Blackpool (with Hurley contributing an own goal) and that was followed by a 6-0 thrashing from Burnley, the newcomer having the misfortune to come up against two future international centre-forwards in Ray Charnley and Ray Pointer respectively. After such a baptism of fire, things could only get better and Hurley became a colossus for the Wearsiders, adopting an approach that was firm but fair. His last appearance in the red and white stripes was at Turf Moor, Burnley, in April 1969, before he joined Bolton Wanderers on a free transfer. When Hurley left Sunderland, fans held an abdication party for 'The King' at a local ballroom.

Hurley stayed at Bolton until 1971, making 43 League appearances. He then turned his hand to management at Reading, remaining at Elm Park for five years, during which time the club gained promotion from the Fourth Division. Fondly remembered wherever he played, Hurley has even been celebrated in verse by poet Peter Goulding:

A centre-half, he was ten foot six,
And he thrilled the crowd with his showboat tricks.
He liked to get his tackles in early,
Tough as old boots was Charlie Hurley.

He lived in a cage and was fed raw meat,
Ate turkey heads for a Christmas treat.
Compared to him, Ron Yeats was a girlie,
Eat your granny, would Charlie Hurley.

Vinnie Jones
Playing the Tough Guy

When Vinnie Jones famously squeezed Paul Gascoigne by the testicles, he took man-marking to unprecedented levels. At the time most people assumed it was a trick he had dreamed up himself to further his hard man image, but it transpired that Jones had actually been taught it by the coach of the schoolboy team for whom he had played as an 11-year-old. Then, Jones was turning out for Bedmond, near his hometown of Watford, but as he was a small boy competing against much bigger and older lads, his coach had a few words of advice on how to even up the score. One suggestion was that after knocking an opponent over, Jones should pick him up with a smile but make sure that he pulled under the armpits at the same time. The second piece of advice was that if Jones was being marked too closely, he should reach back, grab the boy by the testicles and twist, because 'they won't mark you too closely next time!' An award-winning photograph was born.

Love him or hate him, Vinnie Jones certainly left his mark on the game – and on opponents' bodies. In a career littered with disciplinary indiscretions, ranging from biting the nose of a reporter in Dublin to accusing foreign players of 'squealing like pot-bellied pigs', he was sent off 13 times and was twice booked within five seconds of the kick-off. After being cautioned for a three-second foul on Sheffield United's Dane Whitehouse, Jones remarked: 'I must have been too high, too wild, too strong or too early, because, after three seconds, I could hardly have been too late!' He also received a suspended six-month ban and a £20,000 fine for his 1992 video *Soccer's Hard Men*, which offered advice to budding hatchet men, yet he continued to revel in his notoriety, boasting: 'The Football Association have given me a pat on the back because I've taken violence off the terraces and on to the pitch.'

The players who have been on the receiving end of his bone-jarring tackles no doubt have mixed feelings about the fact that Vincent Peter Jones was very nearly lost to the professional game. Released by Watford as a teenager, he became a labourer on a building site before he landed a job as groundsman at Bushey College, white-lining the pitches. Wealdstone used to train there and one day in 1984, short of players, they asked the 19-year-old to make up the numbers. He impressed to such an extent that he was signed permanently. Two years later he joined the Swedish club Holmsund, arriving in Scandinavia with all his worldly possessions in a bin bag. He helped the part-timers reach the semi-finals of the Swedish Cup before returning to England as the craziest member of Wimbledon's 'Crazy Gang'.

Playing for Wimbledon in the late 1980s would have felt rather like being with 20 Jeremy Beadles. Some of the players' initiation ceremonies would have been rejected by the British Army for being too extreme, while virtually every day there was a new prank to be tried out. Nobody was safe – the manager, the training staff, and even visiting journalists were targets. In fact, especially visiting journalists. Staying in hotels on away trips, players would routinely have water-filled waste paper bins hurled at them, their bed linen tied in knots and their clothes dumped in a bath full of water. In one of their most elaborate jokes, Jones and team-mate Wally Downes moved all of the furniture out of manager Dave Bassett's Portugal hotel room and carefully rearranged it in the hotel lobby. In his autobiography, Jones recalled how on the night before his first-team debut at Nottingham Forest, the other players brought into his room a stripper who proceeded to sing on his bed. Any benefits of the late-night enter-tainment were not immediately obvious. At half-time the following day Jones asked the team's kit-man how he had been playing. The kit-man replied: 'I'm 85 and if you gave me the number four shirt, I'd do better!' But Jones soon adjusted to the tempo of play in the top flight and after scoring the winner against Manchester United in his second game, he never looked back…apart from grabbing Gazza's goolies.

The enforcer reputation was quick to follow. After Arsenal's Graham Rix had the temerity to criticise Wimbledon's robust, route one style of play, Jones left him in a heap at the first opportunity and was sent off. And when Kenny Dalglish caught him on the shin, Jones snarled: 'If I get near you once I'm going to rip your head off and crap in the hole!' It was a line he had heard in a film – probably not a Disney one. The message was clear: nobody messed with Wimbledon, they were family. The formidable team spirit fostered within the club took them to their greatest triumph in 1988 when they defeated the aristocrats of Liverpool in the FA Cup final. Jones's contribution to the occasion may not have been spectacular but he won his personal midfield battle by flattening Liverpool hard man Steve McMahon early on. After that, McMahon exerted minimal influence on the game.

However, the publicity seemed to be going to Jones's head, where many felt it would have led a lonely existence. During 1988–89 he was sent off in pre-season, ended the career of Tottenham defender Gary Stevens with a horrendous tackle, and was also accused of head-butting Everton's Kevin Ratcliffe. Wimbledon's new manager Bobby Gould decided that Jones had become a liability and sold him to Leeds, a move that infuriated Elland Road legend Johnny Giles who raged: 'In Don Revie's day he wouldn't have got through the door, let alone pulled on a Leeds shirt.' Jones made his position clear from the outset. When team-mate Bobby Davison questioned his ability in a training session, Jones flattened him with a punch in the mouth before asking if any of the other players 'would like some'. There were no takers. He subsequently settled down at Leeds under the guidance of manager Howard Wilkinson, receiving just three yellow cards in the whole season, and in the process helped the club gain promotion to the First Division.

Following short spells with Sheffield United and Chelsea, Jones returned to Wimbledon in 1992 for a fee of £640,000, and celebrated by being sent off on his Dons debut. It was actually his first dismissal since being sent off for them five years earlier. Somehow Jones and Wimbledon seemed to bring out the worst in each other. Amid widespread derision he was selected to play international football for Wales (having qualified through his paternal grandfather) and was even named captain, but in 1995 he was given a five-month ban after being sent off against Georgia for scything down an opponent and then standing on him. Those who deemed Jones unfit for international football were proved right.

After making more than 250 League appearances in his two spells with Wimbledon, he left in 1998 to become player-coach of Queens Park Rangers, but when he was overlooked for the vacant managerial post, he announced his retirement from the game. Since then, he has gone on to develop a successful career as an actor, principally in tough-guy roles in films such as *Lock, Stock and Two Smoking Barrels*.

No one can dispute that Vinnie Jones has made the most of the talent at his disposal, often putting to shame more gifted players who put in markedly less effort. He might not have known a step-over from a comb-over but he fulfilled a vital role, doing the dirty work in midfield. He made no apologies for his style. 'I adopted that attitude that said: "I am from Watford, I'm off the building site and I'm representing the ordinary working-class folk of this country."'

Following that ball-squeezing incident, Gazza had a red rose sent to Jones in the dressing room. So at least somebody loved him. And it is worth remembering that despite his dreadful disciplinary record, he does a lot of unsung work with children's charities. Saint Vinnie? Maybe not quite yet, but stranger things have happened. If Carlton Palmer can play for England, anything is possible.

Fred Keenor
Local Hero

When Cardiff City lifted the FA Cup in 1927 to take the trophy out of England for the first and, to date, the only time, their captain Fred Keenor became the toast of Wales. In many respects, Keenor was an unlikely Welsh sporting hero. He did not possess the skills of Ryan Giggs – nor even, in truth, those of Vinnie Jones – and was described as having the worst shot in the Football League plus a complete inability to run with the ball. But what he had in abundance was courage. He battled back from a career-threatening leg injury sustained in the First World War to make over 500 appearances for Cardiff and win 32 international caps, his greatest attributes being his commitment and his uncompromising tackling. At 5 feet 7 inches, he was not the most physically imposing figure in the half-back line, but his strength, fitness levels and sheer energy amply compensated for his lack of inches. Team-mate Ernie Curtis said of Keenor: 'He was one of the hardest tacklers in the game, some said he was dirty but he was just hard. Nobody took liberties with old Fred. He could run all night, he couldn't run with the ball mind you.'

The son of a bricklayer, Keenor was born in Cardiff in 1894 and, after making his name in schoolboy football, was snapped up by Cardiff City at the age of 17, first as an amateur before quickly turning professional for a weekly wage of 10 shillings. No sooner had he begun to establish himself in the first team than war broke out. Keenor served in the 17th Middlesex Battalion (the Footballers' Battalion), where a sergeant-major told him he was the worst rifle marksman he had ever seen. His inability to shoot straight would spill over into his football career. Wounded at the Somme, his prospects of returning to the sporting arena looked slim but he recovered and, after working on a milk round following demobilisation, he was able to rejoin Cardiff City when professional soccer started up again in 1919.

Keenor wasted little time in rebuilding his strength and in that same year sparred with the former European featherweight boxing champion, Jim Driscoll. Being fond of a beer and a smoke, Keenor had to train harder than most, so while his team-mates were concentrating on their ball skills, Keenor could be seen doing lap after lap of the Ninian Park pitch in a pair of old army boots, just to work off the previous night's ale.

The 1920s saw Cardiff develop into one of the strongest teams in the land. Promoted to the First Division in 1921, they missed out on the League title three years later to Huddersfield by a fraction of a goal (position, in those days, being decided on goal average as opposed to goal difference). They reached the FA Cup final in 1925, going down narrowly to Sheffield United, before gloriously making amends in 1927 with a single-goal success at the expense of Arsenal. Keenor, the local boy made good, was at the very heart of City's rise. Charles Buchan, the defeated Arsenal captain, was moved to describe him as having 'a store of energy which seemed inexhaustible in defending his goal and supplying his forwards with crisp passes'. A chronicler of the time said Keenor was 'a leader in every sense of the word, he commands respect of colleagues and sets an inspiring example by his whole hearted enthusiasm'.

His leadership qualities were also recognised at international level. He won his first cap in 1920, helping Wales to the British International Championship, a feat they repeated in 1924 and 1928, even though many English clubs were reluctant to release players for these games. Indeed, the side that faced Scotland in Glasgow in 1930 was tagged 'Keenor and the 10 unknowns' because it was composed chiefly of players from minor leagues. Yet thanks largely to Keenor's drive and relentless encouragement, which was so forceful that he was almost sent off for swearing at his own team-mates, the Welsh snatched a 1-1 draw. The 1929 fixture between the two nations had witnessed another demonstration of Keenor's remarkable bravery. He injured his neck on the morning of the match but, with Wales unable to call up a replacement in time, Keenor agreed to play with his neck strapped. Under strict instructions not to head the ball, he endured the pain for the sake of his country.

In common with most of soccer's hard men, Keenor's popularity among his own supporters was not replicated with opposing fans. He was constantly booed during games and, while playing for Crewe Alexandra towards the end of his career, he was assaulted at the end of one match then followed to the train station. Eventually he needed a police escort to guarantee his safety. He not only put the fear of God into the opposition, but sometimes into his own team-mates too. When Tom Farquharson, the Cardiff goalkeeper, was lobbed from the half-way line in a Cup tie against Blackpool, Keenor showed his displeasure by running back and shaking him violently. In his later years with the club, he became increasingly belligerent, forever involved in altercations with staff and players.

In the wake of the Cup triumph, Cardiff's decline was swift and four years later Keenor found himself captain of a team relegated to the Third Division (South). He had always prided himself on his bond with the club's fans – strengthened by the column he put his name to in the matchday programme. Even though he was by now well paid for running the midfield, he was still viewed by the thousands who poured into Ninian Park on a Saturday afternoon as very much their Fred, a working-class hero. Whereas others departed for richer pickings in England, Keenor remained loyal to his hometown club – but City were keen to trim the wage bill and the ageing Keenor was top of the list. In 1930 they told him he would have to take a £2-a-week wage cut, probably half-hoping that he would demand a transfer, thereby enabling them to offload him without angering the fans. To the club's surprise, Keenor agreed to the pay cut, but the parting of the ways was drawing ever nearer.

Keenor's reserves of energy were seemingly exhausted, his old legs no longer able to cover every blade of grass on the pitch. The same fans who had worshipped him for so many years now held him partly responsible for the team's relegation from Division Two, and when he was released at the end of the 1930–31 season, there were few complaints in the local press. If he had been a horse, he would have been turned into glue; instead he went to Crewe.

There, he revived his career to the extent that he won another Welsh cap at the age of 38. As late as 1934, by which time he was nearly 40, Crewe chose not to announce that an injury would prevent Keenor from playing in a match, for fear of reducing the gate. On leaving Crewe, he became player-manager of Oswestry Town and then Tunbridge Wells, where he combined the role with a job as a poultry farmer. Then in 1937 he was admitted to hospital, suffering from diabetes, having managed to keep the disease a secret for some time. Keenor was still remembered with such fondness in South Wales that an appeal was launched, with a collection blanket being carried around Ninian Park by former players. He recovered sufficiently to return to Cardiff as a builder's labourer in the late 1950s. The hero had returned home, and when Fred Keenor died in 1972, the news made the front pages of the local newspapers. Ernie Curtis led the tributes. 'I would have liked to see him against today's fancy dans with their elbowing, shirt-pulling and poking out tongues,' said Curtis. 'Fred would have tackled them once – they wouldn't have come back for more.'

Brian Kilcline
The Killer

Brian Kilcline has been described as looking like a cross between Billy Connolly and a Viking, and it is certainly not difficult to picture him at the head of a longboat, leading his fellow warriors ashore for an evening of pillage. The long flowing hair, the moustache, the 6-foot 4-inch, 14-stone-plus frame all conspired to make Kilcline the most fearsome looking defender in Britain. If anything, his nickname of 'The Killer' seemed to understate his persona.

Forwards riled him at their peril. Ian Wright, who could certainly look after himself, said: '"Killer" was one of the most frightening defenders you'll ever come up against; he must have been about 20 feet tall with muscles on his breath, let alone his legs.' Wright's introduction to Kilcline came in a game between Crystal Palace and Coventry City. When Wright, a newcomer to the Palace side, jumped for the first time in the match, Kilcline clattered into him from behind with a force that Wright likened to a speeding juggernaut. Wright said: 'I flew – and that's the only word for it – about 20 yards, landed in a heap and looked up to see "Killer" with a little smile on his face as if to say, "Welcome to the real world, son."'

Kilcline had always been a big lad. At the age of 14 he was already 6 feet tall and he claims he had the beginnings of a beard! As a schoolboy his physical attributes were put to use in attack, but when he joined his local club Notts County as a 17-year-old in 1979, he was converted into a central defender. He was sold the positional switch with a message from one of the club staff: 'Try kicking them instead of letting them kick you.'

In 1981 the giant defender helped County gain promotion to the First Division and his performances earned him two England Under-21 caps. County's relegation in 1984 prompted Coventry manager Bobby Gould to splash out £60,000 to secure the services of Kilcline, who three years later led the team out at Wembley for the FA Cup final against Spurs. Injuring himself while making a typically forthright tackle on Gary Mabbutt, Kilcline had to be substituted a minute before the end of normal time but had the satisfaction of seeing his side win 3-2 in extra time. It was a limping Kilcline who led the players up the Wembley steps to receive the trophy for the first time in Coventry's history. Just as his proudest moment came in the FA Cup, so did his most humiliating when, just two years later, Coventry were knocked out of the competition by Sutton United.

In 1991 Kilcline joined newly promoted Oldham Athletic for £400,000 but stayed only a year before Kevin Keegan made 'Killer' his first signing in his bid to rejuvenate Newcastle United. Kilcline was immediately installed as club captain and Keegan subsequently went on record as saying that he was the most important player he had ever brought to Newcastle. Kilcline's tenacity in the tackle, aerial supremacy and willingness to stick his head in where it hurt made him a great favourite with the Geordie fans who were willing to overlook the occasional deficiency in the more artistic aspects of the game. Kilcline always looked as if he meant business; even on the coldest of Newcastle nights it is impossible to imagine him wearing gloves on the pitch.

In 1994 he joined Swindon Town for an ill-fated season in the top flight, and then dropped down the League with Mansfield Town and out of it altogether with Halifax Town. However, he managed to steer Halifax back into the Football League before finishing his career with Altrincham in 1999.

Kilcline, who once emerged without a scratch after writing off a Mercedes in a 120mph crash, admits that he used to live up to his image. 'When I started, I often had eight pints – and the rest – on a night out. One rule I had was not to get involved in punch-ups. There were plenty of morons wanting to take me on in pubs but I always walked away.' Drink can certainly make people behave irrationally, and what could be more irrational than wanting to challenge Brian Kilcline to a fight?

In 2002 he featured in arm-wrestling contests with ex-footballers on Sky and took part in abseiling and white-water rafting competitions with former players in Malaysia. Generally, however, he leads a quieter life, renovating houses in Holmfirth, the West Yorkshire town famous for the TV series *Last of the Summer Wine*. Nora Batty might finally have met her match.

Dave Mackay
A Born Fighter

Jimmy Greaves has said of his Tottenham colleague Dave Mackay: 'He was the greatest professional I ever played with. If ever he was missing from the Tottenham line-up, the rest of us had to work twice as hard to make up for it. We always used to say that Dave was on nodding terms with every blade of grass on the White Hart Lane pitch. He tore into opponents and he tore them apart. Playing against

Dave must have been like walking through a lion's cage wearing a three-piece suit made of sirloin!'

To anyone familiar with Sixties football, Dave Mackay was a true giant of the game, rarely mentioned in the press without the words 'square-jawed', 'barrel-chested', 'hard-tackling' or 'fearsome' appearing in close proximity. His name was a byword for courage, since he had recovered from breaking the same leg twice in the space of nine months, and for hard but fair play. When Dave Mackay tackled you, you stayed tackled; but he was never nasty and was never sent off in his entire career.

His sheer physical presence was awesome, yet he stood a modest 5 feet 8 inches tall. But that compact framework housed muscular thighs like tree trunks and a chest that was as broad as a barn door. One soccer writer noted: 'The man tackled like a granite avalanche, exuding a passionate will to win and apparently consumed by a devilish, ruthless relish for his work.' Another wrote: 'His tackling could have earned him a good living felling trees.' If Danny Blanchflower was the brains of that great Tottenham side, Mackay was its heart. From his favoured position of left-half, the combative Scot would drive his men forward, linking defence and attack, typically winning the ball, flicking a pass, then surging forward for the return. When he did come within sight of the opposition goal, that left foot could cause some damage, as he proved with a hat-trick against West Ham in 1962. He was also the pioneer of the long throw, possessing the ability to hurl the ball 40 yards into opponents' penalty areas.

However, Mackay was more than just a powerhouse. He had an exquisite touch, superb ball control and a range of precise passing. In training he used to astonish team-mates by volleying the ball continuously against a wall from 15 yards. And when he led the Spurs team out as captain, he would run on to the pitch, kick the ball high in the air, then control it perfectly on his instep. The routine sent out an instant message to the opposition: that Dave Mackay and his team were a class act.

Mackay was born in Edinburgh on 14 November 1934. A Scottish schoolboy international, he joined his local club Hearts from junior side Newtongrange Star, making his debut for the reserves in a 6-6 draw at Montrose. He stayed at Hearts for seven years, during which time he inspired the Tynecastle club to their first Scottish League title of the century and was voted Scottish Footballer of the Year in 1958.

He also progressed to the full international team (winning the first of his 22 caps), before Spurs manager Bill Nicholson snapped him up for £32,000 in 1959 after failing to land Swansea's Mel Charles. Nicholson admired Mackay's hugely competitive nature (there was no such thing as a friendly game of snooker to Dave), but even he questioned the player's approach in the latter stages of a 1960 FA Cup replay against Crewe. The first match had ended 2-2 but in the replay at White Hart Lane, Spurs romped to a 13-2 victory, and right to the final whistle Mackay was as committed as ever. Nicholson felt that for once Mackay could have taken his foot off the gas and told him so after the match. 'Dave,' said Nicholson, 'I don't expect to see you going in on tackles like that, risking injury to yourself and others, and getting booked or sent off. Anyone would have thought we were 10 goals behind not 10 goals up!' But Mackay could not play the game any other way.

Defeat was not part of Mackay's vocabulary and, being a fierce patriot, defeat in a Scotland shirt hurt even more. Jimmy Greaves acknowledged: 'Defeat was always painful for him – but defeat by England was worse than death.' So Mackay was devastated to be part of the Scottish side that lost 9-3 at Wembley in 1961. Afterwards Greaves asked Tottenham centre-forward Bobby Smith, who had been a member of the victorious England team, if he was going to rib Mackay on their return to White Hart Lane. 'I don't think so,' said Smith, himself no shrinking violet. 'I like my face the way it is.'

Fortunately, defeat was not something Mackay had to experience often at club level. He helped Spurs to their epic League and Cup double in 1961, followed by further success in the FA Cup in 1962 and the European Cup Winners' Cup in 1963, although he missed the European final because he was laid low by a severe stomach upset. It was a brave bug that dared to upset Dave Mackay. Then just when he appeared to be at the top of his game, his world came crashing down. Playing in a European tie against Manchester United at Old Trafford in December 1963, Mackay broke his left leg in a challenge with Noel Cantwell. The injury was so serious that the surgeon warned Mackay that he might never play again. But Mackay defied the odds and made his comeback in a reserve team game against Shrewsbury in September 1964, only to break the same leg again. A lesser man would have called it a day there and then. The papers had already prepared their career obituaries but Mackay's unquenchable spirit spurred him on. Team-mate Alan Mullery recalled: 'Sheer guts got him back. I used to see him gritting his teeth as he ran up and down the White Hart Lane terraces, pouring strength back into that left leg. It was like Everest to him.'

Mackay did make a second comeback but it was his continued concern for his leg that led to that famous clash with Leeds' Billy Bremner in 1966. Bremner kicked his Scottish team-mate on his newly healed left leg and Mackay reacted with uncharacteristic fury. 'He could easily have broken my leg for a third time,' said Mackay. 'I was enraged. For a couple of seconds, I lost my rag and was temporarily capable of breaking his neck in return. I grabbed him by the front of his shirt and lifted him from the ground. Our faces almost touched as his legs dangled in the air.' Tellingly, afterwards the pair went for a drink, and to this day, Mackay hates the famous photograph of that incident because he believes it wrongly depicts him as a bully.

Mackay's return was crowned the following year when he captained Spurs to victory in the FA Cup final. By now he was operating in a mainly defensive role, the years of patrolling the midfield having taken their toll. He began to feel ready for a fresh challenge. 'Spurs were no longer a great side,' he admitted, 'and frankly I felt I was no longer good enough to be able to do something about it.' In 1968 he was sold to Derby County for a knockdown £5,000 (in recognition of his service to Spurs). Derby's new young manager, Brian Clough, would later describe signing Mackay as the best day's work of his life – 'a bit like getting Laurence Olivier down to the village hall to act for 30 bob'.

Mackay formed an almost impregnable central defensive pairing with Roy McFarland and took Derby to the Second Division title in his first season at the Baseball Ground. His efforts were recognised when he shared the Footballer of the Year award for 1969 with Manchester City's Tony Book. In 1971 Mackay took up the challenge of becoming player-manager of Swindon Town. This was followed by a brief stint in charge of Nottingham Forest before he succeeded Clough at Derby in 1973. Mackay did not win any popularity polls in the East Midlands that winter. The Forest fans were livid that he had left them for their bitter rivals, while the Derby fans were angry because they wanted Clough back. Leaflets were handed out at home games, comparing the managerial records of

Clough and Mackay, and with good reason since in Mackay's first two months in charge, Derby failed to win a game and plummeted from third in the table to 15th. The writing appeared to be on the wall – all over the town in fact, and most of it read BBC ('Bring Back Clough'). Calls for Mackay's head intensified but he stood firm with characteristic fortitude and the team gradually turned the corner. The following season he took Derby to the League Championship. Clough was but a distant memory.

Following a poor start to the 1976 season, Mackay was dismissed (the newspaper headline 'Mackay sacked' featured in the TV comedy series *Porridge*). Subsequent spells in charge of Walsall, Kuwait, Doncaster Rovers and Birmingham City brought him only moderate success.

However, nothing can diminish Dave Mackay's standing as a player, a man who in 40 Cup finals at all playing levels never once finished on the losing side. His old Tottenham team-mate Cliff Jones put Mackay's strength in a nutshell: 'He was the ball-winner. You hardly ever saw him come out of a tackle without it.'

Roy McDonough
Red Card Roy

Even though the majority of his playing career took place in the 1980s, Roy McDonough was very much an old-fashioned centre-forward – a throwback to the days of the Fifties and Sixties when robust strikers used strength and aggression to scare the life out of the opposition. Players such as George Kirby and Pat Terry were commonplace in the lower divisions, using their arms, shoulders, elbows and a fearsome heading ability to batter centre-halves and goalkeepers into submission. McDonough was from a similar mould. 'I'm not the sort who'll hurt people on purpose,' he once said, 'but if it gets a bit naughty, it brings out the best in me.'

It also brought out the beast in him, as he was sent off no fewer than 21 times in his career (which is believed to be some sort of record), including 13 in English League football. But whereas other hard men were at least revered by their own club's fans, if not by the opposition's, McDonough sometimes managed to alienate both sets of supporters. At Southend (208 games and six sendings-off), he was described as a love-hate figure, but that made him a positive god compared to the treatment he received during a brief spell as player-manager of Chelmsford City. He was so unpopular at Chelmsford that when he scored for them in a Cup replay against Heybridge, he was actually booed by his own fans!

Born in Solihull in 1958, McDonough made only two appearances for Birmingham City before joining neighbours Walsall in 1978. The 6-foot 1-inch striker's next port of call was Colchester United, where he remained for three years, scoring 24 times in 88 appearances. In 1983 he moved to Southend, followed by short spells at Exeter City and Cambridge United before returning to Roots Hall in 1985 where he played the bulk of his football…that is, when he was not suspended.

By now his disciplinary record ensured that he was a marked man in the eyes of referees. His reputation went before him and could probably count itself lucky that McDonough didn't scythe it down from behind. Most chairmen would have given him a wide berth but in 1990 he was appointed player-manager of Colchester in succession to his pal Ian Atkins. Colchester had just been relegated to the Conference and McDonough was seen as the type of determined character needed to help the club regain Football League status. In 1992 he did just that, winning not only the Conference but also the FA Trophy, despite spending just £1,000 on players.

The Conference that season was an acrimonious affair, developing into a two-horse race between McDonough's Colchester and Martin O'Neill's Wycombe Wanderers. The seeds of loathing were sown as early as September when Colchester won 2-1 at Wycombe thanks to a last-minute wind-assisted kick from their goalkeeper Scott Barrett. The ball sailed over the head of his opposite number, Paul Hyde, and into the net. The match had been marred by crowd trouble with Colchester hooligans allegedly attacking children in the Wycombe end. McDonough did little to ease the tension afterwards and was quoted as saying: 'It takes two to fight, one to punch, the other to stand there and be punched.' McDonough decided that if it came down to psychological warfare, he was going to be armed to the teeth. 'The rivalry between us was strong,' he admits. 'I made a couple of remarks in the local paper saying they would bottle it and they got back to Martin who called me and wanted to know why I was winding people up. In December we beat them 3-0 at home and when we were 3-0 up with 20 minutes to go, the ball went out and a ball boy threw it back to me. I looked at Martin on the bench and shouted to my players, "No more goals, let's play keep-ball." We must have strung nearly 30 passes, and Martin knew then we were taking the piss. The following week we played Wycombe again in the Bob Lord Trophy, which was a Mickey Mouse competition. So I played myself as sweeper and put the defenders up front. Wycombe won 6-2 and the Conference wanted to fine me £500, but they couldn't because I had played my first team...merely out of position. We made it to the FA Trophy final that year as well and Martin was the commentator for Sky. He called me an arrogant so-and-so on live TV.'

Keeping the war of words going to the bitter end, McDonough reportedly declared that his team could turn up in fancy dress and still beat Barrow in their final Conference game. In the event, United wisely chose to keep their normal strip and won 5-0 to pip Wycombe to the title on goal difference. Not surprisingly, the animosity between the two clubs continued when Wycombe followed Colchester into the Football League a season later. When they met at Wycombe in a Third Division encounter in 1993–94, the Adams Park faithful had not forgotten Roy McDonough. He says: 'We beat them 5-2 and I put a left-footer in the top corner. Afterwards I waved goodbye to the Wycombe fans, who were going mental, and Alan Parry, the TV commentator who is a director there, tried to get me arrested for starting a riot.'

Yet Wycombe were to have the last laugh. They won promotion that season while all McDonough got was the sack. Nevertheless, he remains something of a cult hero at Layer Road, not only for leading the club back into the League but also because he was rumoured to be able to drink a pint of lager while standing on his head.

After making nearly 500 Football League appearances and falling four short of a century of goals, McDonough drifted through the lower leagues, turning out for Dagenham & Redbridge, Canvey Island and Braintree Town. In May 1996 McDonough took charge at Chelmsford, but following mounting criticism from fans, he and the club soon parted company. In April 1998 he became player-manager with Ryman League side Heybridge Swifts, but he was dismissed six months later and went on to combine scouting with his job as a car salesman.

Roy McDonough was even a firebrand as a spectator. Watching his brother play in a fiercely contested Sunday League match, he took exception to a challenge on his sibling and ran on to the pitch to take issue with the opposing centre-half. His intervention sparked a 22-man – or rather, 23-man – brawl, which led to the referee abandoning the match. Afterwards, Ian Atkins tried to smooth the troubled waters and apologise for McDonough's behaviour. McDonough says: 'Ian went to see the referee in his room and said, "I'm ever so sorry, ref, he comes to watch us every so often." The ref looked at him and said: "Bollocks, I know who he is – that's Roy McDonough. He's a raving lunatic."'

Stuart Pearce
Controlled Aggression

For many, it was the defining moment of Euro '96. England's quarter-final against Spain had gone to a penalty shoot-out and walking up to the spot was Stuart Pearce, whose saved kick six years earlier had led to England's heartbreaking exit from the World Cup. Everyone remembered the tears that Pearce – one of the hard men of English football – had shed that night in Italy, and they knew of the pain he had endured since. As he placed the ball on the spot, a nation held its breath, silently praying that he would finally be able to exorcise the memory of that semi-final with Germany. We need not have worried. Summoning all the strength at his disposal, Pearce ran up and lashed the ball low into the bottom corner of the net. The Spanish keeper dived the right way but had no chance. Even if he had got in the way, the sheer force of the kick might conceivably have propelled him to Wembley Park station. The relief was instant. Arms pumping, eyes bulging, veins throbbing, Pearce turned to the crowd, bellowing defiance and encouragement. 'Psycho' was back.

The fact that he volunteered to take that kick speaks volumes for the man. The pressure on him was enormous, but he wanted to do it – partly for his own peace of mind but chiefly for his country. Few players have worn the Three Lions with greater pride. Furthermore, he repeated the feat four days later in the ultimately unsuccessful semi-final against Germany. Pearce recalled: 'Barry Davies said on the commentary, "What a penalty! What a great penalty!" It was not a great penalty, it was a shit penalty, but the goalkeeper had gone the wrong way.'

Pearce has always been the most unassuming of heroes. When he first joined Nottingham Forest, he still advertised as an electrician in the club programme, just in case he ever needed the work. It was the same with the 'Psycho' nickname: he never took it seriously. When his daughter's soft toy briefly brought him luck in his job as Manchester City manager in the autumn of 2006, she asked whether Beanie the Horse could sit next to him on the touchline in future matches. Pearce explained patiently: 'It's difficult to tell a seven-year-old that this is the Premiership and that I'm known as Psycho, I'm a hard man.'

Given that Brian Clough was his manager for much of his club career, it is hardly surprising that Pearce's feet remained firmly on the ground. When Pearce was called into the England squad for the first time, Clough told him with characteristic bluntness that he was not good enough to represent his country. Pearce did not throw his toys out of the pram; instead he just set about proving Clough wrong... 78 times over.

Born in Hammersmith, London, in 1962, Pearce's early career gave little hint of a glorious future. Rejected by Queens Park Rangers, he turned down an offer from Hull City, preferring instead to work as an electrician and plumber while playing non-League football for Wealdstone. Pearce had always been able to look after himself. A schoolmate at primary school remembers him suffering a nasty gash to his head on the playing field and calmly walking back to class with blood pouring everywhere. And so it proved on the football pitch, with the result that Wealdstone's raw, rugged left-back was soon attracting attention from bigger clubs. Coventry manager Bobby Gould went to watch him on a miserable night at Yeovil. 'After eight minutes,' recalled Gould, 'he put in a thundering tackle and the Yeovil winger landed in my wife's lap. I said to her: "That's it. I've seen enough. We're going home.'" Shortly afterwards Gould paid £30,000 (a lot of money for a non-League player in 1983) to take Pearce to Highfield Road. Pearce stayed at Coventry for two years before Clough took him to Forest, ironically as the makeweight in a £300,000 deal that also included City centre-back Ian Butterworth. The latter struggled at the City Ground but Pearce spent 12 years there, becoming club captain and a huge favourite with the fans who christened him 'Psycho', partly because of a perceived physical similarity to Norman Bates but also because the tag suited his aggressive style of play.

Pearce would listen to his favourite punk rock music in the dressing room before a match and then take to the field baying for blood. Occasionally he overstepped the mark, but for the most part he played within the laws of the game. Whether it was charging up the left wing like a train or thundering home a free-kick, he could do no wrong in the eyes of Forest supporters. When he scored (and he did so 63 times in 401 League games for Forest), there was no choreographed celebration routine or daft dancing, just a stony-faced expression. As Terry Venables once said of him: 'He's got one hell of a lot of aggression inside him – but it's all under control.' The one time he allowed his emotions to pour forth at a goal was following the first penalty at Euro '96, but that was entirely understandable.

His relationship with Clough was interesting. In his early days at the club, Pearce used to do electrical repair jobs for the manager, who would regularly bring in something from home that needed mending. But he was never intimidated by Clough and when a contract dispute dragged on, he was strong enough to snub the manager for months – something nobody else at the club would have dared to do. Clough's bully-boy tactics reduced most players to nervous wrecks in his presence; Pearce was an exception. Despite his loyal service to Forest, all Pearce had to show at the end of it were a couple of League Cups and a Simod Cup. In fact, he was always one of football's nearly men. When he made his England debut against Brazil in 1987, he was the 999th player to receive an England cap, and as a 39-year-old in his last-ever match, he missed two penalties for Manchester City, thus leaving him stranded on a career goals total of 99.

And of course he nearly appeared in a World Cup final, only for Germany's Bodo Illgner to save his penalty at Italia '90. No matter that Chris Waddle's subsequent missed penalty was far worse or that Peter Shilton did not exactly cover himself in glory with his attempts to stop the Germans – Pearce was inconsolable because he believed he had let his country down. As the players left the pitch, Thomas Berthold asked him to swap shirts. 'Not here,' said Pearce. 'I'll do it in the dressing room, but I'm not walking off this pitch with a German shirt on.'

At the 1992 European Championships, Pearce again proved himself a model professional and master of self-restraint. Despite being head-butted by France's Basile Boli – a blow that left blood pouring from Pearce's face – he did not retaliate. Instead, after having his face cleaned up, he planned to exact revenge via the free-kick. Alas, he crashed it against the bar and France survived. His face swelled up but he still refused to 'grass' on Boli, claiming the collision was accidental. Boli later faxed a letter of thanks to him. Even a lorry was unable to crush Stuart Pearce. It crushed his car, but Pearce climbed out of the wreckage and simply walked away.

When the Italians complained bitterly about Pearce's roughhouse tactics in the 1997 international friendly tournament *Le Tournoi*, he simply told them: 'I don't do friendlies.'

Pearce left Forest that year to join Newcastle before finishing his career with first West Ham and then Manchester City. He broke his leg twice in six months in his later years, the second time for West Ham against Southampton in March 2000. Typically, he refused to be stretchered off and limped to the Upton Park medical room, where X-rays confirmed that his left leg was broken. Two serious injuries in such a short space of time would have finished many younger players but the old warhorse battled back.

After briefly tasting the manager's life as caretaker at Forest in the mid-1990s (when in his first team selection his wife pointed out that he had forgotten to include a goalkeeper), Pearce was keen to try his hand again and got his chance at Manchester City in 2005. His honesty won respect but not enough games, with the result that he was sacked in 2007.

His predecessor at City, Kevin Keegan, marvelled at the way Pearce's enthusiasm for the game remained undiminished right up to the very end of his playing career. 'Two days after a hamstring strain that would have kept anyone else out for a fortnight, on a freezing day when we were all training in bobble hats and gloves, he emerged, running out of the mist, wearing nothing but a pair of underpants and a towel wrapped round his head. That's why they call him Psycho.'

Tommy Smith
The Iron Man of Anfield

Before a League game at Anfield, a fan threw a piece of raw meat on to the pitch at Tommy Smith's feet. Smith looked suitably mystified until the fan shouted: 'It's just to make sure yer get fed!' Smith always had the image of being a caged animal and when he went out on to the pitch, he did little to dispel it, crunching into tackles with little regard for life or limb, particularly those of his opponent. Of all the hard men around in football at the time, Smith looked the least advisable to upset; with his craggy face and steely expression, he made Chelsea's Ron 'Chopper' Harris look like a choirboy.

He certainly had the respect of his peers. Jack Charlton, another player you would not want to meet on a dark night, said: 'Tommy Smith was easily the hardest player I faced. I ran into him once and he knocked every ounce of breath out of me. I tried to get up and look like he hadn't hurt me, but he had.' Meanwhile, Manchester United's Martin Buchan acknowledged: 'With 11 Tommy Smiths you would not only win the European Cup, you would fancy your chances against the whole Russian Army.'

And when the old Everton hero Dixie Dean had a leg amputated and went to a rehabilitation centre where there were a dozen patients without limbs, he asked the physiotherapist: 'Blimey, has Tommy Smith been let loose in here?'

Smith admitted at the end of his career that he spent 12 months building a tough-guy reputation and 12 years trying to live it down. He recalled a conversation following a reserve game at Anfield against Preston that was part of his rehabilitation from injury. 'I was approached by a chap and his wife as I left the ground. I asked if I could help them and they simply thanked me for not kicking their son. He had been playing inside-left for Preston. It showed the value of reputation. I'd had absolutely no intention of doing anything to this kid but my reputation had obviously not only got to him but to his parents as well.'

Smith claims that he was hard but fair, presumably in the same way that Vlad the Impaler was hard but fair. Some of his opponents might care to disagree with this assessment, not least Everton's Roy Vernon who was clattered by Smith in the opening minutes of a Merseyside derby and sidelined for several weeks as a result. Prior to the game, Liverpool manager Bill Shankly had identified Vernon as the major threat to his side. Shankly was quick to exploit Smith's reputation, reinforcing it whenever possible with one-liners such as 'Tommy Smith could start a riot in a graveyard.' It let opponents – particularly those from the south – know that they would be in for a hard game and often gave Liverpool a psychological advantage before the team had even set foot on the pitch. Smith explains: 'Shankly would always be looking for whatever it was that would give us the edge. In those days reputation was a big thing. If you could win a game before you went out, win it. Some players were good dribblers, others good headers, I was a hard tackler, and I used it to gain that edge that Shanks was looking for.'

The ploy worked, causing opponents to tread warily when within snapping distance of Smith. Jimmy Greaves recalled his pleasure at winning a 50-50 challenge with him, only to be warned by a Koppite: 'You'll wish yer hadn't done that, Greavsie. Now Tommy's going to eat yer for dinner!' Greaves admitted: 'He didn't get the chance. I gave him a wide berth for the rest of the match.'

As the legend grew, so did the stories. One surrounds George Best's first appearance at Anfield. Best liked to let the hard men know he was no pushover and decided to make his presence felt by clattering Smith.

'If you do that again,' said Smith, 'I'll break you in half.'

Best turned to the referee: 'Did you hear what he just said?'

'Yes,' replied the ref, 'but I think he's talking to you.'

The story may be apocryphal but it illustrates Smith's standing in the game. His tongue could be as sharp as his tackling and he frequently indulged in verbal spats with referees, which led to the majority of his bookings. Curiously, he was never sent off, but then again, referees did tend to be more lenient in the Sixties. Nowadays he would probably miss half of the season through suspension.

Smith was born within spitting distance of Anfield on 5 April 1945 and, contrary to Shankly's assertion that 'Tommy was never a boy – he was born a man', he starred in local schoolboy teams. When he was 15, his mother took him to Anfield and told Shankly to take good care of her son. Smith remembers one of his first steps in football education. 'I was playing in a five-a-side game at the Liverpool training ground. I nutmegged Gerry Byrne and scored, and I was on top of the world. A couple of minutes later a ball dropped between us, I went to head it and Gerry headed me and I went down with a gashed eye. As I lay on the ground covered in blood, Bill Shankly strolled across, looked down at me and said: "Lesson number one, never nutmeg Gerry Byrne, son, and think you can get away with it!"'

The incident taught Smith the value of reputation, although in his early years he was a forward rather than an iron-man defender. He made his first-team debut in the final game of the 1962–63 season but did not fully establish himself in the side until 1965, when Shankly decided to baffle opponents by putting him in the number 10 shirt while instructing him to play at the back. That year, he was a key member of the Liverpool team that lifted the FA Cup – the first of a host of club honours that would come his way, although he was only ever capped once by England. He was appointed Liverpool captain in 1970 and retained it for three years until he fell out with Shankly after being dropped from the starting XI. The two men patched up their differences and Smith was a member of the team that beat Newcastle in the 1974 FA Cup final. The occasion was particularly satisfying for Smith, as earlier in the season Malcolm Macdonald had scored a hat-trick for Newcastle against Liverpool at St James' Park. Macdonald had to be carried off later in that game following a collision with Liverpool keeper Ray Clemence and as he left the field on a stretcher, Smith walked over to him and growled: 'Right, that's yer lot, you'll never score another goal against Liverpool while I'm on the same pitch.' Smith was as good as his word. Despite Macdonald boasting about how he was going to destroy Liverpool in the final, he barely had a sniff of goal and Liverpool won 3-0 in a canter.

With three League Championship and two UEFA Cup winners' medals to his name, Smith announced that the 1976–77 season would be his last. It started with him being left out of the side for several months, but ended with his greatest triumph. Having already clinched another League title, Liverpool reached the final of the European Cup against Borussia Moenchengladbach, and Smith powered home a header from Steve Heighway's corner for Liverpool's second goal in their 3-1 victory. Smith had a superstition before every big game whereby he wrapped his false teeth in a strip of bandage and handed them to trainer Ronnie Moran. He would then collect them at the final whistle to avoid looking too scary in photographs. At the end of that European final in Rome, Moran was pictured hoisting Smith in the air. Everybody thought the expression on Smith's face was one of jubilation but he was actually saying to Moran: 'Put me down, you big soft bugger. I want me bloody teeth!'

After that memorable night, Smith decided to play on for one more season, but in 1978 (having made 633 appearances and scored 48 goals for Liverpool) he joined Swansea City for the curtain call on his career, helping the Swans to promotion from Division Three. His one regret was that, in his last year at Anfield, he missed out on the chance to be part of the team that retained the European Cup. Smith had been ruled out of contention a month before the final after dropping a hammer on his foot at home. In true Tommy Smith tradition, it is said that the hammer winced.

Nobby Stiles
The Unlikely Lad

While the Luftwaffe were bombing Manchester on 18 May 1942, a baby boy was born in the cellar of a terraced house in the city's Collyhurst district. Little could anyone have guessed that the infant, Norbert Peter Patrick Paul Stiles, would exact a glorious revenge on the Germans 24 years later.

Nobby Stiles, as the baby would become known to football followers throughout the world, was an unlikely hero. He had dreadful eyesight, wore dentures after losing his front teeth in a match, was small in stature at a time when clubs routinely rejected players for being too short, and as a toddler he was run over by a trolley bus. He was the human equivalent of a mole but his saving grace was that he could tackle like a tiger.

The son of an undertaker, Stiles played for England Schoolboys and in 1957 joined the team he supported, Manchester United, as an amateur. He cleaned the boots of his heroes – Duncan Edwards and Eddie Colman – and as a youth player vividly remembers sitting in the Old Trafford dressing room that afternoon in February 1958 when the trainer said that the team plane had crashed in Munich. At the time he thought that the injuries were probably only minor, but his mood changed when he saw the newspaper headlines. 'I felt sick. We'd been laughing about this crash back in the dressing room, saying maybe somebody had broken a leg, maybe the big chance had come for one of us.'

Stiles eventually made his senior debut in 1960 at full-back against Bolton Wanderers. With his simple but effective passing game and tenacious ball-winning skills, he was soon converted into a defensive midfielder whose job was to man-mark and stifle the opposition's most creative player. However, in his early years at Old Trafford his eyesight was so poor that he often lost players he was supposed to be marking and found that he was relying almost solely on guesswork when it came to timing the ball. He wore thick glasses off the pitch but obviously this was not an option on the field of play. For fear of losing his place in the team, Stiles did not admit to his problems until Harry Gregg, United's Northern Ireland goalkeeper, spotted that something was amiss on an away trip. The players were enjoying the usual game of cards, but Stiles kept putting down the wrong card. Gregg encouraged him to seek help, as a result of which Stiles decided to have contact lenses fitted. They were very much a novelty then and Stiles discovered that they were by no means perfect. 'One of the problems with contact lenses in that early stage of their development,' he said, 'was that after a while your eyes dried out with the lack of oxygen. I used to get rings around my eyes like a panda and if a match went into extra time I would have problems under the floodlights.'

These teething troubles manifested themselves in alarming fashion when Stiles was chosen to play for England Under-23s against Scotland in February 1965. He was so excited that in his rush to leave for Aberdeen, he forgot the fluid for his contact lenses. At half-time the England manager, Alf Ramsey, instructed him to sort out Charlie Cooke who had been causing England problems all evening. Stiles took the orders on board and early in the second half duly whacked his victim, leaving him lying in a crumpled heap. Mission accomplished thought Stiles…until Norman Hunter quietly informed him that he had taken out Billy Bremner by mistake.

As little more than a destroyer, Stiles was not everybody's idea of a natural contributor to the beautiful game. Placing him alongside Bobby Moore was like putting Pot Noodle next to the finest smoked salmon. Even his England team-mate Jack Charlton (not renowned for his ball skills himself) acknowledged: 'When it came to the more artistic side of the game, Norbert was not the kind of bloke to stand out in a crowd.' However, Ramsey's England was very much a functional machine and he saw the little Mancunian as a vital cog. So it was that Stiles found himself in England's 1966 World Cup squad, but the adventure nearly ended in tears. In England's final group game, Stiles brutally scythed down France's Jacques Simon directly in front of the royal box. Condemnation was instant. Vastly respected figures such as Joe Mercer, Billy Wright and Danny Blanchflower slaughtered Stiles, Mercer suggesting that the foul had brought shame to English football. The press weighed in, too, with only Jimmy Hill standing up for the player, saying that Stiles should not be criticised for one mistake. So concerned were FA chiefs about the effect on England's reputation for sporting fair play that they ordered Ramsey to leave Stiles out of the next game.

Ramsey called Stiles over during training and asked him about the tackle. 'Did you mean it?' asked Ramsey.

'Course not, Alf,' replied Stiles.

'That's good enough for me,' said Ramsey, and the matter was dropped.

Ever supportive of his players, Ramsey resisted all calls for Stiles's head and threatened to resign if he was not allowed to pick him. The FA caved in and Stiles played against Argentina at Wembley, where he was greeted by a banner reading 'Nobby For Prime Minister'. The nation had forgiven him. He made no attempt to tone down the on-field aggression. 'I played hard,' he says, 'but I also tried to operate on some kind of rough sense of justice.' Before the semi-final against Portugal, Ramsey instructed him: 'Put Eusebio out of the game.' To which Stiles responded: 'For tonight or for ever?'

Stiles maintained a curious ritual during that World Cup run. After England's opening win against Mexico, he insisted on wearing the same shirt, tie, shoes, socks and underpants every day around the training camp…although thankfully he did get them laundered. But it was for wearing an England shirt, performing that toothless jig, clutching the Jules Rimet Trophy in one hand and his dentures in the other, that he will always be remembered. Stiles, who had actually lost his false teeth in the Old Trafford mud during a match the previous year, says the famous victory dance was purely spontaneous. 'I don't know what I was thinking,' he laughs. 'I'm a bloody awful dancer anyway.'

Stiles's international form dipped after the World Cup and Ramsey did drop him the following year, but it was on the manager's own terms. He finished with 28 caps – the lowest total of any member of the triumphant 1966 team. But there was plenty of compensation at club level, with Stiles playing a key role in United's 1968 European Cup success against Benfica. Although he managed to shackle his old adversary, Eusebio, reasonably effectively in the final, it was his performance in the semi-final against Real Madrid that delighted the United fans and infuriated the Spanish. In the second leg at the Bernabeu, Stiles hammered Real star Amaro Amancio in an off-the-ball incident, as a result of which the man who had been causing United all manner of problems faded quietly from the action. Stiles was hit on the head by a bottle for his pains, but he knew that extreme fan reaction came with the territory when playing abroad. He was hissed and spat at in Italy and described as an assassin and a bandit in South America. United's World Club Championship first leg against Estudiantes of Argentina in Buenos Aires in 1968 was a particularly volatile occasion. After being pulled up for offside, Stiles moaned to Bobby Charlton that the referee was blind. When the referee ran over and asked him what he had said, Stiles turned to Charlton and said: 'He's fucking deaf as well!' Stiles was sent off for dissent and felt the full wrath of the Argentine crowd. Afterwards, as he emerged from the stadium into the dark night, he heard something thrust into his back and a voice whispering: 'Now then, El Bandido.' 'I thought my end had come,' admitted Stiles, 'until I realised it was Brian Kidd!'

After 392 matches and 19 goals for United, Stiles was sold to Middlesbrough for £20,000 in 1971. Two years later, he became player-coach at Preston during Bobby Charlton's brief tenure as manager. In 1977 Stiles himself was appointed manager at Deepdale, holding the post for four years before joining Vancouver Whitecaps as coach. In 1985 he returned to England as manager of West Bromwich Albion but was sacked five months later following a string of poor results. He later revealed how he had struggled with depression while in the job. In 2002 he suffered a heart attack on the eve of the World Cup, brought on, he believes, partly by his heavy smoking. As a manager, he once got through 40 cigarettes during a match.

More than 40 years after England's finest hour, Nobby Stiles is still recognised wherever he goes. 'Grandparents stop me in the street and tell their grandkids that this is the chap with no teeth on the telly with the World Cup.' Ah yes, the teeth. Even they were part of his World Cup superstitions. 'When I met the Queen before the opening game against Uruguay I kept my teeth in and I then gave them, wrapped in a handkerchief, to Ian Callaghan to take back to the dressing room. We drew 0-0 and we got panned by the press. I vowed after that if we got to the final there would be no way I'd wear my teeth. My wife has never forgiven me.'

Charlie Williams
The Trailblazer

An uncompromising centre-half for Doncaster Rovers, Charlie Williams was one of the first black players in British football after the Second World War. When his playing career ended, he entered the world of entertainment and enjoyed even greater success as the first black comedian in Britain to achieve nationwide fame on television, daringly making fun of his colour and delivering punchlines in his broad Yorkshire accent. Lenny Henry has cited Williams the comedian as one of his inspirations. Williams the footballer was equally inspirational, although appearing in front of an audience of 10,000 as opposed to 15 million made this a much better-kept secret. Yet enough Doncaster fans retained fond memories of Williams to vote him the club's all-time cult hero in the 2004 BBC *Football Focus* poll.

Charlie's father had come to England from Barbados in 1914 and had served with the Royal Engineers in the First World War. After the war he had settled in Royston, a small mining village near Barnsley, where he sold groceries from a horse and cart and married a local girl. Charlie was born in 1929 and on leaving school at 14, worked down the mines at Upton Colliery. He played football for the colliery team and after being spotted by scouts from Doncaster Rovers, he signed for the Belle Vue club in 1948. He made his first-team debut at home to Tranmere Rovers in a Third Division (North) fixture on 3 May 1950, but after that he remained in the reserves for over four years, not making his second senior appearance until the 1954–55 season. However, once he was given another chance, he seized it with both hands and firmly established himself in the team over the next four seasons, making 171 appearances and scoring one goal – in a local derby at Barnsley in March 1956. Among his team-mates was goalkeeper Harry Gregg, who went on to star for Manchester United and Northern Ireland.

'I suppose I made my mark,' reflected Williams in later years. 'We went from the Third Division (North) to the Second Division, and I'm not saying Donny were poor but the only automatic sprinkler we had for the pitch was the club cat! Football was a man's game and we got stuck into it. I recall playing at Bury in a rainstorm and the pitch was a quagmire. I said to the captain, "If you win the toss, stick with the tide!" We drew 4-4 so you can tell what kind of game it was.'

He continued: 'I wasn't a big man for a defender – 5 feet 11 inches, 11½ stone – but I was extremely fit. Summer months, I used to run miles on the road in a tracksuit for the sheer love of it. I was a hard player, although I wasn't dirty. I was never a fancy player but I could stop them buggers that were.'

Among 'them buggers' was Brian Clough, then a young centre-forward with Middlesbrough. Williams recalled: 'I stuck that close to Cloughie that he said, "If I go for a cup of tea will you follow me?" I told him, "I won't follow thee, lad, but I'll be waiting here for thee when tha comes back!"'

In January 1958 Doncaster were drawn at home to Chelsea in the FA Cup, a game the visitors eventually won 2-0. Williams remembered:

'I was up against young Jimmy Greaves that day. He twisted and turned me so many times, I came off that pitch suffering from spiral blood. And Ron Tindall hit a shot that was so powerful our goalkeeper caught pneumonia from the draught the ball created as it flew past him on its way into the net.'

As one of only a handful of black footballers, Williams was viewed as a novelty but he never responded to any racial abuse that was hurled at him from the terraces. 'Several times I heard the shout: "Get back to your own country, you big black bastard!" I had to laugh. It were only two pounds on t' train back to Barnsley!'

He was frequently referred to in the press as 'the coloured player' and strangely, when the 1956 *Encyclopedia of Association Football* was published, there was no mention of Williams even though he had been ever-present in the 1955–56 season.

After 12 years with Doncaster he was put on the transfer list and joined Skegness Town, where he actually found himself better off financially. At Doncaster he was paid £20 a week in the first team, whereas at Skegness he got £15 a week but he also took a job that paid him £10. Then in 1962 he was offered a job as player-coach with the Australian club Auburn, based near Sydney, but when the Australian immigration service saw from his passport that he was coloured, he was refused entry to the country. After the British press took up the story about someone born and bred in Yorkshire being barred, the Australian authorities had a sudden change of heart – but Williams told them what they could do with their offer.

Staying in England, he tried his hand as a singer in local clubs, only to discover that his comic patter between numbers went down better with the working-class audiences. Defusing racial tension, he would tell hecklers: 'If you don't shut up, I'll come and move in next door to you.' As his showbusiness career took off, he became one of the mainstays of the popular 1970s TV series *The Comedians* and also presented the ITV game show *The Golden Shot*. Awarded the MBE for his charity work, he died in September 2006, having suffered from Parkinson's disease for some time.

Charlie Williams never pretended to be a great player, but he relished the physical side of the game. And even when he was kicked where it hurt, he was still able to come up with a wisecrack. 'Don't rub 'em,' he told the trainer. 'Count 'em!'

SEVENTIES SWINGERS

Stan Bowles
Gambling Man

Crewe manager Ernie Tagg once famously remarked: 'If Stan Bowles could pass a betting shop like he can pass a ball, he'd have no worries at all.' In truth, Bowles's carefree approach to the game and to life in general ensured that he never did have any worries – he left the worrying to the poor defenders who were trying to mark him and to the equally long-suffering managers who were trying to keep control of him. He was so laid-back as to be almost comatose, and his brilliance on the pitch was matched only by his chaotic lifestyle off it. When it came to getting himself and the people around him into another fine mess, Stan Bowles was on a par with Stan Laurel.

Bowles was born in the Manchester district of Collyhurst on Christmas Eve 1948 and began his career with Manchester City. He has since claimed that he was never really in love with football, that it was simply something that his father had pushed him into. This would certainly explain his sometimes lackadaisical approach and an apparent determination to ruffle as many feathers as possible. At Maine Road he became embroiled in a series of off-the-field incidents, one of which ended in a brawl with manager Malcolm Allison, never a wise man to pick a fight with. Therefore it came as no surprise when, in 1970, after three years and just 17 first-team games for City, Bowles was released.

He joined Bury but lasted only five games and looked destined to drift out of the professional game. Luckily, Crewe boss Ernie Tagg was prepared to give Bowles one last chance to show what he could do. Tagg was a shrewd operator who knew that Bowles enjoyed a flutter (Stan reckons he became hooked on gambling at the age of 15 after winning £24) and the manager even took the precaution of paying Bowles's wages directly to his wife, Ann, before Stan could fritter the money away at the bookies. Bowles repaid him with some dazzling performances, which were clearly way above Fourth

Division standard, and after scoring 18 times for Crewe in 51 games, he was signed by Second Division Carlisle United for £12,000. He proved equally successful at Brunton Park (12 goals in 33 appearances) and in September 1972 his form prompted Queens Park Rangers to fork out £110,000 for his services. Loftus Road was to become his spiritual home.

At Rangers he replaced local hero Rodney Marsh, who, ironically, had been transferred to Manchester City (Bowles's old club) six months earlier. Nobody at QPR wanted to wear the number 10 shirt made famous by Marsh but Bowles had no such qualms, claiming that because he hailed from the north, he had never even heard of Marsh! The yarn bears all the hallmarks of one of Stanley's wind-ups.

Bowles was very much in the Marsh mould: an individualist, a flair player with an abundance of skill but not necessarily someone to be relied upon in the trenches. With his long hair, his deceptively languid style and his shirt hanging out of his shorts, he was every inch a cult hero. He was no respecter of reputations on the pitch but was sometimes grateful to call upon rugged team-mate Dave Webb, who acted as his 'minder' and could be relied on to sort out any opponent that had clattered Rangers' gifted inside-forward. Bowles had more tricks than Paul Daniels, including one that he copied from Marsh, whereby he would win a free-kick by tripping himself up. As it was always done side-on, the referee could never spot that it was a con. 'If you managed to do it right,' says Bowles, 'it looked as though you had been cut in half.' He made up other tricks as he went along, knowing full well that he had the backing of the Loftus Road crowd, who were appreciative of a true entertainer. 'The thing about the QPR fans,' revealed Bowles in a 2004 interview, 'was that if the tricks went wrong, I would hold my hands up, but they would blame somebody else anyway!' Whenever he scored a special goal, he would conduct the applause from the crowd. 'I regarded the crowd as an audience who wanted me to go out and perform for them.' He rarely failed to give value for money.

Opposition fans did not always appreciate his antics. In May 1973, four days after winning the FA Cup, Sunderland entertained QPR in a Second Division match, and the famous trophy was placed on a table by the side of the pitch. At the first chance he got, Bowles set off on a horizontal run and blasted the ball at the Cup, sending it flying through the air. It turned out that he and some of his team-mates had a bet on who could hit the trophy first. The Sunderland crowd did not see the funny side and were even more aggrieved when Bowles scored twice.

His cheek was staggering. During one home game, he was defending the near post at a corner when he spotted someone in the crowd behind the goal holding a copy of the *Sporting Life*. Keen to check whether a horse he had backed was running that afternoon, he grabbed the paper and began thumbing through it, much to the amusement of the crowd. As the corner was swung in, he headed the ball away while still clutching the paper in one hand. Furthermore, Rangers went straight up to the other end and scored.

Along with women, horse racing was Bowles's great passion, although he was usually more successful with the two-legged fillies than the four-legged variety. He claims to have lost £18,000 on the horses in one day. QPR team-mate Frank McLintock said: 'You would seldom see Stan in the dressing room before 2.30. He was usually in the local bookies looking at the 2.30 race.' Bowles had the uncanny knack of being able to wander into the dressing room 10 minutes before kick-off (having watched the 2.45 race), get changed and score in the first minute. He could turn it on just like that – he never needed a team talk. 'I was never nervous before a game,' he says. 'I could play in front of 50,000 people or in front of 15, it didn't bother me. Yet Frank McLintock and David Webb – who had won everything – would be in the dressing room an hour and a half before kick-off being physically sick. I never understood why people got there so early. All you have to do is put your kit on and tie your shoe laces.'

QPR chairman Jim Gregory was eager to keep his greatest asset happy and would sometimes give Bowles cash to cover his gambling debts. By the end of the player's seven-year stay at Loftus Road, Gregory was handing Bowles an extra £200 a week on top of his wages. 'It was my betting money,' said Bowles, 'so it went straight to the bookie.' When team-mate Don Masson, a Scottish international, heard about the extra payment, he demanded the same but Gregory rejected it out of hand, saying: 'You can't play like Bowlesy.'

Bowles was the focal point in Rangers' greatest ever team, the one that under manager Dave Sexton finished League runners-up in 1975–76. His form also earned him five England caps but predictably his international career stalled with Don Revie at the helm. A free spirit such as Bowles was never going to be Revie's sort of player. Bowles attempted to cash in on his soaring status with sponsorship deals, and when Gola and Adidas offered him big money to wear their boots in a match, he decided to appease both parties by wearing odd boots! Gola were offering £200 and Adidas £250, so by wearing both he hoped to make £450. However, when the firms discovered what Bowles was up to, they were not happy and his masterplan was dropped.

Despite his success at QPR, he regularly threatened to quit. By his own estimation he made more than 30 transfer requests but had usually forgotten about them two days later. Short of money in April 1975, he came up with another money-making scheme and decided to announce his retirement from the game in the *Sunday People*. He pocketed the £500 for the article…then two days later announced that he was making a comeback!

There were plenty of off-field scrapes. He and his pal Don Shanks (then with Luton Town) were once wrongly arrested for being in possession of a stolen van. When Bowles appeared in court, the QPR fans in the gallery gave the familiar chant of 'Stanley! Stanley!' He and Shanks were also arrested during Rangers' 1977 pre-season tour of Belgium after getting drunk. His gambling habit was at the root of many of his problems. QPR captain Gerry Francis recalled in Bowles's entertaining autobiography: 'I was invited to his house for a meal one evening after training. Ann cooked a beautiful meal, and we all sat down at the table. Just as we started eating, a knock came on the front door. In came the bailiffs and took the television, three-piece suite, dining-room table and chairs, and anything else they could lay their hands on. We ended up with the dinner on our laps, with no furniture left in the room. You never knew from one day to the next what was going to happen with Stan.'

After 70 goals in 255 appearances with QPR, Bowles joined Brian Clough's Nottingham Forest in 1979 for £250,000. It was always going to be an interesting clash of personalities and they got off on the wrong foot when Clough, in his usual arrogant manner, told him: 'You Cockneys are all the same.' When Bowles pointed out that he actually came from Manchester, Clough was not pleased. Nobody corrects God. From then on, his days were numbered and Bowles departed after just 19 games. At least one person at the City Ground appreciated Bowles's talents, centre-half Larry Lloyd remarking: 'Stan could sell a dummy better than Mothercare.'

He dropped a division with a £100,000 move to Leyton Orient in 1980 and a season later he was down in the Third Division with Brentford, where he stayed until calling time on his professional career in 1984.

Stan Bowles was an anti-hero. When he took part in the TV show *Superstars* (purely for the appearance fee), he made little effort to compete and took great delight in getting the lowest points total ever. His high spot was the shooting event when, with live ammunition, he succeeded in shooting a hole in a table, forcing the instructor to run for cover.

Yet he had a knack of always managing to come up smelling of roses, even with the most tangled of love lives. When his former wife, Ann, took him to court over maintenance payments, he ended up being chatted up by the female clerk of the court. In his auto-biography he wrote: 'So, all of a sudden, I had my wife Ann trying to divorce me and claim maintenance; Jane – the girl I was living with – on at me to marry her; and now I had this clerk of the court in bed, urging me to leave both of them...My life has always been like that – a roller-coaster ride with no one operating the controls.'

Alan Hudson
Missed Opportunities

Alan Hudson is generally regarded as one of the most skilful players to have graced the English game in the past 40 years. An intelligent, creative passer of the ball with an abundance of skill and stamina, comfortable using either foot, he seemed to glide across the midfield at Stamford Bridge, even on the boggiest of pitches. With so much going for him, he ought to have been a permanent fixture in the national team, but instead he finished up with just two caps, courtesy of an ability to press the self-destruct button at precisely the wrong moment. In the final analysis, perhaps the fact that he managed to fall out with no fewer than three different England managers represents his greatest achievement. Certainly it is a more impressive statistic than his career record of a meagre 19 goals in 324 League games in England – and one of those should not have counted.

Born (in 1951) and raised near the King's Road, Hudson used to play football with his friends on a patch of waste land strewn with broken bottles and gravel, conditions that helped him acquire impeccable balance, not to mention courage. Nevertheless, he was rejected by Fulham as a schoolboy on the grounds that he was too small. Undeterred, he joined the Chelsea groundstaff at 15 but a mystery knee complaint sidelined him for six months. He finally made his senior debut in February 1969, Chelsea ending up on the wrong end of a 5-0 scoreline against Southampton.

It was in the following season that Hudson really established himself in a Chelsea side that was overflowing with charismatic, skilful players such as Charlie Cooke and Peter Osgood. 'We had a team at Chelsea that was a delight to watch,' says Hudson. 'The entertainment factor was always well worth the admission money and the skill factor was unbelievable at times. It was a pleasure to play in a team that allowed you freedom to express yourself with the ball. We were encouraged to play. There was never anything negative about our play – why should there be when we had individual skills to kill off any team?' At a time when the best teams in the land, Arsenal and Leeds, were not exactly renowned for demonstrating the virtues of free-flowing football, Chelsea were a breath of fresh air. They certainly had players who could mix it with the best – Ron Harris, Dave Webb, Eddie McCreadie, Ian Hutchinson, Osgood – but there was also a welcome flair, and Hudson slotted in perfectly, specialising in short, sharp passes as 'long passes are so much easier to defend because defenders have got time to see them coming'.

Chelsea finished third in the League in 1970, helped by a Hudson shot against Ipswich that brushed the side netting, hit the back stanchion and rebounded into play. Convinced that the ball had gone between the posts, referee Roy Capey insisted on awarding a goal, much to the amusement of the Chelsea players. Even Hudson tried to persuade him to disallow it, but Mr Capey was not for turning. Chelsea also lifted the FA Cup at the expense of Leeds, although Hudson missed the final through injury. He did, however, excel when the club won the European Cup Winners' Cup the following year.

Hudson's outstanding form caught the eye of Alf Ramsey, who selected him for the England squad for the 1972 home internationals. Bobby Moore had tipped him off that he would be playing against Northern Ireland, so when Ramsey read out the team and Hudson's name was not in it, the Chelsea man was bitterly disappointed. Also overlooked for the Scotland game, he felt that Ramsey had treated him poorly. Accordingly, when the manager phoned a week later asking him to go on an Under-23 tour of Eastern Europe, Hudson refused. As a result, he was banned from international football for a year.

Worse was to follow at club level when Hudson broke his right ankle following a terrible challenge from George Best. That evening at a nightclub Hudson bumped into Best and asked him why he had done it. Best explained that in a mêlée where legs were flying he had intended to exact retribution on his old adversary Ron Harris but had accidentally gone for the wrong leg. That was of little comfort to Hudson who missed three months of the season. To add insult to injury, on his return to the first team he was shifted by manager Dave Sexton from his favoured central midfield position to wide right. With the international ban still in force, Hudson's mood darkened. 'I felt I'd been stripped of everything,' he said. 'I dreaded every match. It was like knowing I was going to have toothache every Saturday.'

To numb the pain, he began drinking heavily. That Chelsea team had a reputation, built up over years of practice, for partying, so Hudson had plenty of role models. One day he would wake up and decide to have a vodka day, the next maybe a brandy day. Yet despite knocking back a bottle and a half of spirits, washed down by six pints of beer, he still shone at training, demonstrating both the stamina for cross-country and the speed for sprints. After a particularly long Sunday, he used to cry off sick for training on a Monday morning, whereupon his team-mates would find him in a pub at lunchtime. He later admitted: 'I just drank more and more to enjoy myself.'

Whilst being one of the most gifted coaches of his generation, manager Sexton was a taciturn, somewhat dour character who found himself increasingly at odds with the cavalier approach of Hudson and Osgood. Additionally, the building of the new West Stand at Stamford Bridge had cast a shadow of debt over the club, and by January 1974 the zest and vitality that had once made Chelsea FC a symbol of swinging London had been replaced by an air of brooding discontent. Matters came to a head after a game against West Ham, which Chelsea contrived to lose 4-2 despite being two goals up at half-time. Sexton felt that Hudson and Osgood's influence on the second half had been negligible and said that Hudson's breath stank of alcohol. Both men were placed on the transfer list and within two weeks Hudson was sold to Stoke City for £240,000.

Stoke boss Tony Waddington saw the 22-year-old playmaker as the man who could turn his struggling outfit into genuine title contenders and hoped that, away from the bright lights of London, there would be fewer off-field temptations. In Hudson's first practice match, before he had even been introduced to his new team-mates, Waddington handed him a green bib and simply told the rest of the first team: 'Whenever you get the ball, just give it to the green bib.' Hudson repaid his manager's confidence by recapturing his form and helping Stoke to fifth place in the League and a UEFA Cup spot.

The new England boss, Don Revie, was so impressed that he awarded Hudson his first cap. After producing a starring role in a 2-0 victory over world champions West Germany, Hudson kept his place for the 5-0 demolition of Cyprus, but just when things were looking up, the demon drink soured their relationship. Hudson disobeyed orders by going out drinking, and the disciplinarian Revie told him that he was not the sort of player he wanted in his squad. His international career was over almost before it had begun.

In 1976 Hudson was again sold to pay for a stand. The roof of Stoke's Butler Street Stand had blown off and Hudson was moved to Arsenal for £200,000 to pay for the repairs. Although he never really got on with manager Terry Neill, he helped Arsenal reach the 1978 FA Cup final, where they lost to Ipswich. His form resulted in a call from Revie's successor, Ron Greenwood, who wanted Hudson as a late replacement. Instead Hudson told him: 'I thought I should have been in the side anyway. I don't want to get picked just because you've got injuries.' It was the third England manager with whom he had fallen out. Drink may have been Hudson's worst enemy, but he himself ran it a close second.

The Cup final defeat was to prove his last game for Arsenal. On a pre-season tour of Australia, he was caught in breach of a drinks curfew and soon left Highbury to start afresh in the United States with Seattle Sounders. In those days decent players moved to the American

League only at the end of their careers, but Hudson was just 27. If he could have sorted himself out, he still had so much to offer the English game. He did make a nostalgic return to Stoke in 1983, helping them to avoid relegation from the top flight before retiring.

His chequered lifestyle continued away from the game. As well as the drinking, he was declared bankrupt and in 1997 sustained serious injuries (spending two months in a coma) after being hit by a car. He was not expected to walk again but fortunately this one chapter in his life story had a happy ending and he recovered, albeit with a limp. Bobby Moore once said: 'Alan Hudson could have conquered the world, but there was no guarantee he was going to conquer his temperament.' That pretty much sums up the man who not only epitomised the spirit of the Seventies but also drank it.

Rodney Marsh
That's Entertainment

R odney Marsh was one of the game's great mavericks – a free spirit with the ability to delight and frustrate in equal measures. He possessed all the skills and more, and had the cheek and supreme self-confidence to support his unquestionable ability. Whenever he received the ball, there was a buzz of anticipation among the crowd. Would it be a drag-back, a nutmeg, a dummy or something else from his box of tricks? Would he run at defenders in that deceptively languid way of his, leaving them looking foolish as they tackled thin air, wrong-footed by a sudden shimmy? Or would he simply disappear down a cul de sac of his own making, leaving better-placed team-mates shaking their head in despair?

His Queens Park Rangers manager Alec Stock, a shrewd judge of a footballer and a confirmed Marsh fan, used to say: 'He would run at fellas, looking at them and chatting to them while dribbling the ball between his heels. If you whacked him, he didn't take umbrage, he just came back at you with the ball, pushed it between your legs or over you or under you or through you.'

Marsh was a big man. Over 6 feet tall, he was good in the air and, as Stock described, a real handful when running at defenders. But his showmanship could be his undoing. 'The trouble with Marshy,' said QPR team-mate Frank McLintock, putting the case for the prosecution, 'was that he'd rather put the ball through someone's legs one more time.' He could be murder to play against and almost as bad to play with.

Born in Hatfield, Hertfordshire, in 1944, he started out as a left-back with Hackney Schools but switched to a forward role when the usual left-winger forgot to bring his boots to a match. Marsh went on to play for West Ham's youth team but was released because the club said they had a more promising youngster coming through the ranks. His name was Geoff Hurst. Marsh was quickly picked up by Fulham and made an instant impression on manager Bedford Jezzard during a reserve match against Birmingham City. When Fulham's goalkeeper was injured, Marsh volunteered to take over between the posts, but when his first corner came over, instead of trying to catch it, he attempted to turn the ball over the bar with an extravagant bicycle kick, only to smash it into his own net.

'What the hell were you trying to do?' raged Jezzard afterwards.

'Entertain the punters,' replied Marsh.

'If I wanted players to do that, I would have signed some clowns!'

'Why bother? You've got a first team full of them already.'

It would not be the last time that Marsh's quick wit landed him in hot water.

He eventually broke into Fulham's first team in March 1963 against Aston Villa, replacing the injured Johnny Haynes, and in typical Marsh fashion he scored the winner. But six months later another winning goal nearly ended his career. Rising to head home against Leicester City, he was caught on the side of the head by defender John Sjoberg – a clash that left Marsh with a fractured jaw and skull and permanent deafness in his left ear. He was sidelined for nearly 10 months and after falling out with new manager Vic Buckingham, he was offloaded to Third Division QPR for £15,000 in March 1966.

Loftus Road was the perfect stage for Marsh's talents. Under Stock, Rangers were an exciting side that played attractive, flowing football, and Marsh was given the freedom to express himself. In his first season there, he scored 44 goals in 53 games as Rangers became Third Division champions and won the first Football League Cup final to be staged at Wembley, battling back from two goals down to overhaul First Division West Bromwich Albion 3-2. Naturally, Marsh conjured up a moment of magic for the equaliser – despite revealing in his autobiography that on the night before the final, many of the players partied with strippers in a hotel room until 1am.

The chants of 'Rod-neee, Rod-nee' continued to ring down the Loftus Road terraces the following season as Rangers swept through Division Two and into the top flight, but there the fairytale ended. Unprepared for life in Division One, they were relegated with a meagre 18 points. The jury was still out on whether Marsh could hack it at the highest level.

Marsh himself entertained no such doubts. In one game for Rangers he casually beat two defenders, leaving just one defender and the keeper to beat, and with the team's big, somewhat cumbersome striker, John O'Rourke, completely unmarked and screaming for the ball. Instead of passing to his better-placed team-mate, Marsh took on the last defender and lost the ball. At half-time, captain Terry Venables demanded to know why he had not passed to O'Rourke. 'Because,' replied Marsh, 'I think I had a better chance of scoring with one defender to beat than John did with none.'

When Gordon Jago took over as QPR manager and gave a long pep talk, Marsh decided to inject a little humour into the proceedings by raising his hand and announcing: 'Mr Jago, I'd just like to say on behalf of the lads, we're 40 per cent behind you.' Jago almost certainly appreciated the joke and it must have been pure coincidence that a few weeks later, in March 1972, Marsh was sold to Malcolm Allison's Manchester City for a club record of £200,000. At the time City were four points clear at the top of the table but ended up finishing fourth, Marsh's style clearly not fitting in with that of the rest of the team. City's general manager, Joe Mercer, remarked frostily: '£200,000 is a lot of money to spend to throw away the Championship.'

Even so, Marsh won over the fans with 19 goals in 1972–73 and led the club to the League Cup final in 1974. They loved his individualism, particularly when he was showboating at the expense of their neighbours. In one derby at Old Trafford, City were leading 3-1 with the seconds ticking away when Marsh collected the ball and ran towards the corner flag to waste more time, hotly pursued by a snorting and raging Nobby Stiles. Just before he got there, Marsh stopped and dragged the ball back, the move sending Stiles careering onto the running track. Standing at the flag with the ball at his feet, Marsh put one hand on the corner post and looked at an imaginary watch on his other wrist and shouted at the United fans: 'How long to go?'

Marsh had made his England debut in 1971, and although not exactly Alf Ramsey's kind of player, won nine caps before another joke backfired. Ramsey warned him before the 1973 match against Wales: 'If you don't work harder tonight I'll pull you off at half-time.' To which Marsh replied: 'Christ, Alf, we only get a cup of tea and an orange at City!' The straitlaced Ramsey did not see the funny side and Marsh was never selected again for his country.

Marsh was eventually transfer-listed at Manchester City for telling chairman Peter Swales that manager Tony Book was useless. Seven thousand fans sent letters to the club urging them to keep Marsh but, after 36 goals in 118 League games for City, he joined Tampa Bay Rowdies in America before being reunited with Alec Stock at Fulham. With George Best and Bobby Moore in the same side, it was carnival time by the Thames. Marsh particularly remembers a 4-1 victory over Hereford United. He had already scored twice but his chances of a hat-trick were being wrecked by Best who was monopolising the ball to such an extent that finally Marsh felt compelled to tackle his own player. The crowd roared their approval and Best later returned the compliment by tackling Marsh.

In 1977 he returned to Tampa Bay, where he was held in such high esteem that he was asked to sign the underwear of the Rowdies' 12 cheerleaders. He said: 'I had to sign the girls' knickers while they were wearing them!'

He stayed in Florida for two years and teamed up again with his old QPR boss, Gordon Jago. The pair had a good working relationship...until Jago substituted him 10 minutes before the end of his final game. It was the first time in his career that Marsh had ever been substituted for any reason other than injury and he was furious.

Hurling his shirt to the ground, he yelled: 'Gordon. It's my last game. Why have you taken me off?'

'To be honest, Rod,' answered Jago, 'I thought we needed a bit more pace up front.'

Marsh was dumbfounded. 'Gordon, how long have you known me? Fifteen years? With 10 minutes of my career left you've realised that I'm not fucking quick enough?!'

Upon retirement, Marsh became an outspoken pundit with Sky Sports. At the start of the 1999 season, he said that newly promoted Bradford City had no chance of surviving in the Premier League and offered to have all his hair shaved off if they stayed up. City did avoid relegation and Marsh honoured the bet by having his locks shorn in the centre circle of their Valley Parade ground. But after 11 successful years at Sky, in 2005 he made one joke too many, an ill-advised on-air pun in the wake of the Asian tsunami disaster. He joked that David Beckham had turned down a move to Newcastle United because of trouble with the 'Toon Army in Asia'. In truth, the joke had been doing the rounds on the Internet for weeks and was very much at the expense of Beckham rather than those affected by the tragedy. Marsh was sacked over the remark, although most thought he had been harshly treated. To his credit, Marsh stated that although he disagreed with Sky's stance, he respected their right to dismiss him. In many ways, the episode encapsulates Rodney Marsh's career: sometimes one joke too far, one defender too many...

Peter Osgood
The Wizard of Os

Peter Osgood always had a swagger about him. At the height of his powers, he was London's most recognisable footballer, playing as he did for what was then the capital's most glamorous club, Chelsea. Whereas Fulham's most famous supporter was Radio 1 disc jockey David 'Diddy' Hamilton, the Stamford Bridge stands were home to a vast array of celebrities, including, or so it seemed, virtually every member of Equity. Along with Dickie Attenborough, who is still a vice-president at Chelsea, the likes of Michael Caine, Michael Crawford, Honor Blackman and Terence Stamp were regular visitors to the Bridge, and the showbiz connection even encouraged visitors from Hollywood who probably wondered why the ball was not oval. John Wayne, Paul Newman, Steve McQueen, Raquel Welch and

Robert Redford all attended Chelsea home games. And the player they all wanted to meet was Osgood.

When Ossie came off the field after scoring his 100th goal for Chelsea, Steve McQueen was waiting to greet him in the dressing room. And Raquel Welch, who had reputedly taken a shine to the lean, mean, goal machine, once ran up the touchline at Stamford Bridge waving at him. She was also seen wearing a T-shirt that read 'I scored with Osgood', although it is by no means certain that she understood the meaning to be anything other than sporting. Whatever, it must have seemed mightily impressive to a kid who was once rejected by Reading.

Appropriately for someone who went on to be known as the 'King of the Bridge', Osgood was born in Windsor, on 20 February 1947. After being turned down by Reading, he tore up a letter from Arsenal inviting him for a trial because he thought he was sure to be rejected. He eventually joined Chelsea in 1964 and, having scored 30 goals in 20 reserve games, was given his first-team opportunity in December of that year, scoring both goals in a League Cup victory over Workington. A further 12 goals in eight games on a summer tour of Australia prompted manager Tommy Docherty to predict that the 6-foot-1-inch forward 'could become one of the all-time greats.' Selecting Osgood for the start of the 1965–66 season, Docherty told the youngster (already a father at 18) that he would give him a run of 10 matches in the first team, no matter how he played. 'It took only the first 10 minutes to realise he was there to stay,' recalled Docherty.

Even at that age, Osgood combined strength with a change of pace and nimble footwork that was unusual in someone of his size. Docherty remembered a goal against Burnley where Osgood 'threaded through the defence, passing four players as if they had been sitting in the dressing room. Then, just as I thought he was going to dribble round the goalkeeper, he cracked in a rifle shot from the edge of the box. When Adam Blacklaw picked the ball out of the net, he then joined in the applause which was roaring Osgood back to the centre circle.'

Docherty also discovered that Osgood could be quite a handful off the pitch. Fined for being late for training, the 'Wizard of Os', as Chelsea fans had christened him, simply dismissed the punishment with a laugh. However, it was no laughing matter when he suffered a broken leg in a challenge with Blackpool's Emlyn Hughes in October

1966, an injury that caused him to miss that season's FA Cup final. Without him, Chelsea lost 2-1 to Spurs.

On his return, Osgood added real bite to his play, developing the ability and willingness to mix it with the toughest of defenders. He had a rebellious streak, which contributed to his cult status, but also enjoyed a laugh with the lads. Once, he, Terry Venables and George Graham put on their smart Chelsea blazers and posed as customs officers at an airport. They were so convincing that they managed to persuade an American tourist to open her case and reveal what she was bringing in to the country. He also liked a drink and the company of beautiful women (he was eventually married three times), and fulfilled the Carnaby Street image to the letter. But as his new manager, Dave Sexton, lamented: 'He didn't know when to be a good lad or Jack-the-Lad.'

He was integral to Chelsea's success in the early Seventies, scoring in Cup finals in three successive years – the 1970 FA Cup final replay, the 1971 European Cup Winners' Cup final and the 1972 League Cup final. Only the third ended in defeat. He was a member of England's 1970 World Cup squad but, despite having scored 31 First Division goals that season, was left out of the key games by Alf Ramsey. Osgood was so angry when Ramsey brought on Jeff Astle instead of him against Brazil (Astle famously missed a sitter) that he got drunk, missed training the following day and was not picked again for four years. A total of four caps was a scandalously poor return for such talent.

As Chelsea's fortunes declined, so did his relationship with Sexton, who, like Ramsey, disapproved of Osgood's playboy lifestyle. At Osgood's instigation, he and Sexton nearly came to blows on at least one occasion, and when Osgood and Alan Hudson were dropped and failed to attend training before a 1974 FA Cup tie against Queens Park Rangers, they were placed on the transfer list. While Hudson went to Stoke, Southampton signed Osgood for £275,000. His finest hour on the south coast was when the Saints sprang a surprise to defeat Manchester United in the 1976 FA Cup final. At the end of the night-long celebrations, Osgood found himself in possession of the famous trophy. His team-mate Mick Channon recalled: 'He nicked the Cup and took it home with him. And he even finished up in the early hours of that morning flashing it at a motorway café before eventually bringing it back, safe and sound, to The Dell.'

Despite his extrovert nature, doubts began to creep into Osgood's game as he realised that his best days were behind him. 'I'm not the player I was and I know that better than anyone,' he said. 'I started thinking about turning it all in when my mum and my sisters decided to go and watch Southampton play at Chelsea while I was with the reserves at Birmingham. When your biggest fans desert you, you are really in trouble.'

He left Southampton a year after the Cup triumph, joining the American exodus with a move to Philadelphia Fury, where he managed just one goal in 23 games for a team that also included Johnny Giles and Alan Ball. In December 1978 he made a surprise return to Chelsea, who were struggling at the wrong end of the table. He again scored on his debut for the club but Chelsea crashed 7-2 to Middlesbrough and ended up being relegated. After a total of 150 goals in 380 appearances for the Blues, he retired from playing in 1979.

After an ill-fated venture running a Windsor pub with his former strike partner Ian Hutchinson, Osgood worked as a hospitality host on matchdays at Stamford Bridge. On 1 March 2006, just three weeks after receiving a standing ovation when presented to the Chelsea crowd at half-time of a match, he collapsed and died of a heart attack while attending a family funeral. The setting might have appealed to his quirky sense of humour. In a memorial service attended by more than 2,500 fans, his ashes were laid to rest under the penalty spot at the Shed end of Stamford Bridge. 'Osgood Is Good' proclaimed those same fans' banners back in the Seventies. He was better than that.

Frank Worthington
Elvis Impersonator

Frank Worthington scored prolifically both on and off the pitch. His career total of 234 League goals was matched only by a success rate with the ladies that rivalled even George Best and made most other professional footballers seem like Trappist monks by comparison. He had more models than Airfix. Judging by the tales from his aptly titled autobiography, *One Hump or Two?*, Worthington rarely ventured out in public without a blonde on each arm, but it was this hedonistic lifestyle that almost certainly cost him a dream move to Anfield in 1972.

After six successful years with Huddersfield Town, he was all set to sign for Liverpool until a medical revealed that his blood pressure was exceptionally high. Bill Shankly advised him to take a holiday abroad and then come back for a second medical. But, being Frank, the relaxing break proved just the opposite. Although he was dating Miss Great Britain at the time, he pulled a young woman on the plane to Majorca, where he also enjoyed a threesome with two Swedish tourists (mother and daughter), and a romp with a busty Belgian. Supposedly reinvigorated, he returned for the medical, which he promptly failed again, leaving Shankly with no option but to call off the deal. In a moment of rare sombre reflection, the player himself attributed the failed medical to 'living a little bit too much in the fast lane'.

But did Worthington have any regrets? Probably not. He much preferred life in the fast lane to the bus lane, and although he never again had the chance to play for one of the country's very best sides, he did go on to win eight England caps and turn out for 11 different English League clubs in a career spanning 22 years. And that's no mean feat for someone with high blood pressure. Besides, countless bland players have turned out for Liverpool over the past four decades, but there has never been any footballer quite like Frank Worthington.

Above all, he had style. Instantly recognisable with his long swept-back hair and huge sideburns that made Engelbert Humperdinck's look restrained, he once turned up for an England Under-23 tour of Eastern Europe dressed in cowboy boots, red silk shirt, black trousers and a lime green velvet jacket. Alf Ramsey, for whom Dunn & Co gents outfitters was a little racy, looked predictably horrified. Of course, Worthington's hero was – and still is – Elvis Presley. He never needed any excuse to burst into song, although, as Worthy started to lose his hair towards the end of his career, Graeme Souness remarked that he could be 'the first bald guy ever to do impressions of Elvis.' Not everyone appreciated Frank's singular devotion to the King. When Bolton Wanderers were on a summer tour of Germany, Worthington decided to treat the team bus to nine hours of non-stop

Elvis tapes. Eventually it proved too much for manager Ian Greaves, who marched to the front of the coach and hurled the cassettes out onto the autobahn. Worthington refused to speak to him for a week.

It was at Bolton that Worthington enjoyed the moment that defined his career: one of the finest individual goals ever seen on an English League ground. Playing against Ipswich on 21 April 1979, he received the ball with his back to goal on the edge of the penalty area. Controlling it with his head, he juggled the ball twice on his left foot, flicked the ball over his shoulder, swivelled, and then drilled it left-footed past the keeper and into the corner of the net with his fourth touch. Not once did the ball hit the ground. It is difficult to think of many other players having the nerve, let alone the ability, to execute the move, but that was Worthington: always the individualist, always the entertainer. He openly admitted that his own individual performance was more important to him than the team result. 'I would rather lose a match 5-4,' he said, 'and give all the supporters entertainment than win 1-0 and bore everyone to death.' It almost goes without saying that Frank was never really cut out for football management.

Frank was born into a footballing family near Halifax in 1948. 'My father, mother and both of my brothers, Dave and Bob, took up the game at some level or other,' he says. 'I honed my football skills in the streets around our home. We had a makeshift goal in the street outside the house. My dad, Eric, would always encourage me to aim for the corner of the goal to make sure I beat the keeper.' Frank started out with Huddersfield in 1966, and although he could sometimes appear lazy on the field, his sweet left foot earned him a legion of admirers, while his ball skills were simply breathtaking. However, his manager there, the same Ian Greaves who would later take charge of him at Bolton, was frustrated at his selfishness and one day after training planned to give him a dressing down. 'He was talking to me,' said Greaves, 'and his eyes never left mine, but he must have flicked the ball up 47 times. He flicked it up and caught it behind him on his neck, down the back of the neck, hoofed it over his back and caught it on his foot, something I could never do if I played forever. I thought, "How do you give him a telling-off when he's doing that?" That's why fans used to turn up early for games – just to watch Worthington practise his ball juggling skills in the warm-up.'

He scored 41 times for Huddersfield in 171 League games, and after the Liverpool move fell through, he joined Leicester City. The Foxes' side of the Seventies under Jimmy Bloomfield was arguably the most attractive in the club's history, boasting exciting, skilful players such as Keith Weller, Alan Birchenall and Jon Sammels, so Worthington found himself in good company. Over the next five seasons with Leicester he rattled in 72 goals at a rate of one in every three games, mesmerising defences even when suffering from a hangover. His social life never seemed to affect his ability to deliver on the pitch. When he signed for Southampton in 1983, Saints' boss Lawrie McMenemy, fully aware of Worthington's reputation, told him: 'I don't care how you train just so long as you perform for me on a Saturday.'

As well as his addiction to beautiful women, Worthington occasionally snorted cocaine and smoked dope. 'It was all part of the crazy scene at the time,' he says. Needless to say, he enjoyed a flutter too. Following a 1974 England win in Bulgaria, several of the players became involved in a marathon game of three-card brag that ended at nine o'clock the following morning – and then only because the team had to set off for the airport to fly to their next match in Yugoslavia. Worthington reckons he finished £1,500 up on that card game. His England career flourished briefly under the genial, adventurous Joe Mercer but inevitably ground to a halt once Don Revie took charge. There was no place for flamboyant individualists in Revie's world.

Worthington had not endeared himself to Revie's Leeds while playing for Leicester. He remembers a match that Leicester were winning 1-0 when he found himself with the ball down near the corner flag, hemmed in by Johnny Giles. 'I flipped the ball over my shoulder and over his head. He just turned to me and said, in a very cold, calculating, matter-of-fact sort of way: "If you ever take the piss out of me or Leeds United again, I'll break your legs."'

Both on and off the pitch, Worthington came alive after dark. 'I always loved playing under floodlights – at Leicester they called me Badger because rumour had it I only came out at night.' Always one for keeping up appearances, he used to groom his hair while waiting for corners to be taken, and when he moved to Bolton in 1977 he took to wearing a red headband, as if he needed something else to make him stand out from the crowd. His two years at Burnden Park were highly productive. *That* goal against Ipswich was one of 24 he scored in 1978–79, winning him the coveted Golden Boot for the First Division's top scorer. Two games against Manchester United brought him four goals and the need to seek refuge in a Chinese restaurant after being chased by angry United fans.

After Bolton, the clubs came thick and fast: Philadelphia Fury, Birmingham City, Tampa Bay Rowdies, Leeds United, Sunderland, Southampton, Brighton, Tranmere Rovers (where, unlikely as it may seem, he briefly tried his hand at being player-manager), Preston and finally Stockport County. That he carried on playing until he was 39 is testament either to his fitness or to his amazing powers of recovery.

Frank Worthington will always be remembered as one of soccer's great showmen, but this should not detract from the fact that he possessed remarkable talent. He was not a scorer of ordinary goals but he revelled in the spectacular and on his day was a match for any defender in the land. As Manchester United's Paddy Crerand once said: 'There was only one way to play Frank – kick him as soon as you can.'

MANAGING TO
BE DIFFERENT

Martin Allen
Mad Dog

With some justification, Martin Allen hates his nickname of 'Mad Dog'. It was originally given to him when he shaved his head as a combative midfielder with West Ham and has dogged him ever since he turned to management. Unfortunately for Allen, some of his antics as a manager have lent weight to the view that if not certifiably insane, he definitely has an eccentric streak. After all, this is a man who has been known to feed his players greasy fry-ups before a game; who has stood in shirtsleeves watching them play in sleet and rain to help team bonding; and who has developed a habit of jumping naked into dirty, freezing rivers before important matches.

His first skinny dip took place shortly after he had been appointed manager of Brentford in 2004. 'It was my first away game in charge, against Hartlepool,' he remembers. 'They were in a play-off position, we hadn't won away for God knows how long. We went to train in a little park when we got up there and as we were jogging along, I heard the players challenge each other. They said they'd have a whip-round – £10 a man – for anyone that dived into the river. But no one would. I stopped them eventually. I said, "I've been listening to you for 20 minutes and no one's been man enough to take the challenge. I'll show you."

'I walked round to the other side of the river over a bridge, stripped off my clothes and took a deep breath. There were Coke cans and crisp wrappers and holes in the river bank where the rats were. I dived in, swam as hard as I could to the other side and walked into our hotel dripping wet in my shorts. I came down at 7.15 in a collar and tie. All the players went silent. I asked the captain for the money and he handed me 160 quid.' The next day Brentford beat Hartlepool 2-1.

As a motivational exercise, the stunt had proved so successful that before the Bees' fifth-round FA Cup tie at Southampton the following season Allen decided to jump naked into the Solent. 'I nearly had a heart attack at Southampton it was so cold,' he admits. 'When I jumped in the Solent there was a tanker, bigger than St Mary's Stadium, a hundred yards from where I was, and I did question my sanity.' Even so, after Brentford had earned a 2-2 draw, he did promise to swim in the Thames if they reached the sixth round. To the relief of the river's fish population, Brentford lost the replay 3-1.

Martin's behaviour has caused amusement and admiration in equal parts among other members of the famous Allen footballing dynasty. Cousin Clive – the former Tottenham and England striker – says: 'He was quite a character as a player and it hasn't surprised me that he's taken that into management. But there's a method in his madness in terms of his management skills. He gets respect from the players and he gets a response from them.'

Martin Allen was born in 1965 in Reading, the town where his father Dennis was a free-scoring inside-forward. When it looked as though Martin, then an apprentice at Queens Park Rangers, might not follow the family tradition and make it as a professional, his father enrolled him at a boxing gym to build him up. The extra training produced a fiercely competitive midfielder who enjoyed six seasons at QPR before falling out with manager Trevor Francis, who harshly fined him two weeks' wages for missing a match to attend the birth of his son. Shortly afterwards, in 1989, Allen was sold to West Ham for £675,000 and developed a reputation as someone who would kick lumps out of opponents on the field and wear pink baseball boots off it. In 1995 he went on loan to Portsmouth, making the move permanent the following year. He finally hung up his football boots in 1999 at the end of a career spanning 449 games and 57 goals.

On retirement he coached Portsmouth reserves, and when he was sacked made ends meet by working as a gardener. 'I was collecting leaves in Gerrard's Cross in black bags in people's gardens for ten pounds an hour.' Alan Pardew rescued him by asking him to become Reading's reserve coach, and from there he moved on to his first managerial post at Barnet and then Brentford. When interviewed for the job at Griffin Park, he was asked what he wanted as a salary.

He replied that he wanted a car and six tickets every match – he would leave the salary up to the board. 'The wife went mad,' he confesses, 'but I just want to be happy in my work.' Sometimes he would put tickets in an envelope in the name of his late father and leave them at the ticket window. 'To me, he's here every game.'

Money was tight at Brentford and with the club facing administration, Allen raised £22,000 by cycling from Maidenhead to Brentford. 'I could have sat at home and had 10 points deducted or I could have done something,' he says. He chose the latter option and his selfless determination won him new admirers (Sir Alex Ferguson sent him a personal cheque for £450) and the London Sports Personality Award for 2005, in which he beat, among others, fellow West London manager José Mourinho. Allen's unconventional style established tremendous team spirit at Brentford – he even used to join in snowball fights with the players.

After leading the club to the fifth round of the FA Cup in successive seasons and to the First Division play-offs, Allen quit in 2006 to take charge at Milton Keynes Dons. When the Dons' team coach broke down on the way to a game at Lincoln, Allen, inventive as ever, made the players practise on a roundabout! He guided the Dons to the Second Division play-offs, where they lost to Shrewsbury Town, and in May 2007 was appointed manager of Leicester City. Allen immediately livened up Leicester's pre-season training with a seven-a-side 'World Cup', the players divided into teams representing France, Bulgaria, England and Australia. The winners received a Mars Bar each, while the player of the tournament – striker Matt Fryatt – was presented with a £3.99 set of barbecue utensils. Alas, Allen lasted just 96 days at the Walkers Stadium after falling out with high-profile chairman Milan Mandaric.

Allen had feared that his reputation might prevent him landing a job with a big club, which is why he is keen to emphasise his attributes of hard work and organisation rather than any wild eccentricity. 'They say there is a fine line between madness and genius,' he says, 'and I'd like to be the nutty professor, not a mad dog.'

Malcolm Allison
The Man With Big Ideas

As a forecaster, Malcolm Allison was not quite in the same league as Nostradamus. After his Manchester City team won the League in 1968, he predicted: 'We will win the European Cup. European football is full of cowards and we will terrorise them with our power and attacking football.' City were knocked out in the first round by Turkish side Fenerbahce. In December 1975, with his Crystal Palace side well clear at the top of the table, Allison declared: 'We're the best team there's ever been in the Third Division.' They finished fifth that season. Then in 1979, by which time he was back at Maine Road, he signed Steve Daley from Wolves for a British record fee of £1,437,500 and predicted that Daley would become one of the world's great players. He didn't. Not by a long way.

It was all typical Allison: his clubs may not have got many points when he was in charge but they always got plenty of publicity. The fedora hat, the sheepskin coat and the fat cigar were vintage 'Big Mal', all designed to cement his image as the most flamboyant manager of his day. He was so flash he should have carried a health warning. Who else would have encouraged a soft porn actress to jump naked into a bath with his players for a *News of the World* photo shoot?

The media loved him because he could always be relied upon to produce a controversial statement; players liked him, too, because he was an innovative coach; fans were divided because although his teams were usually exciting to watch, they did not always find winning easy. His finest hour was with Manchester City in the late Sixties, but there he had the wise head of Joe Mercer for support. Allison himself admitted that he would sweep through a place, ruffling everyone's feathers, leaving Mercer to soothe wounded pride and pick up the pieces, rather like the man who follows the horses with a dustpan, brush and bucket at the Horse of the Year Show. Without an old hand to guide him and left to his own devices, Allison could run amok, especially in the transfer market, where his judgement was sometimes questionable to say the least.

Consequently, all too often his big words were not mirrored in his achievements.

Allison was born in Dartford in 1927, playing for Erith & Belvedere before joining Charlton in 1945. Over the next six years, he made just two first-team appearances at The Valley and so when West Ham came looking for a new centre-half, he did not need much persuading to move to Upton Park. Even in those days he was considered by some to be extravagant, attempting to clear the ball with spectacular, continental-style overhead kicks while facing his own goal. They were not always successful, resulting in Allison ending up flat on his back and the ball ending up in the back of the net. However, he was always thinking of ways to improve his game. He pioneered cut-down, lightweight boots and streamlined shorts and played a big part in the development of the young Bobby Moore. 'He made you really think,' admitted Moore. 'He'd tell you to ask yourself through the game, "What will I do if the ball comes to me now?" and to try and keep a mental picture of where everyone was on the park.' Allison is also said to have changed the team's tactics without the manager's knowledge. The story goes that manager Ted Fenton walked into the dressing room after one match and demanded to know what the 4-2-4 formation was all about. Under Allison's orders, they had been playing it for the past six games.

Sadly, in 1958 Allison was struck down by tuberculosis, which necessitated the removal of a lung and effectively ended his playing career after 238 League games for the Hammers. He decided to put his ideas into practice in management with Bath City, whom he duly led to the Southern League title. In 1964 he left for Plymouth Argyle and was keen to sign his Bath full-back and captain, Tony Book. Unsure whether the Plymouth board would be happy to sign a 30-year-old with no League experience, the ever resourceful Allison told Book to alter the date on his birth certificate from 1934 to 1936. He later took Book, his trusted lieutenant, with him to Manchester City, too.

Always outspoken, Allison soon fell out with the Plymouth board and joined Manchester City as Mercer's right-hand man, helping to build a fine team around the likes of Colin Bell, Mike Summerbee and Francis Lee in what turned out to be a golden era at Maine Road. Allison was desperate to sign Bell from Bury but City had to take out a bank loan to finance the £45,000 fee. Knowing that other clubs were interested, Allison made a point of telling coaches and scouts that Bell was over-priced, anything to put rivals off the scent. The ruse worked, and as soon as the money was available, Allison snapped up his man. Allison always liked to do things in style. After winning a European game in France, he celebrated by ordering champagne all round. Some hours later with the drink still flowing, the head waiter quietly informed him that his bill was more than £1,000. 'Is that all?' said Allison, puffing on his cigar. 'You insult me. Don't come back until it's double that!'

In 1973, after a brief period in sole control at City, Allison took over as boss at struggling Crystal Palace, partly because he had been having a fling with *Playboy* Bunny Girl, Serena, who wanted him to move to London. But his promises of a great future for the club began to sound hollow as he led them to two successive relegations. As Palace found to their cost, lower division opponents always liked to cut Allison down to size. In 1975–76 he donned a fedora hat to a Cup tie at Scarborough and, always on the lookout for a new gimmick, wore it for the rest of the Cup run, which saw Palace reach the semi-finals. The Palace shop sold more than 3,000 replica fedora hats that season. Meanwhile, he invited former *Playboy* model Fiona Richmond to the training ground for a tabloid feature. After going in goal for penalties, she appeared in the dressing room, wearing only a fur coat, which she promptly removed before jumping in the players' communal bath, along with Allison. While more photos were being taken, a few embarrassed players kept their heads under the water so that their wives would never see the pictures. Allison landed in hot water over the photos. It was a publicity stunt too far and that, coupled with Palace's poor League form, saw him sacked in May 1976.

His thirst for the champagne lifestyle took him briefly to Turkish club Galatasaray and then on a return journey to Plymouth, where, appealing against yet another touchline ban, he quipped: 'I've served more time than Ronnie Biggs did for the Great Train Robbery.' Next he tried to rekindle former glories at Maine Road, but the signings of players such as Daley and Kevin Reeves for hugely inflated fees meant that whilst the fans still chanted Allison's name, it was invariably followed by the word 'out'. They soon got their wish and, with his reputation on the slide, he rarely lasted more than a year at his remaining posts – Crystal Palace (revisited), Sporting Lisbon,

Middlesbrough, the Kuwait national team and Bristol Rovers. In fairness, he was particularly unlucky in Portugal, having taken Sporting to a League and Cup double.

In 2001 he was admitted to hospital, reportedly suffering from alcoholism. His son Mark said: 'If he goes into a pub, someone there will buy him a drink and then they get one of his great stories.'

He had a fund of stories and sayings. One of his favourites was: 'You're not a real manager unless you've been sacked.' If that were the sole qualification for good management, Malcolm Allison would have been a very good manager indeed.

Ron Atkinson
When the Champagne Went Flat

Like 'Big Mal', 'Big Ron' was never one for hiding his light under a bushel. However, whereas Allison's self-confidence often bordered on arrogance, Ron Atkinson adorned his with a nice line in self-deprecating humour that saw him succeed Tommy Docherty as the king of the one-liners. He memorably described Devon Loch as a better finisher than Carlton Palmer, adding for good measure: 'Carlton Palmer can trap the ball further than I can kick it.' On signing 39-year-old Gordon Strachan for Coventry, Atkinson remarked: 'There's nobody fitter at his age, except maybe Raquel Welch.' And in a post-match interview he informed reporters: 'I never comment on referees and I'm not going to break the habit of a lifetime for that prat.' It was the way he told them.

Atkinson is one of those men whose career rubbishes the theory that you have to be a great player to become a great manager. Born in Liverpool, he failed to make the grade at Aston Villa and joined non-League Oxford United in 1959. Anyone who saw him fill every inch of Oxford's gold shirt during his 500 games for the club would not instantly have marked him down as somebody who would one day be pitting his wits against the cream of European football. Nicknamed 'The Tank' – on account of both his build and his acceleration – he was a combative, if limited, right-half, but even in those days his leadership qualities stood out as captain of the Oxford side that rose spectacularly from the Southern League to the Second Division in just seven seasons.

When he retired from playing in 1971, he became manager of Kettering Town, where he quickly imposed his idiosyncratic style. After every away win, he made a point of stopping the team bus and buying all of the players a drink at a convenient pub. He also bought a box of cigars by way of celebration and made it a club rule that every player must smoke one. He stayed at Kettering for three years, gaining valuable insight into the world of management wheeling and dealing at the lower levels (he once sold one of his reserves to Stevenage in return for a lawnmower). Money was still tight at his next club, Cambridge United, where he sold full-back Billy Baldry to Barry Fry's Dunstable for a crate of champagne, an early sign that Atkinson was beginning to develop a taste for the high life. Under his astute charge, Cambridge won the Fourth Division title in 1977 and were on their way to a second successive promotion when First Division West Bromwich Albion came calling.

It was at The Hawthorns that Atkinson really made his mark. He developed an exciting team built around the talents of full-back Brendan Batson (whom he signed from Cambridge), winger Laurie Cunningham and striker Cyrille Regis, the first trio of black players to feature simultaneously in an English team and who became known collectively as the Three Degrees in reference to the female vocalists of the same name. Atkinson steered Albion to third place in the League in 1978–79 before his success and charisma came to the attention of Manchester United, a big club in need of a big manager. Whereas his taciturn predecessor, Dave Sexton, was always uncomfortable dealing with the press, Atkinson positively revelled in the media spotlight. On taking over at Old Trafford in 1981, he told journalists: 'You're welcome to my home phone number, but don't ring me during *The Sweeney*.'

Atkinson lived the part at Old Trafford – the champagne lifestyle, the permanent suntan (he kept a sun bed in his office), the expensive suits and the flash gold jewellery that made him a pioneer of bling when Snoop Dogg was still a puppy. Gordon Strachan, who joined United in 1984, remembers his first match under Atkinson. When the manager turned up carrying a briefcase, Strachan assumed it contained tactical notes. Instead, when Atkinson opened it, the only items were a can of hairspray and a bottle of aftershave.

But there was substance behind the image. Atkinson led United to two FA Cup triumphs and to the semi-finals of the European Cup Winners' Cup, while League finishes of third, third, fourth and fourth raised hopes of a long overdue First Division championship in 1985–86. A run of 10 victories on the trot put United in a commanding position before their form dropped away badly and they again could finish no higher than fourth, prompting mutterings that neither the team nor the manager had the stamina necessary for a concerted title push. Atkinson was popular with most of the players – even Ray Wilkins, whom he christened 'The Crab' because he only passed sideways. They liked his humour and enthusiasm, which always manifested itself in five-a-side matches. Although he was now in his early forties, ample of girth and never the most skilful of players even in his prime, he evidently saw himself, with echoes of Brian Glover's schoolmaster in *Kes*, as Michel Platini in practice matches, and always hated finishing on the losing side. He would actually try and impersonate Franz Beckenbauer, Pele or Maradona in these matches and invite his players to guess his identity. It was all a bit like *Stars in Their Eyes*. However, his critics cited a growing drinking culture within the club, hinting that discipline wasn't always Atkinson's strong point. Ron himself later admitted in his autobiography that what started out as a dressing-down for captain Bryan Robson on an end-of-season tour to Hong Kong turned into a five-and-a-half-hour drinking session, during which the pair got through six bottles of champagne. Atkinson was no soft touch but that just happened to be his method of man management; he was never likely to be confused with Ron Saunders.

Yet the murmurings of discontent became a deafening clamour as United started the 1986–87 season disastrously. In November, with the club languishing fourth from bottom, Atkinson's tenure was brought to an end. He returned to West Brom for a year before making a high profile move to Atletico Madrid where, after just six months in charge and in spite of the fact that Atletico were lying third in the table, he fell foul of the club's president, Jesus Gil, who was renowned for eating managers for breakfast. Reflecting on his Spanish experience, Atkinson later remarked wryly: 'I see Atletico Madrid just sacked another manager before the season has even started. He must have had a bad photocall.'

Atkinson did not remain out of work for long, taking over at Sheffield Wednesday in February 1989. Relegation from the top flight was followed by instant promotion in 1991 and a memorable League Cup final triumph, all the sweeter because Wednesday's opponents were Manchester United. At the end of the season, however, he was on the move again, tempted by an offer from Doug Ellis at Aston Villa.

It was a marriage made in hell. 'Deadly Doug' not only had a reputation for hiring and firing with bewildering regularity, but he was considered – by the Villa fans at least – to have such a tight hold on the purse strings that it was tantamount to a vice-like grip. They were two strong characters. Behind the genial smile and the wisecracks, Atkinson was a tough cookie. At West Brom he had argued bitterly with a director who appeared to be blocking the signing of defender Chris Whyte. Atkinson told the director that if the deal didn't go through, 'I'll be round to your house and give you a whack you will remember for the rest of your days.' The deal went through.

Atkinson wanted to elevate Villa to a place among the country's top clubs and, to that end, steered them to second spot in the inaugural Premier League and, in 1994, to League Cup success, but his lofty ambitions resulted in frequent clashes with Ellis over transfer targets. Under fire from the Villa Park faithful, Ellis tried to deflect the criticism by inserting self-congratulatory comments into Atkinson's programme notes. Atkinson recounted how he was ordered by fax to write what a wonderful chairman Ellis was and how he often used Ellis as a sounding board for tactics and team selections. Naturally, Atkinson was distinctly unimpressed by Ellis's demands and showed the offending fax to the press. This scarcely improved relations between manager and chairman.

Atkinson was equally frustrated by his namesake Dalian, a gifted but languid striker. He used to say: 'I always make sure I write Atkinson D. on the team sheet. Sometimes I wonder if I'm making a mistake!' After a goalless draw with Chelsea in February 1994, Ron deliberately provoked a fight with Dalian in an attempt to get the player to demonstrate some passion. There was a brief bout of fisticuffs, after which Ron straightened his tie and jacket and went directly into a BBC interview with John Motson. As Ron later wrote: 'If he (Motson) had only known what had happened just a few seconds earlier and barely 10 yards from the site of the interview, he would have had quite a story to tell *Match of the Day* viewers!'

The inevitable parting of the ways at Villa came in November 1994. Atkinson went on to have short spells at Coventry, Sheffield Wednesday (again), and Nottingham Forest, where he marked his first match in charge by clambering into the wrong dugout. Following a humiliating 8-1 home defeat to Manchester United, he told reporters that he hoped everyone enjoyed 'that nine-goal thriller'.

Atkinson's gift of the gab made him a natural for television, and as a co-commentator on ITV he introduced a vocabulary all of his own, which became known affectionately as 'Ronglish'. His favourite terms included 'early doors' (early in the game); 'reducer' (a strong tackle made early on to reduce a skilful player's contribution); 'give it the eyebrows' (make a glancing header with deliberately minimal contact, usually by attackers at near post corners); 'spotter's badge' (a plaudit given to a player for making an accurate pass); and 'lollipop' (a trick where a player passes his foot over the ball to fool a defender, from the rhyming slang 'lollipop stick' meaning 'trick'). These endearing terms combined with his wealth of knowledge made Atkinson a favourite fixture at ITV...until his world imploded on 21 April 2004.

At the end of a Champions League tie, mistakenly believing his microphone to be switched off, he made a racist remark live on air about Chelsea's black defender Marcel Desailly. Although transmission in the UK had finished, the comment was broadcast to various countries in the Middle East. A contrite Atkinson resigned immediately. Never a slave to political correctness (his views on the role of women in football could scarcely be called enlightened), he had overstepped the mark this time. In his defence, Atkinson claimed that the Desailly remark was an aberration and strongly denied that he was racist, supporting his argument by correctly reminding people that he had done more than anyone to encourage black players in the English game. His plea for forgiveness did little to diminish the public condemnation. Overnight, one of football's most familiar faces had become a pariah.

Although work has started to come in again, his rehabilitation has been slow. As Atkinson himself once remarked, tongue firmly in cheek: 'It's bloody tough being a legend.' The trouble with legends is that it can be a long fall from grace.

Jack Charlton
An Irish Legend

Whether by design or by accident, Jack Charlton in his management days appeared to cultivate the image of an amiable buffoon. He never seemed able to remember the names of his Republic of Ireland players. Paul McGrath was forever 'John' and, more alarmingly, Liam Brady was 'Ian'. He would rarely attempt to pronounce foreign players' names and if he did, he made them all sound like Mussolini. When Alan McLoughlin turned up for an international in Dublin, Charlton looked at him and asked: 'What are you doing here?' A bemused McLoughlin replied: 'You picked me.'

It had been much the same story at Middlesbrough, where players were always 'You there' or 'Thingy' because he was unable to remember their names, even after four years. At Sheffield Wednesday, he once wrote the team's names down on the back of a cigarette packet, and before a Cup semi-final with Brighton, the Wednesday team bus left the hotel without two of the players. Charlton was unaware of their absence and the pair had to dash to the ground by taxi.

He was no better in his media work and once nearly missed a live match at Birmingham after falling asleep in his vehicle in the St Andrews car park. The late ITV commentator Brian Moore wrote in his autobiography: 'Jack Charlton is a champion of many parts, but he is not an advertisement for self-organisation.' Moore recalled how Charlton had phoned him in a panic from Stockholm airport during the 1992 European Championships, saying that he had mislaid vital documents. On Moore's advice, Charlton rang lost property, then called back.

'Yes, Brian, they had it,' he said. 'Can't tell you how relieved I am. Now, shouldn't we be getting along to the match?'

Moore replied wearily: 'Jack, the match is tomorrow.'

Yet Charlton denies he has a bad memory for names and claims that he was just feigning absent-mindedness for amusement. Or perhaps the image was created so that the opposition would underestimate Charlton and his team, because, let's face it, amiable buffoons do not get to be World Cup winners, feared centre-halves or the most popular person in Ireland apart from the Pope. Jack Charlton may have enjoyed playing the fool from time to time, but there is little doubt that he is a very shrewd operator.

A nephew of Jackie Milburn and elder brother of Bobby Charlton, Jack was born in Ashington, Northumberland, in 1935. Quitting his job in a coal mine after only a day, he applied to join the police, but was then offered a trial by Leeds United who had seen him playing as a centre-half in an amateur match. The trial game clashed with the police interview, and Charlton chose the former. He impressed them sufficiently to be taken on as an apprentice at Leeds, for whom he signed professional terms in 1952. Before his first-team debut against Doncaster Rovers the following year, Charlton remembers waiting for instructions from manager Raich Carter. Finally, at five to three as the players left the dressing room, Charlton asked: 'What do you want me to do, boss?' Carter answered: 'See how fast their centre-forward can limp!'

It was a policy Charlton was often encouraged to adopt during his 21 years with Leeds, and at 6 feet 3 inches tall (hence his nickname of 'The Giraffe'), he had the physique to back up the attitude. After Southampton's bruiser of a centre-forward George Kirby had flattened Charlton, the referee said: 'Give it five minutes, Jack.'

'For what?' asked Charlton, puzzled.

'Before you try to get your own back,' said the referee.

In 1970 Charlton sparked outrage when he revealed in a television interview: 'I have a little black book with players' names in it. If I get the chance to do them, I will.' The prospect of Charlton roaming pitches the length and breadth of the land wreaking revenge for past misdemeanours had the authorities in a lather, but Charlton later insisted that the book did not really exist.

By then of course he had a World Cup winners' medal to his name. He remembers how in the last minute of extra-time in the 1966 final, when Bobby Moore got the ball, he yelled at him to get rid of it. Instead, Moore coolly looked upfield, spotted Geoff Hurst in acres of space and played a perfect pass for his West Ham colleague to score the fourth goal. Charlton says: 'I remember looking at my captain (Moore) and thinking, "I will never be able to play this bloody game."'

Charlton may have been a hero that afternoon alongside brother Bobby, but as a key cog in the Leeds mean machine of the early

Seventies, he was definitely cast in the role of villain. When Don Revie had succeeded Carter as manager in 1961, Charlton thought his days were numbered as the two had clashed as players. In fact, he was all set to join his brother Bobby at Old Trafford but the asking price was too high. Instead, Charlton stayed and Revie built his uncompromising defence around him. Part of Charlton's remit was to go forward for corners and free-kicks and make life as uncomfortable as possible for the opposing goalkeeper by generally getting in the way. Many questioned the legality of this tactic but it reaped enormous dividends for Leeds, bringing them a string of honours. Team-mate Billy Bremner, no shrinking violet himself, said of Jack: 'He was a one-man awkward squad. There was a time when he was ready to feud and almost to fight with anyone who crossed his path.'

After an impressive 96 goals in 773 games for Leeds, Charlton retired from playing in 1973 to become manager of Middlesbrough, whom he immediately led to the Second Division title by such a margin that he was named Manager of the Year, the first time the award had been given to a manager outside the top division. He quit Middlesbrough in 1977 and, after failing to land the England job vacated by his old boss Revie, he took over at Sheffield Wednesday. His will to win was still very much to the fore at Hillsborough; he once called a priest to the ground to find out whether a player was lying about a disputed goal in a five-a-side practice game. He left Wednesday in 1983, and following a brief return to Middlesbrough and a short stint at Newcastle, he was appointed manager of the Republic of Ireland in 1986.

The Irish had always had decent players but rarely a decent team. Charlton set about remedying that by fostering togetherness in the dressing room and by recruiting players with the most tenuous of Irish links. Charlton himself used to joke about it and once asked Paul Gascoigne if he had an Irish wolfwound.

'No. Why?' asked Gazza.

'Because,' replied Charlton, 'if you had an Irish wolfhound, you could qualify to play for Ireland.'

After acquitting themselves admirably at the 1988 European Championships, the Irish qualified for the World Cup final stages for the first time in their history. Their style of play was not always easy on the eye but they played to their strengths and relished the role of underdogs. Charlton appeared supremely comfortable on the world stage, his bluntness and wit proving a refreshing change from the usual tame platitudes delivered by managers and coaches. Charlton's love for the Irish lifestyle made him a national hero. During Italia '90 he and the players were granted an audience with the Pope at the Vatican, at which even the Pope addressed Charlton as 'the boss'. The unfancied Irish eventually went out narrowly in the quarter-finals to the hosts but won thousands of new friends the world over. Back home, Charlton was so popular that thousands would turn out to greet him wherever he went and he drew bigger crowds than Nelson Mandela in Dublin. Even his cigarette butts were collected by fans. He was awarded the OBE, given honorary Irish citizenship...as well as the freedom of any bar in the land. Indeed, he once admitted: 'The honour that pleased me most of all was when the House of Commons voted me Beer Drinker of the Year.'

Ireland qualified again for the 1994 finals, reaching the second round, but his team was starting to show its age. After failing to qualify for Euro '96, Charlton resigned to spend more time on his favourite hobby, fishing. He had always said that football was not everything to him. 'I won't die at a match. I might die being dragged down the River Tweed by a giant salmon, but a football match, no.' In one of his last press conferences as manager, he mocked the assembled media by asking, after a disappointing display against Northern Ireland: 'Can I go storming out now, please?'

Charlton's strength with Ireland was his man management. He fostered a wonderful team spirit and recognised the benefits of the occasional communal drinking session. He was very loyal to his players and repeatedly covered up defender Paul McGrath's drinking problems. McGrath said: 'He has always defended me no matter what the weight of evidence against me. He's been like an old mongrel; no matter how many times you kick him, he will always come back on side.'

Even when a player did something he totally disapproved of, Charlton would usually offer his support. During the 1994 World Cup in the United States, striker Tony Cascarino met a girl in a bar and took her back to his hotel room. Charlton was livid when he found out and threatened to send Cascarino home. But at the last minute he relented, muttering as he walked away: 'Well, I hope she was fucking worth it!'

Brian Clough
Old Big 'Ead

There have been few more complex, contradictory characters in football than Brian Howard Clough. He was a strict disciplinarian yet he encouraged his players to go out drinking before big European ties; he treated the press with contempt, keeping reporters waiting for hours and being downright rude to them, yet he was more than happy to take newspaper money in return for writing columns; he was widely praised for launching a campaign to stop Nottingham Forest fans swearing during matches though he himself swore like a trooper; he was an authoritarian figure but despised authority; he insisted on players being smartly dressed and detested 'shabby appearance', yet he himself wore that same green sweatshirt day after day and once attended tennis at Wimbledon in a tracksuit; he could be a vindictive, heartless bully but he could also be compassionate and would arrange for flowers to be sent to a player's family in times of trouble.

'He was a man for all seasons,' says Stuart Pearce. 'He had a reputation as being a hard taskmaster, which he was when it was needed. But there were other times like when I came back from the 1990 World Cup under a bit of a cloud and he was there with an arm around the shoulder. He knew exactly what to do at the right times.'

Clough's management style was unique. In training at Forest he would call a halt to a practice match after just 15 minutes if he couldn't be bothered with it. Once he made the entire squad run through a huge patch of stinging nettles and on another occasion he had them scouring the hedgerows at the training ground for mushrooms. As part of one training session, he arranged a competition to see how many players would fit into a five-a-side net. His players and staff never knew what to expect from one day to the next, but it certainly kept everybody on their toes.

He seemed to be at his most unpredictable when travelling in the team coach. On the way to a match at Luton, he made the coach driver pull over because they were running early. Consequently, the Forest players were left wandering around on the hard shoulder of the M1 for half an hour. For a game at Millwall, he ordered the Forest players off the coach half a mile from the old Den and forced them to walk through the hostile crowd to the ground. En route for another match in London, he spotted a truck driver stuck on the hard shoulder, peering into the engine of his lorry. Clough immediately told the team coach driver to pull over, whereupon football's most famous manager climbed down carrying the plate of sandwiches that had been prepared for after the game and, offering nourishment to the stricken lorry driver, asked if he could help in any way. Fortunately, the driver declined and Forest were able to resume their journey. Even more bizarre was the episode when, having arranged a club trip to Spain in two weeks' time, he ordered the Forest coach to pull off the M1 at junction 24 so that the players could drive past East Midlands Airport and wave...

Clough was a firm believer in the family unit, an attitude stemming from his own happy childhood in Middlesbrough. The sixth of nine children, he was born on 21 March 1935. His father worked in the local sweet factory and his mother toiled all hours looking after the large family. She was a major influence on him and even when he lived in a large house in Derbyshire courtesy of his manager's wages, Clough displayed his mother's old washing mangle in the front room, to remind him of his roots. The scroll naming him a Freeman of the City of Nottingham was placed incongruously on top of the mangle.

The arrogance that would become such a feature of his managerial career was there right from his playing days. His job was to score goals and nobody was allowed to get in his way, particularly his Middlesbrough team-mates. He would yell 'Out of the way' at colleagues as they were shaping to shoot, and would then steal the ball from them and score himself. Once he went so far as to barge team-mate Arthur Fitzsimmons off the ball before running on to score. Challenged about the incident afterwards, Clough replied simply: 'I'm better at it than he is.' In fairness, he had the statistics to back up the self-belief – 204 goals in just 222 starts for Middlesbrough, followed by 63 goals in only 74 appearances for Sunderland. He later described himself, with suitable immodesty, as 'the finest goalscorer in the country and one of the best the game has ever seen', conveniently forgetting that virtually all of those goals were scored in the Second Division. What really irked him was that he earned only two England caps – in 1960 against Wales and Sweden. But the truth is that he under-performed in both matches at a time when there were plenty of good English goalscorers (Jimmy Greaves and Bobby Charlton to name but two) playing at the highest level.

Sadly, any public bar arguments about his non-selection were rendered immaterial on Boxing Day 1962. Playing for Sunderland against Bury on an icy Roker Park pitch, Clough pursued a loose ball and collided with the onrushing Bury goalkeeper. Among the Bury line-up that day was Bob Stokoe, later to become manager of Sunderland. Thinking Clough was feigning injury, Stokoe yelled at him to get up and get on with the game. Clough never forgave him. The young striker was stretchered off with torn cruciate ligaments, and although he attempted a comeback 18 months later, he played only three more games before being forced to retire at 29. The cruel curtailment of his career would serve to drive him as a manager.

Clough's first chance in management came in 1965 at the distinctly unglamorous setting of Hartlepools United, as the club was then known. The strict dress code with no players being allowed long, unkempt hair had been inherited from his old Sunderland manager, Alan Brown, but the abrasive style was all Clough's own. As his assistant, Clough recruited Peter Taylor, who had been a goalkeeper with him at Middlesbrough and who had since managed Burton Albion. The first of many battles with chairmen was fought at the Victoria Ground. Hartlepools chairman Ernie Ord wanted to sack Taylor and when Clough stood up to him, Ord tried to sack him, too. But Clough refused to go and after an emergency board meeting, it was Ord who departed instead.

In 1967 Clough and Taylor joined Second Division Derby County, where they employed guile and resourcefulness to sign the players they wanted. Midfielder Archie Gemmill was procured after Clough won over Mrs Gemmill by turning up at their home and washing the dishes, while centre-half Roy McFarland was signed from Tranmere Rovers after the dynamic duo launched a midnight raid on his Merseyside home. They knocked on the door of the family house in the middle of the night and asked McFarland's parents to get the youngster out of bed. As a bleary-eyed McFarland staggered downstairs in his pyjamas at two o'clock in the morning, Clough told him: 'Take as much time as you want, but we're not leaving this house without a decision.' Within half an hour McFarland had signed.

Clough only wanted people around him who were winners. He is said to have had two of the Derby tea ladies sacked because he heard them giggling after a home defeat. His ruthlessness paid off as he took Derby first to promotion and then, in 1972, to the League Championship for the first time in the club's history. But his frequent outspoken comments about the people running football and club directors in particular led to clashes with Derby chairman Sam Longson. In 1973 Clough and Taylor sensationally resigned from the Baseball Ground and decamped to Brighton & Hove Albion. There, the magic deserted them. Results were dismal, a 4-0 home defeat by Walton & Hersham in the FA Cup being only marginally more embarrassing than an 8-2 home drubbing by Bristol Rovers.

Clough did not hang around for long and the following year moved alone to Leeds as successor to Don Revie, who had accepted the England job. To say the least, Clough was a surprising appointment since he had always been highly critical of Revie's Leeds. And he had no intention of softening his stance, telling the Leeds players in his opening speech: 'Gentlemen, the first thing you can do for me is throw your medals and your pots and pans in the dustbin because you've never won anything fairly. You've done it by cheating.' For once, Clough had bitten off more than he could chew; he might have been able to intimidate ordinary players but the likes of Billy Bremner, Johnny Giles and Norman Hunter were another matter. He lasted just 44 days at Elland Road.

In 1975 he pitched up at Nottingham Forest, where he was joined a year later by Taylor. Together they revitalised another provincial club, bringing unprecedented success to the City Ground in the form of a League title and two European Cup triumphs. His methods were as quirky as ever. His team talks were rarely tactical and he hardly ever discussed the opposition. He would give players whisky or brandy just before kick-off to calm any nerves, while his pre-match talk for one big game consisted of him singing 'Fly Me to the Moon' and then telling his players: 'I'm a good singer and you're good footballers. Now go out and win.'

Before the second leg of a 1978 European Cup tie at Anfield, he plied his players with drink at lunchtime and sent them to bed in the afternoon. The plan worked as Forest held out for a 0-0 draw to go through on aggregate. On the night before the 1979 League Cup final against Southampton, he ordered a dozen bottles of champagne and kept the players up until one o'clock in the morning. It took them 45 minutes to shake off the hangover the following afternoon before Forest fought back to win 3-2 – one of four League Cup successes under Clough. He celebrated one Wembley triumph by taking the League Cup home and putting it on top of the television set while his family sat around eating fish and chips. Before the victorious 1980 European Cup final against Hamburg, he took the players on holiday to Majorca for a week – no training, just drinking and relaxing. One player said: 'No one who saw us stumbling around the streets in the early hours would ever have dreamed we were about to play the most important match of our lives.'

Sometimes on the morning of a big game he would take the players for a walk and, coming across a tree, would suddenly announce: 'This is a punch tree. You have got to punch it. It's lucky.' On other occasions he simply did not bother going to the game, preferring to stay at home and tend his roses.

He continued to rule largely by fear, finding the Forest players more compliant in this respect than those at Leeds. Any hint of dressing room dissent was dealt with summarily. When he was at Derby, he outlined his approach to quashing player unrest: 'I'll invite him in, we'll sit down and talk about it for 20 minutes, and then we'll decide that I was right.' Perhaps because he was a centre-forward himself, he seemed to reserve the greatest humiliations at Forest for his strikers. Upon becoming Britain's first £1-million footballer, Trevor Francis was ordered to clean his team-mates' boots and consigned to the third team. Later at an awards' ceremony, Clough told him very publicly to take his hands out of his pockets. Garry Birtles was once thrown off the team coach and told to find his own way to the airport after making the mistake of complaining about an early start. Clough derided Justin Fashanu, another million-pound man, as his worst-ever signing ('when I buy a player, I don't expect to have to teach him to play football'), and when Nigel Jemson threatened to display an ego that matched that of his manager, Clough asked him: 'Have you ever been punched in the stomach, young man?' Jemson replied that he hadn't, whereupon Clough fulfilled the threat with the words, 'Well, now you have.'

Worse still was the withering put-down he delivered to Darren Currie. A month after signing the striker from Barnsley, Clough realised he had made a mistake. In front of the whole team, he asked: 'Hey, son, have you got yourself a house yet?'

'No, boss, not yet,' replied Currie cheerfully.

'Well, don't bother,' sneered Clough.

Within weeks Currie was on his way out of the City Ground.

Clough was a none-too-benevolent dictator at Forest. The players, the board, the fans, even visiting managers were all in awe of him, although in some instances it was more a fear of being kissed by him. As he became increasingly eccentric, he took to kissing everyone in sight, including hard-bitten newsmen. When Forest fans invaded the pitch to celebrate a League Cup victory over Queens Park Rangers, an angry Clough whacked two lads around the ear and dragged them off the pitch. He realised he had overstepped the mark this time and decided to make up with the pair by persuading them to give him a kiss in front of the TV cameras. He also punished Everton players who, disappointed at losing a League Cup tie, had trashed their City Ground dressing room. Knowing they were due back three days later for a League match, Clough instructed the cleaners to leave it as it was.

His great gift was in being able to turn average players into world-beaters. John Robertson, the overweight winger, was a case in point. Clough said of him: 'He didn't look anything like a professional athlete when I first clapped eyes on him. In fact, there were times when he barely resembled a member of the human race. Whenever I felt off-colour, I'd sit next to him because then I looked like Errol Flynn.' Yet he turned Robertson into a match-winner, to the extent that talented team-mates such as Martin O'Neill were instructed to give the ball to the Scot at the first opportunity...or risk the wrath of Clough.

In all this time his one big gripe was that he was overlooked for the England job in favour of Ron Greenwood, although Clough could understand, to a point, why the FA reached its decision. He said: 'Ron is a charming man who wouldn't hurt a fly and couldn't fall out with his wife if he tried. They just didn't want any trouble. They were shrewd, because they were thinking I was going to take over the FA. And they were right! They didn't want an England manager who was prepared to call the Italians cheating bastards. They failed to understand that I would have curbed my language and revelled in the relief from the day-to-day grind of club management.' The snub would continue to rankle and Clough left anyone who asked in no doubt that he would have made a great England manager. 'I could manage England part-time and still walk the dog,' he proclaimed. And when there was talk of him being in line for the Republic of Ireland job, he joked: 'It's easy enough to get to Ireland. It's just a straight walk across the Irish Sea as far as I'm concerned.' Clough was certainly not above poking fun at himself and always claimed that his OBE stood for 'Old Big 'Ead.'

While the one-liners continued, the success didn't. In 1982 Peter Taylor took charge at Derby and infuriated his old partner by poaching John Robertson without informing Clough. The pair had a massive fall-out, with Clough growling: 'We pass each other on the A52 going to work most days of the week. But if his car broke down and I saw him thumbing a lift, I wouldn't pick him up – I'd run him over.' The bitter feud had not been repaired by the time of Taylor's death in 1990, although Clough and his family did attend the funeral and he subsequently spoke in glowing terms about his old friend – as well he might, because without Taylor, Clough struggled at Forest just as he had done at Leeds. His roses might have flourished, but the Forest garden slowly died of neglect.

In 1993 Forest were relegated and Clough announced his retirement from management. When one director, free at last of the Clough tyranny, broke ranks and revealed details of Clough's heavy drinking, Clough reacted with typical bluster, calling him a liar and threatening to sue. No writ was forthcoming, Clough instead choosing to confirm his alcoholism in print...for money. He was also heavily implicated in the 'bungs' scandal that hit English football in the 1990s, but the FA conveniently decided that he was too ill to face any charges.

Clough became increasingly frail but the ego was still rampant. 'I wouldn't say I was the best manager in the business,' he stated, 'but I was in the top one.'

He died of stomach cancer on 20 September 2004, and former colleagues queued up to pay tribute to this extraordinary character. Martin O'Neill summed up Brian Clough's personality with typical eloquence. 'He was absolutely sensational and I don't think Brian would disagree with that. He would be the first to say he was the greatest of all time. He had unbelievable charisma. Outwardly he had this fantastic self-belief and self-confidence but in truth I think sometimes he was as vulnerable as all of us.'

Inevitably, the old question about whether Clough should have been offered the England job resurfaced. His devotees say it was a scandal that he was ignored, but while he was undoubtedly a great club manager, his increasing dependency on alcohol mixed with more than a dash of xenophobia and a problem with handling big-name players would surely have made for an unpalatable cocktail.

Brian Clough was a flawed genius, but tellingly very few of his former players have ever had a bad word to say about him. As Martin O'Neill said: 'I've seen big men hide in corridors to avoid him. He was egocentric, sometimes a bully, often impossible. But I wouldn't have missed a moment of it because, in the end, as a manager he was magical.'

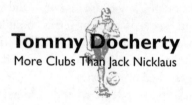

Tommy Docherty
More Clubs Than Jack Nicklaus

Tommy Docherty had a wisecrack for every occasion – whether it was to mark a success, a scandal (of which there were plenty) or a sacking (of which there were even more). Controversy was virtually a constant companion to the doughty little Scot in a career in which he managed 13 different clubs (two twice) and one country. There was a high-profile court case, a high-profile love triangle and countless bust-ups with chairmen. Only Rome was sacked more often than Docherty. As Matt Busby, who was a director of Manchester United when Docherty was manager during a typically turbulent reign, once remarked: 'Tommy Docherty didn't make news, he *was* the news.'

Thomas Henderson Docherty was born in the tough Gorbals district of Glasgow on 24 August 1928. After representing the British Army football team while doing his National Service, he was offered a contract with his beloved Celtic in 1947. He found first-team opportunities restricted at Parkhead and two years later moved to Preston North End, where he developed into a solid, dependable wing-half, making 323 League appearances for the club and winning the first of his 25 Scottish caps. In 1958 he joined Arsenal for £28,000 and effectively finished his playing career at Highbury, although he did go on to make a handful of appearances for Chelsea, whom he joined as player-coach in 1961. When Ted Drake stepped down as manager, with Chelsea staring relegation in the face, Docherty was appointed his successor – and although he was unable to keep the club in the top flight, he set about building for a brighter future.

Docherty got rid of a lot of the old guard, replacing them with emerging youngsters such as Terry Venables, Bobby Tambling, Peter Bonetti and Barry Bridges. He backed these up with shrewd signings, such as left-back Eddie McCreadie from Scottish minnows East Stirling. Docherty remembered the boardroom there being 'so small, someone had to step outside to make way for me'.

His bright young Chelsea team won promotion back to Division One at the first attempt and finished a highly creditable fifth the following year. Docherty's bubbly personality brought out the best in his players although McCreadie later noted: 'He could get angry if he felt you weren't putting it in on the field. He once came into the dressing room at half-time and it was like the first 20 minutes of *Saving Private Ryan*.'

In 1964–65 Chelsea were in line for an historic treble of League, FA Cup and League Cup. They won the League Cup (beating Leicester City over two legs), but lost to Liverpool in the semi-finals of the FA Cup. However, Docherty's relationship with some of his players – notably his captain, Venables – had become strained, and when eight of them broke a curfew before a vital match at Burnley, he sent them home. Chelsea were just two points behind Manchester United at the time but the weakened side lost at Turf Moor to end any hopes of bringing the title to West London. Venables was sold to Spurs and, ironically, was a member of the side that beat Docherty's Chelsea in the 1967 Cup final. Five months after that Wembley defeat, Docherty sensationally resigned.

The following month he took charge at Second Division Rotherham United, which, by anyone's estimation, was a far cry from the bright lights of Stamford Bridge. Prior to accepting the job, he was given a tour of Rotherham's Millmoor Ground by chairman Eric Purshouse. As they turned a corner at the back of the main stand, Docherty noticed a dilapidated wooden hut.

'Well, that eyesore will have to go for a start,' he told the chairman. 'That's your office,' said Purshouse.

A year later he was back in London with Queens Park Rangers. Reflecting on his time in Yorkshire, he said: 'I made a promise to the chairman that I would take Rotherham out of the Second Division. I did. I took them straight into the Third!'

He lasted just 29 days at Loftus Road before quitting in frustration at not being able to persuade chairman Jim Gregory to sanction signings. In December 1968 he enjoyed the dubious distinction of becoming Doug Ellis's first manager at Aston Villa. As results stuttered, Docherty received the dreaded vote of confidence. 'Doug Ellis said he was right behind me. I told him I'd sooner have him in front of me where I could see him.' His worst fears were realised in January 1970 when, with Villa bottom of the Second Division, Ellis sacked him.

Next he tried his luck in Portugal with FC Porto but stayed for just four months. He returned to England in July 1971 to take up the post as assistant to Terry Neill at Hull City, but two months later Docherty was appointed caretaker-manager of the Scottish national team, the position soon becoming permanent. However, in December 1972 the lure of Old Trafford proved too powerful to resist and 'The Doc' took charge of Manchester United, promising to restore the ailing patient to good health.

The parallels with his time at Chelsea were uncanny. As at Stamford Bridge, he had no qualms about upsetting stellar reputations. Denis Law was given a free transfer and George Best was eventually sacked, although Docherty did fear the public backlash if he got rid of Bobby Charlton – fortunately Charlton saved him the trouble by announcing his retirement. In their place came a host of promising youngsters (including wingers Steve Coppell from Tranmere Rovers and Gordon Hill from Millwall) to create a fearless, buccaneering side that restored the feel-good factor to Old Trafford. Even the team's fortunes followed a similar pattern to Chelsea's in the Sixties – relegation, instant promotion and a losing Cup final. But this time Docherty followed up with a second Wembley appearance a year later, in 1977, which brought victory over Liverpool. The realisation that he was a winner suddenly hit him when he went for a jog in Hyde Park the following morning, causing him to do cartwheels in celebration. However, once again a Wembley appearance was swiftly followed by a sudden exit. When news broke that Docherty had been having an affair with the wife of United physiotherapist Laurie Brown, he was sacked as manager amid sensational tabloid headlines. 'I have been punished for falling in love,' he complained. 'What I have done has nothing at all to do with my track record as a manager.' To complete the Chelsea analogy, he was replaced as manager by Dave Sexton, the same man who had succeeded him at Stamford Bridge.

Docherty was later asked whether he had ever received any death threats at Old Trafford. 'Only the one,' he replied deadpan. 'A supporter wrote to me and threatened that if I picked goalkeeper Paddy Roche again, he'd kill himself.'

Docherty did not remain out of work for long. Two months after being ousted from Old Trafford, he took over the reins at Derby County but this, too, ended in a blaze of unwanted publicity. Against his better judgement, he was persuaded to sue former Manchester United captain Willie Morgan and Granada Television for libel, but the case was eventually dropped after Docherty admitted he had lied in court. The end of the court case coincided with the end of Docherty's time at Derby.

But a month later, in May 1979, the irrepressible Scot was back in management at Queens Park Rangers, the club he had walked out on 11 years earlier and where Jim Gregory was still chairman. The two were soon at loggerheads and Docherty was sacked almost immediately, only to be reinstated. Then in October 1980, with the team struggling for form, Gregory summoned Docherty to his office.

'Things are not going well around here, Tommy,' he said. 'There will have to be changes.'

'You can't walk away now, Jim,' urged Docherty. 'You're doing a great job!'

Docherty was out. Looking back on his time at Loftus Road, he said: 'I sacked Queens Park Rangers once and they later sacked me twice.'

Following a short spell in Australia coaching Sydney Olympic, he came back to England to manage Preston but was sacked after a few months. 'They offered me a handshake of £10,000 to settle amicably. I told them they would have to be a lot more amicable than that.' The only good news for him in 1981 was that he was cleared of perjury charges arising from the Morgan trial.

Still the jobs kept on coming, Docherty himself admitting, 'I've had more clubs than Jack Nicklaus.' First it was South Melbourne, followed by another spell at Sydney Olympic, and then in 1984 Wolverhampton Wanderers. The once-mighty (for those with a long memory) Wolves were in freefall, plunging down the divisions at an alarming rate. Their financial position was equally dire. Due to non-payment the milkman was refusing to deliver any milk to the club, the local garage had cancelled the club's petrol account and even the electricity was cut off at Molineux at one point. On one away trip Docherty had to pay the hotel for the players' pre-match meal out of his own pocket because the hotel feared that the account would not otherwise be settled. Meanwhile, results were so bad that Docherty quipped: 'We don't use a stopwatch to judge our golden goal competition now, we use a calendar.' Before a vital game with Blackburn, Docherty cheekily sat in on the Blackburn team talk and then calmly stood up saying: 'Don't worry about our lot; they're crap.'

Naturally, the fans were restless. Following a 5-1 defeat at Brighton, Docherty saw a Wolves supporter with a clipboard and pen. When he walked over to him and asked what he was doing, the supporter's face went white.

'I'm collecting signatures for a petition to get you out of the club,' he stuttered.

'Here, give me that petition,' said Docherty. 'I'll sign it myself.' And he did.

Days later he and the club parted company as Wolves were relegated to Division Three. He said afterwards: 'It was stated that I had left the club by "mutual consent" and for once that was true. The club wanted to get rid of me and I couldn't wait to go.'

His last stab at management came at Altrincham in 1987. Walking into the dressing room, he turned to physio Jeff Warburton and asked with a twinkle in his eye: 'How's the wife?' The remark was vintage Docherty – he was even able to turn his biggest scandal into a joke. Altrincham also afforded him the chance of one final dispute with a board. When chairman Geoff Lloyd told Docherty that there was a clash of personalities between them, Docherty responded: 'Impossible. You haven't got one.'

Docherty appeared to thrive on confrontation. In a comment scarcely designed to endear him to his employers, he once said: 'The ideal board of directors should be made up of three men: two dead and the other dying.' Unfortunately, these frequent fall-outs have sometimes overshadowed his very real ability as a manager. At both Chelsea and Manchester United he created teams that were good enough to challenge for honours while playing attractive, open football. But being Docherty, the adventures were bound to end in tears and recrimination. Whatever anyone says about him – and he has stepped on plenty of toes in his time – life with him in charge was never dull.

Barry Fry
The Del Boy of Football

Some people are born to manage international superstars but Barry Fry knows his place. 'I've made my career by getting players nobody else wanted and getting them to believe that they are the bollocks,' he says in his own inimitable style. If Sir Alex Ferguson is the Donald Trump of the football world, Barry Fry is the Del Boy.

The chirpy Fry is a compulsive wheeler-dealer. He played the transfer market like City dealers play the stock market. In his three years at Birmingham City in the mid-1990s, more than 100 players came and went. In one season alone he used 46 players, breaking the English League record of 43…held by Fry and Birmingham the previous season. When he was asked in the club programme what he would buy if he won the National Lottery, he replied: 'Twenty-seven new strikers.' He was only half joking. Fry's frenzied activity led comedian Jasper Carrott, a lifelong Birmingham supporter, to suggest that Fry 'was probably trying to sort out the unemployment problem single-handed'. Fellow managers were also sometimes less than complimentary, Mark McGhee saying of Fry: 'His management style seems to be based on the chaos theory.' But it was all water off a duck's back to 'Bazza' who would continue to manage the only way he knew.

To see the portly Fry these days, it is hard to imagine that he was once a lively winger with Manchester United. Born in Bedford in

1945, he never made the grade at Old Trafford (hardly surprising as George Best was blocking his route to the first team) and left to try his luck at Bolton, Luton and Leyton Orient before being forced to retire prematurely due to injury.

In 1973 he was appointed manager of Dunstable Town. His first game in charge drew 34 paying spectators and the second 42, because Fry's family came. After that he recommended that instead of the team changes being announced to the crowd, the crowd changes should be announced to the team! However, in businessman Keith Cheeseman, Dunstable had a chairman with lofty ideas and the financial clout to match them. Fry never knew exactly what Cheeseman's business entailed but his suspicion that it was not entirely above board was reinforced when Cheeseman later became a guest of Her Majesty. Cheeseman's goal was to put Dunstable on the map as more than a junction off the M1. Fry was told to recruit big-name players and he responded by bringing in former West Bromwich Albion and England striker Jeff Astle and none other than George Best. 'How can you put in words what it means signing George Best for Dunstable?' trilled Fry. 'It will be a bigger boost for the club than having Frank Sinatra sing at half-time.' Although Best only played three games for the club and was a shadow of his former self, his name was sufficient to add hundreds to the gate.

Nevertheless, Fry was not prepared to allow his star players to have an easy ride. He recalls: 'In one game we were 3-0 down at half-time. Jeff Astle came in and was looking for a cup of tea. I gave him one – all over his shirt! The rest of the team got the same treatment and went back out on to the pitch. We ended up winning 5-3 and Jeff got a hat-trick.' Fry's propensity for hurling liquid eventually cost him his job when he was sacked for throwing a glass of whisky over Cheeseman's successor, Bill Kitt.

In 1979 Fry took over at Barnet, a post he would occupy for the next 14 years apart from a nine-month break to manage Maidstone United in the mid-1980s. Money was tight at Barnet so when a Boxing Day fixture with Wealdstone – which was expected to attract a bumper crowd – was put in jeopardy because of a frozen pitch, the manager took matters into his own hands. At one o'clock on Christmas morning he was out rolling the pitch on a tractor, singing carols in the pitch dark, but following complaints from neighbours, the police arrived to arrest him. 'When I said I was the manager,' recalls Fry, 'the policeman replied, "Yeah, and I'm George Best!"' He eventually talked his way out of it but had only been able to roll half of the pitch and the other half was in such a state that the referee called the game off. All Fry's efforts had been in vain.

Never one to hide his feelings, the ebullient Fry once tipped a bucket of ice-cold water over a linesman who had upset him, but on a more serious note he suffered the first of two heart attacks while trying to push the broken-down Barnet team bus at Gateshead. His blood pressure could not have been helped by having to deal with another rogue chairman, ticket tout Stan Flashman. Their relationship was more like Tom and Jerry than Starsky and Hutch. They would row, rant and rage, Flashman would sack him (something he did at least eight times) and then reinstate him a few hours later. Flashman constantly argued with Fry over team selection, going so far as to threaten to have his 'boys' attack one player, Harry Willis, with baseball bats if he ever set foot on the pitch again. Fry defied his chairman and picked Willis, who went on to score a hat-trick, whereupon Flashman claimed the threats had all been part of his motivation technique. When Barnet were finally promoted into the Football League and reached the Division Three play-offs in 1992, Flashman and Fry had another furious fight, which predictably ended in the manager being sacked. Equally predictably, Flashman quickly backtracked and when a radio reporter asked why Fry had been fired, Flashman hit him over the head with his microphone.

The following year the pair did finally part company, with Fry deciding to join Southend United. Fry was always game for a laugh and would seemingly do anything for publicity. After an Italian opponent had threatened Southend winger Ricky Otto with a hammer, Fry chased Otto into the centre circle at the next home game, wielding a huge inflatable hammer! Despite his popularity with the media, Fry left Southend under a cloud by accepting an offer to become manager at Birmingham City.

He spent three turbulent years at St Andrews, with rarely a week going by without a major fall-out between manager and board. On live television he accused the club owner David Sullivan of not knowing a goal-line from a clothes line, causing a watching Sullivan to spill his drink in the boardroom. Once again, the media revelled in Fry's outspoken comments – his disarming honesty and colourful turn of phrase livened up many a post-match interview. He loved to play to the cameras and when Birmingham took the lead in a televised match against Huddersfield Town, he leapt from the dugout and charged down the length of the touchline flailing his arms around like a windmill. It became his trademark goal celebration, although he did not get the chance to use it as much as he – or the Birmingham fans – would have liked. For despite the board backing his almost daily dips into the transfer market, the results were largely disappointing. After the club were relegated to the Second Division in 1994, Fry lamented: 'Even if you are the worst manager in the world, you should win at least once in three months.'

He did take Birmingham back up but was sacked in 1996 as the season started to fall away alarmingly. Not only did his revolving door transfer policy create inconsistency, but his tactics frequently left something to be desired. He loved all-out attack but all too often this left gaping holes at the back. One of his many strikers, Steve Claridge, commented: 'You could write Barry's knowledge of tactics on a stamp…but first of all you'd have to fold the stamp in half!'

In 1996, he became chairman-manager of Peterborough United, which at least prevented him from falling out with himself. However, he suffered a second heart attack, which caused him to remark in 2000: 'These days I no longer run down the touchline when we score. I just waddle a bit.' After two relegations and a promotion, he stepped down as manager in 2005 by popular demand and relinquished his role as chairman a year later. In 2007 he served as the club's Director of Football.

Barry Fry has certainly had his critics but, with his cheerful disposition in the face of adversity, it is impossible to dislike him…unless perhaps you happen to be a supporter of one of the clubs he has managed.

Ian Holloway
Barking Mad?

In an age when most managers trot out the same clichés and criticisms in their post-match interviews, Ian Holloway is a glorious exception. He is no more likely to describe himself as being 'sick as a parrot' or refer to 'a game of two halves' than Sam Allardyce is to recite a few lines from Wordsworth. And when Holloway's Queens Park Rangers team beat Cardiff City in 2006, he did not profess himself to be 'over the moon'; instead he told reporters: 'I couldn't be more chuffed if I were a badger at the start of the mating season.'

Holloway specialises in convoluted metaphors and analogies. After QPR had struggled to beat Chesterfield, he delighted journalists with the following assessment: 'To put it in gentlemen's terms, if you've been out for a night and you're looking for a young lady and you pull one, some weeks they're good looking and some weeks they're not the best. Our performance today would have been not the best-looking bird but at least we got her in the taxi. She weren't the best-looking lady we ended up taking home but she was very pleasant and very nice, so thanks very much, let's have a coffee.'

He was equally inventive in praise of his veteran striker Paul Furlong. 'Paul Furlong is my vintage Rolls-Royce and he cost me nothing. We polish him, look after him, and I have him fine-tuned by my mechanics. We take good care of him because we have to drive him every day, not just save him for weddings.'

Nor is Holloway found wanting when it comes to debating the finer points of positional play. He summed up the role of the defensive midfield player thus: 'It's all very well having a great pianist playing but it's no good if you haven't got anyone to get the piano on the stage in the first place, otherwise the pianist would be standing there with no bloody piano to play.' And of strikers: 'You can say that strikers are very much like postmen: they have to get in and out as quick as they can before the dog starts to have a go.'

Holloway's ramblings have made him something of a national treasure, with entire websites devoted to what have become known as 'Ollyisms'. In 2005, when he was manager at QPR, he was voted

15th in *Time Out*'s list of the 50 funniest Londoners, beating Paul Merton and Ali G among others – no mean feat since Holloway comes from Bristol. Although the words of wisdom keep pouring from his mouth and he admires great orators like Churchill, he feels slightly uneasy with his new-found fame and prefers not to be viewed as madcap. 'It upsets me a bit, to be honest,' he says, 'because things make sense when I say them.'

Born in 1963, Holloway turned professional with his local team, Bristol Rovers, in 1981. At 5 feet 8 inches he describes himself as a 'rottweiler trapped inside a terrier's body', and made a sufficient impression in Rovers' midfield to earn a £35,000 transfer to Wimbledon in 1985. The move did not work out and after 14 games he was loaned first to Brentford and then Torquay before returning to Bristol Rovers. He spent the next four years with Rovers, scoring 26 times in 179 League appearances, but in 1991 when Rovers' manager Gerry Francis moved to QPR, he took Holloway with him for a fee of £230,000. 'I was 29 and I'd never played in the top flight,' says Holloway. 'But Gerry said I was an infectious little git and he wanted to take me with him. He said I probably wouldn't play, that he just wanted me around for my attitude in training and in the dressing room. But I ended up playing 150 games in five years there.'

In 1996 he moved back to Bristol Rovers as player-manager, taking his total number of appearances for the club to over 400. So passionate was he about the blue half of Bristol that he banned all vehicles in red (the colour of rivals Bristol City) from the training ground. His excellent work at Rovers attracted the attention of struggling QPR in 2001, and he returned to the London club, where his honesty, commitment and quirky character endeared him to the fans. However, after twice failing to gain promotion back to the Championship, he was aware that they could turn against him. After a much-needed win, he reflected: 'In football there is no definite lifespan or time span for a manager. After a while you start smelling of fish. The other week it looked like I was stinking of halibut!' Promotion was eventually secured in 2004 and Holloway was determined to savour the moment. 'They say that every dog has his day and today is woof day. I want to go and bark.'

Rangers wagged their tails quite contentedly in the Championship for two seasons until Holloway was suddenly placed on gardening leave amid rumours linking him to a vacancy at Leicester City. In the summer of 2006 he became manager of Plymouth Argyle instead, an appointment he marked with a characteristically creative metaphor that started promisingly before drifting into surrealism. 'I want to try and spread the support with my Bristol connection,' he said. 'Rovers are in the bottom division so why can't I try and convert some of them into Argyle fans? We're in the West Country so it's not that far away. Only two and a half hours away in a slow car, an hour and a half in a fast one – or 10 minutes in a rocket! As long as you aimed it right, you'd be down here really quickly. Don't land it on the pitch, though, because you'd ruin it!' After Plymouth won 3-2 at Sunderland, he offered to buy a drink for every one of the 700 fans who had made the 805-mile round trip, and further cemented his popularity by leading the club to the quarter-finals of the FA Cup. After defeat to Watford, he sighed: 'We threw everything at them. The kitchen sink, golf clubs, we emptied the garage and threw it at them. Unfortunately, it was not enough, but at least my garage is tidy.' In view of the entertainment value he had provided both on and off the pitch, Argyle fans were understandably upset when Holloway was lured to Leicester City in November 2007.

It is not just in terms of his quotations that Ian Holloway is an inspirational figure. He nursed his wife through a battle with cancer and three of their four children are deaf. It helps him to put football into perspective. 'I love dealing with people,' he says, 'and I've got a huge enthusiasm for life.' As for his chances of managing a top club, he doubts that any Premier League chairman would want to hire 'a bumpkin from Bristol.' But he concedes that he can never know what lies around the corner. 'I am a football manager, I can't see into the future. Last year I thought I was going to Cornwall on my holidays but I ended up going to Lyme Regis.' As Eric Morecambe used to say, there's no answer to that.

José Mourinho
The Special One

The recent influx of foreign managers into the Premier League has included the courteous (Claudio Ranieri), the thoughtful (Arsène Wenger) and the unassuming (Rafa Benitez). It has also brought José Mourinho, a man who can be courteous, is often thoughtful, but never knowingly unassuming. Mourinho is not given to false modesty, which has led to accusations of arrogance, something he firmly denies. This evaluation of his personality arose in 2004 when, after winning the Champions League with Porto, he arrived at Stamford Bridge and told a press conference: 'I'm European champion and I think I'm a special one.'

Right up until his surprise departure from Chelsea in September 2007, he occupied more newspaper column inches than any other manager in British football. Every day seemed to herald a fresh vendetta, outburst or rumour, Mourinho appearing to take the view that as long as the press were writing about him, it was taking the heat off his players. There is no doubt about it, Mourinho became a national fascination, but even the most diehard of Mourinho-watchers cannot be sure how much of his occasionally eccentric behaviour is genuine and how much is an act. Is he really that paranoid? Does he truly see conspiracies at every turn, or is it all part of an elaborate game? He is, after all, an intelligent man. Even journalists are divided. Some believed him to be a breath of fresh air in the English game, but others became irritated by his displays of petulance. Patrick Collins of the *Mail on Sunday* wrote scathingly: 'Mourinho is to flouncing what Tiger Woods is to short-iron play; it's what he does best.'

Mourinho's tactics seem designed to get under his rivals' skin. If so, they have certainly worked: Alex Ferguson, Wenger, Benitez – he fell out with them all at some point, to the extent that it was suggested that the League Managers' Association should employ the services of Relate. Yet he also demonstrated a keen sense of humour and his smouldering looks won the hearts of numerous female fans. Even at the height of Manchester United's success, there were no reports of Alex Ferguson being seen as a sex symbol.

Mourinho's impact on these shores – and indeed the world of football – was all the more remarkable in view of the fact that he never played the game professionally, let alone at the top level. Born in Setubal, Portugal, in 1963, he wanted to be a footballer (his father Felix is a former Portuguese international goalkeeper) and he drifted around a few of the smaller clubs but eventually realised that he would never make the grade. So at the age of 23, on the advice of his mother, he signed up for business school. He stayed only one day before enrolling at a physical education college. With qualifications to his name, he was employed as a fitness trainer at various lower League clubs, but his big break came when he worked as Bobby Robson's translator at both Sporting Lisbon and then FC Porto. In 1996 he followed Robson to Barcelona, and when the Englishman left for Holland, Mourinho stayed at Barcelona and worked with Robson's replacement, Dutch coach Louis van Gaal. There, his immense self-confidence and organisational ability carved new openings for him and he began contributing significantly to coaching sessions and management meetings, eventually rising to coach Barcelona's B team.

In 2000 his chance in senior management came at Benfica but internal politics led to his departure after just nine games in charge. He spent the next season with unfashionable Uniao Leiria where he proved so successful that he was appointed manager at Porto. In 2003 he led Porto to a treble of League, Cup and UEFA Cup, following it up in 2004 with the Champions League. English fans had their first taste of him when Porto knocked out Manchester United and Mourinho celebrated by running along the touchline pumping his fist.

A month after his Champions League triumph, he was entrusted with the responsibility of spending Roman Abramovich's millions at Chelsea. In his first three seasons he demonstrated his worth with five trophies, including the club's first League Championship for 50 years. He repeated the feat the following year, 2006. The restocking of the Stamford Bridge trophy cabinet has not been without controversy. When Chelsea equalised against Liverpool in the 2005 League Cup final, Mourinho was escorted from the touchline for allegedly inciting Liverpool fans; he has branded Arsenal manager Arsène Wenger 'a voyeur'; accused defensively minded visitors from Tottenham of 'leaving the bus in front of the goal'; and stated that it is impossible to win a penalty at Old Trafford. Straight-faced he told reporters: 'The circumstances are difficult for us with the new football rules that we have to face. It is not possible to have a penalty against Manchester United. It is not a conspiracy, it is fact. I speak facts.'

However, he went too far in 2005 by hinting at collusion between Barcelona coach Frank Rijkaard and referee Anders Frisk during a Champions League tie. The allegations were shown to be unfounded and Mourinho was handed a two-match suspension and a fine by UEFA for bringing the game into disrepute. So distraught was Frisk at receiving death threats from Chelsea fans that he decided to retire, causing UEFA referees' chief Volker Roth to brand Mourinho an 'enemy of football'. The episode had an intriguing sequel when two national newspapers alleged that Mourinho had beaten the UEFA ban by hiding in a laundry basket. They claimed that he had watched the first leg of the quarter-final against Bayern Munich on TV in a dressing room at Stamford Bridge, communicating his instructions to fitness coach Rui Faria via an earpiece hidden under a woolly hat. Faria was seen fiddling with his hat throughout the match. The papers said that then, 10 minutes from the end, Mourinho clambered into a laundry skip and was wheeled to the Stamford Bridge leisure club, where he was supposed to have spent the entire evening.

Equally riveting was the tale of Mourinho's dog. In 2007 police officers arrived at his London home ready to seize his Yorkshire terrier, Leya, over an alleged breach of veterinary regulations. But while the police waited, the dog mysteriously escaped and was next heard of in Portugal with Mourinho's wife. Mourinho, meanwhile, was arrested and cautioned for obstructing the police. If he had somehow outwitted the Met's finest, it merely added to his image of invincibility.

Mourinho appeared genuinely puzzled by the hostility that he and Chelsea attracted from some quarters. 'Everybody wants Chelsea to lose a game,' he said of his table-toppers in 2005. 'When they do, they should declare a public holiday.' There seems no more chance of him being plagued by self-doubt than there is of Neil Warnock receiving a Christmas card from the Referees' Association or of Iain Dowie enjoying a new career as a Hollywood romantic lead. Indeed, Mourinho's confidence is such that he shrugged off the notion of any pressure attached to management in the Premier League. 'Pressure?

What pressure? Pressure is poor people in the world trying to feed their families. There is no pressure in football.'

Like Brian Clough before him, José Mourinho is a fascinating, complex character, engaging one minute, confrontational the next. What a pity the two men never had the opportunity to share a platform, although it would have needed a room the size of the Royal Albert Hall just to accommodate their egos.

Bill Shankly
Man of the People

Down the years, plenty of football managers have been revered but very few have actually been loved. But Bill Shankly was loved, and more remarkably, the affection was by no means confined to Liverpool FC or even Merseyside, it stretched right across the country, uniting followers of every club from Alloa to Arsenal. Players loved Shankly because he had that priceless gift for making them feel 10 feet tall; the media loved Shankly because he could always be relied upon to deliver a piece of homespun philosophy or a cracking one-liner; and fans loved Shankly because they admired his childlike enthusiasm and felt able to identify with him. He never lost that passion for the grass roots of the game and would often go for a kickabout with youngsters in the local park. If a journalist rang home and asked what time Bill would be back, his wife, Nessie, would reply: 'When he wins, of course.'

Shankly was as much a Liverpool fan as anyone who stood on the Kop; the only difference was that he also happened to manage the club. He sometimes phoned supporters at home to discuss the previous day's game and regularly bought tickets for loyal fans. A poor performance from his team, he thought, was letting down the fans and the people of Liverpool. He used to say: 'I'm a people's man – only the people matter.'

He never lost sight of that philosophy. When a Liverpool scarf that had been thrown at Shankly during a lap of honour was tossed aside by a policeman, Shankly immediately picked up the scarf, wrapped it around his neck and told the officer: 'Don't do that. This might be someone's life.'

An entire industry has been built around Shankly stories. One that perfectly illustrates his desperation to win even in training occurred during a five-a-side match involving Liverpool's first-team squad. Shankly liked to join in these games and was convinced on this occasion that he had scored a goal, but the defenders insisted the ball had not crossed the line. Full-back Chris Lawler, regarded as the quiet man of Anfield and renowned for his fair play, was watching the game from the sidelines.

'Was that ball in, Chris?' yelled Shankly. 'The lads will believe you.'

'It didn't cross the line, boss,' said Lawler.

Shankly threw his arms in the air in despair. 'How about that? That's the first thing he's said since he joined the club and it's a lie.'

He was born in the Ayrshire mining village of Glenbuck on 2 September 1913 into a family of 10 children. One of five brothers who went on to play professional football, he signed for Carlisle United as a wing-half in 1932 but made only 16 appearances before joining Preston North End for a fee of £500 the following summer. Over the next 16 years he made more than 300 appearances for the club and played in two FA Cup finals, losing to Sunderland in 1937 but defeating Huddersfield in 1938. He also won five Scotland caps, being denied only more by the outbreak of war. When he handed over his number 4 Preston shirt to Tommy Docherty at the end of his playing career, he said: 'Just pull it on and it'll run around by itself.'

No sooner had he retired from playing in 1949 than he was appointed manager at Carlisle, but two years later he left, accusing the directors of a lack of ambition. After a failed interview at Liverpool, he took charge at Grimsby Town, moving on to Workington in 1954 and Huddersfield in 1956. Time and again he became frustrated by the lack of boardroom commitment, until in 1959 Liverpool, who had deemed him too inexperienced eight years earlier, decided that his enthusiasm was exactly what they needed. Liverpool were then languishing in the Second Division but within three years Shankly had led them back to the top flight to herald the start of a glorious era, which would bring three League Championships, two FA Cups and the UEFA Cup to Anfield.

One of his first signings was giant centre-half Ron Yeats from Dundee United. Shankly famously invited journalists to walk around Yeats and enthused, 'Christ, son, you must be over seven foot tall!' 'No, I'm only six foot three,' protested Yeats. 'Well, son,' replied Shankly, 'when you turn out for Liverpool you'll be seven foot tall.'

He used the famous Shankly psychology when forward Bobby Graham complained about regularly being named as substitute. Shanks told him: 'Jesus Christ, son, you've no cause to complain. When you started out in this game, you would have settled for being the twelfth best player in the world!'

When Shankly famously declared, 'There are two great teams in Liverpool – Liverpool and Liverpool Reserves', it was his way of making his players feel superior. To this end, one of his favourite pastimes was rubbishing opponents. London teams were a bunch of 'soft southerners', opposition goalkeepers were 'past it' and rival centre-forwards 'couldn't score in a darts match'. He destroyed Manchester United in his team talks. 'Alex Stepney couldn't catch a cold; somebody told me Matt Busby has a bad back, I tell you he's got two bad backs; then there's wee Nobby Stiles – I've got a gnome in my garden bigger than Nobby Stiles, and he's blind as well; as for Bill Foulkes, I've seen a juggernaut turn quicker than him; and Paddy Crerand – now boys, Crerand's deceptive, he's slower than you think! You've only got three players to beat – Law, Best and Charlton. And if you can't do that, you don't deserve to be professional footballers.'

He would come out with all manner of fiction in order to motivate his players. As Liverpool prepared to face West Ham, he told Kevin Keegan: 'Christ, son, I've just seen that Bobby Moore. What a wreck. He's got bags under his eyes, he's limping, he's got dandruff and it looks as if he has been to a nightclub again.' Keegan did score but Moore had a brilliant game. Afterwards Shankly shook his head and said to Keegan: 'Aye, he's some player that Bobby Moore, isn't he? You'll never play against anyone better than him.'

Of course, his most cutting remarks were reserved for Liverpool's neighbours. 'If Everton were playing down at the bottom of my garden,' he growled, 'I'd draw the curtains.' He hated it when they were doing well. On a visit to his barber, Shankly was asked if he wanted anything off the top. Quick as a flash came the reply: 'Aye, Everton.'

If any player dared to reject a move to Anfield, Shankly would let it be known that it was no great loss. After losing out to Manchester United over the signing of Lou Macari, Shankly sent a note to his players saying that he only wanted him for the second team anyway. Lining up full-back Bob McNab from Huddersfield, Shankly gave him the full sales pitch, telling him: 'You're a quality player and you'll be joining the greatest club in the world.' But when McNab phoned a couple of days later to say he was signing for Arsenal instead, Shankly rasped: 'They're welcome to you. You never could play.'

Any criticism of his own players was usually done in jest. He told winger Peter Thompson: 'You're like a racehorse because you're quick, you're like a carthorse because you keep going all day, and you're like a hobby horse because you've got no brain.' After goalkeeper Tommy Lawrence let in a sloppy goal through his legs, he apologised to Shankly: 'I know, boss, I should have kept my legs shut.' 'Nay, lad,' barked Shankly. 'Your mother should have kept *her* legs shut.' Following a rare defeat, Shankly asked skipper Ron Yeats what he had called when he tossed the coin. 'Heads,' said Yeats. 'Och,' said Shankly, shaking his head. 'You should have called tails.' Everyone who played for Shankly had a story to tell about the great man.

He was a wily old fox. After Ian St John had been sent off for fighting shortly before a vital Cup tie, Shankly set about doctoring the evidence. He got trainer Bob Paisley to apply a mixture of gentian violet and black boot polish around the player's private parts and then invited the press in for (not too close) a look. The papers duly ran stories about the brutal attack on St John that had sparked the brawl, but unfortunately, the FA disciplinary committee was not so easily fooled and suspended the player for 14 days.

In the mid-1960s Chelsea manager Tommy Docherty was keen to offload tall striker Tony Hateley. He had once described Hateley's passing as so wayward that it should be labelled 'to whom it may concern'. Shankly was interested but needed convincing, so The Doc waxed lyrical about Hateley's attributes in the hope of pushing the deal through.

'You must admit the boy is fantastic in the air,' enthused Docherty.

'So was Douglas Bader,' replied Shankly, 'and he had two wooden legs!'

Shankly's enthusiasm for the game remained undiminished. During half-time at his testimonial match he played in a five-a-side game but it over-ran and the referee was asked when it was going to end. 'Just as soon as we can get Shankly off the pitch,' answered the referee. 'We've been trying for 10 minutes but he says the score is 4-4 and he refuses to come off until someone's hit a winner!'

In July 1974 Shankly decided to retire. He said that when he went to inform the chairman of his decision, it was like walking to the electric chair. The news came as a bolt from the blue. Distraught fans jammed the club's switchboard and local factory workers threatened to go on strike unless Shankly returned. Even in retirement, Shankly, who was awarded the OBE in November 1974, regularly watched the team train and continued to live in the terraced house that he and his wife had bought when they first moved to the city. He would stop and talk to anyone about football, so much so that Nessie had to take him shopping to Manchester instead.

Sadly, relations between Shankly and his beloved Liverpool began to deteriorate. He felt snubbed by the club and claimed that he was made more welcome at Everton. There was also the suggestion that he could not cope with the even greater success that the club enjoyed under his successor, Bob Paisley. On 29 September 1981 Bill Shankly died of a heart attack, although some believe he really died of a broken heart. 'My life is my work, my work is my life,' he had once said. When that work was taken away, he was left a broken man.

Shankly and Liverpool were a wonderful double act. He used to say: 'Liverpool was made for me and I was made for Liverpool.' And he made sure that the players were fully aware of the honour of playing for the club, that no individual was ever bigger than Liverpool FC. When Tommy Smith told him he was unlikely to be fit for the next match because he had injured his knee, Shankly snapped: 'Take that poof bandage off, and what do you mean, *your* knee? It's Liverpool's knee!'

Jimmy Sirrel

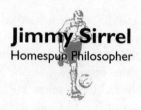

Homespun Philosopher

The term 'canny Scot' could have been invented for Jimmy Sirrel. The down-to-earth little Glaswegian was the complete antithesis to the likes of Malcolm Allison or Ron Atkinson. He was more at home with a mug of Horlicks than a glass of champagne, the only club he was ever likely to be seen in at night would have 'British Legion' over the door, and his favourite suit was a tracksuit. He never courted publicity, was generally too shrewd to risk making rash predictions and what he did say was not always easy to comprehend, partly because of his impenetrable accent and partly because he sometimes appeared to talk in riddles. One of his favourite expressions was, 'I'm never too unhappy about not losing a football match,' which basically meant he was satisfied with a draw. Other examples of his quaint, homespun philosophy are: 'One train disnae make a railway' (a variation on 'one swallow doesn't make a summer'); and perhaps his finest contribution: 'The best team always wins; the rest is only gossip.'

Even the most ardent follower of Notts County – the club he served with distinction for a total of 16 years – could not describe Sirrel as a physically imposing specimen. Author Duncan Hamilton wrote that Sirrel looked 'like a garden gnome who had been roughed up a bit'. His crooked teeth could have opened any bottle and merely served to add to his idiosyncratic demeanour.

He certainly had a style all of his own. He used to go on scouting trips in an old Austin A40 and would explain tactics with the aid of 22 Corona lemonade bottle tops. Another form of preparation involved organising practice matches between the first team and 11 bibs. The bibs, representing that Saturday's opposition, were simply laid on the ground in match-day formation, and Sirrel's chosen 11 would then dazzle these inanimate objects with their skills in a scene reminiscent of the *Monty Python* match between the Bournemouth Gynaecologists and the Watford Long John Silver Impersonators.

After training sessions, Sirrel would often emerge from the tunnel at Meadow Lane, whistle on wrist, and carefully place a ball on the penalty spot. Glancing up at the empty terraces, he would blow his whistle and slot the penalty into the unguarded net, punching the air with joy as he fulfilled every kid's dream. But the routine that his players relished most involved a bottle of tomato ketchup. On away trips, the County team usually stopped at a hotel for a pre-match meal, where Sirrel would order a steak. He would then call out to one of the players at the table, 'Laddee, have you got the red sauce?' They would then fall silent in tense anticipation to see whether, after pouring the ketchup on the plate, Sirrel would then lick the neck of the bottle clean before replacing the top. Rarely did he disappoint.

Some players may have occasionally treated him as a figure of fun, but it did not pay to get on his wrong side for he could be fiery when roused. One writer said of him, rather harshly: 'He had the sharp tongue of a Clydeside shipbuilder, the fantasies of a star struck schoolboy and the social graces of a Brooke Bond chimp.'

'The Squirrel', as he was affectionately known, as much for his build and prominent teeth as for his surname, was born in Glasgow in 1922 and entered the professional game at the end of the Second World War as a tricky winger with Celtic. After four years at Parkhead he moved to Park Avenue, Bradford, in 1949, where he stayed for two seasons before joining Brighton & Hove Albion. In 1954 he signed for Aldershot and as his playing career there drew to a close, he combined it with coaching. He switched to Brentford as a coach in 1960 and seven years later graduated to the post of manager at Griffin Park. The chairman of Brentford at the time was Jack Dunnett, the MP for Nottingham Central, who had grand ideas about merging Brentford and Queens Park Rangers. When opposition from the fans of both clubs caused the scheme to collapse, Dunnett withdrew his interest in Brentford and became chairman of his constituency club, Notts County, taking the Bees' manager, Sirrel, with him.

When Sirrel took over at Meadow Lane in November 1969, County were struggling at the wrong end of Division Four, but in one of his rare public predictions he promised: 'Ask any kid what he knows about Notts County and he'll tell you they're the oldest football team in the world. By the time I've finished he'll know a lot more.' The gate for his first home match was 3,497; two years later Sirrel's brand of winning football had increased the average attendance by 10,000. He said: 'When I arrived at the club, I assessed the situation right – at least almost right. I thought I could get the club into the Second Division within five years but we made it in three.'

As chants of 'Nice One Sirrel' echoed down the Meadow Lane terraces, the manager left no one in any doubt that the club's sudden change of fortune was down to hard work, coupled with a sprinkling of homely advice. 'I tell my players before a match that they'll never live it again. At five o'clock it will be gone forever. That's why they've got to give it everything.'

But the adventure turned sour when Manchester United thugs ran amok at Meadow Lane. At the height of the battle, a raging Sirrel emerged from the trainer's room wielding a tiny bunion scalpel and, waving it at the United fans, yelled in broad Glaswegian: 'Come on, you bastards, I'll have you!' It is doubtful whether even the most hardened hooligan had ever been confronted with such a sight.

To the dismay of the County faithful, Sirrel departed for First Division Sheffield United in 1975 but was unable to stave off relegation. As results failed to improve, he left Bramall Lane in 1977 and returned to Meadow Lane. Blades' fans might argue that his greatest contribution in Sheffield was designing the club badge that is still in use today.

Once again he worked his magic at County, and in 1981 the Magpies were able to enjoy Division One football for the first time in 55 years. Even with promotion close at hand, Sirrel refused to get carried away. 'We're like Lady Di,' he said with reference to the forthcoming royal wedding. 'She's not the Queen yet – she's not even married. But like us, she's nearly placed.' Against all odds, County managed three seasons in the top flight.

Sometimes in the role of general manager, Sirrel remained at the club until 1987, by which time Notts were operating in the Third Division. But his exploits and quirky personality have made him a legend at the Lane, where a stand is named after him. And in May 2006, with County fighting to avoid relegation from the Football League, 84-year-old Sirrel came on to the pitch before the last match of the season against Bury to impart a few of his special words of wisdom. Notts scrambled to safety with a 2-2 draw, but the players had appeared to pay little heed to Sirrel's inspirational address. Or maybe they simply didn't understand a word he said.

When Brian Clough, his neighbour from across the Trent, came to hear about Sirrel's habit of answering a casual remark of 'It's a nice day, Jim' with 'Not if you're dead, it isn't', he smiled: 'Good old Jim. He's more bonkers than me.' There can be no finer recommendation.

Alec Stock
Jumpers For Goalposts

Although a successful manager of the Sixties and Seventies, Alec Stock was a throwback to an earlier era when common courtesy prevailed, people dressed for dinner, and kids in the park used jumpers for goalposts. It is no secret that Stock, with his idiosyncratic syntax, old-fashioned values and dapper attire, was comedian Paul Whitehouse's inspiration for *The Fast Show*'s popular character Ron Manager. Indeed, there was always something theatrical about Stock who, in his cravat, looked more like a member of an amateur dramatics company than a leading football manager.

In fact, he had a military background – rising to the rank of major during the Second World War – and he carried the air of a benign officer (more Sergeant Wilson than Captain Mainwaring) into the world of football. He called players 'old son' and operated a relaxed, liberal regime when the time was right. A notice that he used to hang in the dressing room illustrated his approach to management: 'When we train, we train. When we play, we play. And when we stop and have a beer, we will be bloody good at that too!'

At times – perhaps because he was deaf in one ear – he seemed to be on another planet but players underestimated him at their peril. As Malcolm Macdonald, whom Stock converted from an average full-back at Fulham into a top-class striker at Luton, has testified, he could be a crafty old fox. 'If a player came up to him,' said Macdonald, 'to ask why he wasn't in the team and was looking for a ruck about it, Alec would just walk away. His excuse was that he hadn't heard him, and that he must have talked to him on his deaf side.' His standing in the game also ensured that few players took liberties with him. Such was his durability that he entered League management as the country's youngest boss and left it as the oldest.

Alec Stock was born in the Somerset mining village of Peasedown St John in 1917. The family moved to Dartford, Kent, after the 1926 General Strike and young Alec won a scholarship to a grammar school, where he played rugby and cricket. He began playing football seriously with a village side, Wilmington, and then signed amateur forms with Tottenham Hotspur while working as a trainee bank clerk. In 1936 he turned professional with Charlton Athletic but failed to break into the first team and two years later moved to Queens Park Rangers, for whom he played 30 League games. When war intervened, he served with distinction in the Royal Armoured Corps before being invalided out when he was wounded in Normandy.

Realising that at 29 he was never going to achieve greatness as a player, he began casting his net further afield. His experiences as an army officer had given him a flair for man management, so when his wife Marjorie spotted a newspaper advertisement for the job of player-manager at Southern League Yeovil Town, she encouraged Alec to apply. He landed the job after revealing that he had scored twice for QPR in a friendly that week. 'They thought they were getting some great goalscorer,' he said.

'I set out my stall to be hard but fair. If they needed a rollicking they got one, but if they played well I told them so. Some managers seem to find it very hard to say, "Well played".' When Yeovil were humiliated at Street in the FA Cup fourth qualifying round in 1947, Stock was so angry that after the game he ordered the players straight on to the coach without letting them have a bath. The result created quite a stink in the West Country.

Two years later he used his capacity for military-style organisation to spring one of the greatest shocks in FA Cup history, when little Yeovil humbled mighty Sunderland. Before the game Stock made much of the 10-foot slope at The Huish. The *Daily Graphic* printed it as 14 feet and every subsequent paper added a couple more feet. Stock said: 'By the time match-day came around, everyone must have had the idea we played on the north face of the Eiger!' Beaten virtually before they had started, Sunderland lost 2-1, with Stock, prompting intelligently from inside-forward, scoring Yeovil's first goal.

Naturally, it was not long before Football League clubs came knocking on Stock's door and seven months after the epic Cup tie, he joined Leyton Orient, transforming the fortunes of the London club with an FA Cup quarter-final appearance in 1954 and a Third Division (South) title in 1956. Stock was absent for 53 days of the promotion campaign, having been appointed assistant manager to Tom Whittaker at Arsenal. Although the implication was that he would eventually take over the reins at Highbury, Stock was unhappy at not having the final say in decisions and so after less than two months he returned to Brisbane Road. Ironically, Whittaker died shortly afterwards. Having stabilised Orient in the Second Division, Stock was off again, this time to Italian club Roma. He lifted them to third place in the table, but the language barrier and internal politics proved problematical, leading to another swift return to East London.

He stayed at Orient until 1959, when he moved to Queens Park Rangers. With money to spend, he recruited wisely and his highly individual, occasionally eccentric, behaviour created a marvellous team spirit. With Rangers comfortably in command at half-time in one match, winger Mark Lazarus snatched Stock's pork-pie hat off his head and, singing its praises, announced that he intended wearing it for the second half. 'All right, my lovely lads,' said Stock. 'Let's cool it down. We've not won the match yet. But I'll make you this promise. Go out and win and I'll buy you all a hat each.' Sure enough, the next morning Stock led the players into the nearest gents' outfitters and ordered 'Hats all round.'

After helping Rangers become the first Third Division side to win the League Cup, he guided the club to two successive promotions. The star of the show was Rodney Marsh, who was offered £2,000 to do a newspaper story under the headline 'I'm Ready For England by Rodney Marsh'. The player consulted Stock who urged him not to do it, saying that Alf Ramsey did not approve of players pushing themselves forward. So Marsh declined the offer and was surprised to pick up the paper the following Sunday and see the back page headline 'Rodney's Ready For England by Alec Stock.' Even though Stock pocketed the £2,000, Marsh saw the funny side.

No sooner had QPR reached the top flight than Stock sensationally resigned. Health reasons were given (Stock suffered badly from asthma), but there was a suspicion that ambitious chairman Jim Gregory had eased him out. Stock returned to management in December 1968 with Luton Town, leading the Hatters to promotion to the Second Division before resigning in 1972 because he no longer enjoyed the daily journey from his Surrey home. Within two months he was back in the game with Second Division Fulham, signing Bobby Moore and, in 1975, taking the club to its first ever FA Cup final. He later brought in Rodney Marsh and George Best but in 1976 he was cruelly sacked. Three years later, at the age of 61, Stock took over at Fourth Division Bournemouth, stepping down as team manager in 1980 but continuing as general manager until 1981 and as a director until 1986.

When Alec Stock died in 2001, the game lost one of its true gentlemen, a man with impeccable manners and a wealth of old-world charm. Alas, we may never see his like again.

Harry Storer
The Sergeant Major

After a bitterly fought contest in 1957, Joe Mercer, then manager of Sheffield United, was so angry about the over-physical approach of six Derby County players that he complained to the Rams' boss Harry Storer that they were 'cloggers'.

'Give me their names,' demanded Storer.

'Why, are you going to fine them?' queried Mercer.

'No,' snapped Storer. 'It's the other five buggers I'm after!'

A cultured wing-half in his playing days, Storer the manager was a different beast, calling a spade a shovel and ruling with the ruthlessness of a sergeant major. When he was in charge at Coventry City, the dressing room was essentially a barracks, where the square-jawed Storer kept constant vigil for 'skivers' and 'cissies'. He had no time for the injury-prone or the faint-hearted and would have been appalled by today's pampered stars in their baby Bentleys.

He once gave a trial to a trainee hairdresser. Afterwards he took him to one side and strongly advised him to sell his boots and buy another pair of scissors. On another occasion Storer dragged one of his players back on to the pitch after a match and asked: 'Where is it?'

'Where's what?' asked the bewildered player.

'The hole you disappeared into for 90 minutes,' barked Storer. 'It has to be here somewhere.'

His authoritarian approach meant that few players stormed into his office demanding a pay-rise or wanting to know why they had been dropped, although this may also have had something to do with the presence of Billy, his ferocious-looking dog. Billy used to sit growling outside his master's office, daring any player to step over him and knock on Storer's door. As a method of quelling player unrest, it was probably unique.

Despite Storer's reputation for being almost as fierce as his dog, his captain at Derby, Reg Ryan, was full of admiration for the man. 'If he'd been in the game today,' said Ryan, 'he'd have been one of the outstanding managers. He was a very well-read man who could quote Shakespeare, despite appearing to have a rough exterior. He was supposed to be a real tough nut, but he was quite gentle inside. And his knowledge of football was outstanding.'

He liked to keep things simple and had no interest in coaching theories. Should anyone attempt a technical breakdown of a particular player's strengths and weaknesses, Storer would become impatient and say, 'Yes, but can he play?'

Storer himself certainly could play. He was born in Liverpool in 1898 into a sporting family. His father, also named Harry, kept goal for Woolwich Arsenal and Liverpool and played cricket for Derbyshire. His uncle, William, was a Derby County footballer and cricketer for Derbyshire and England. Harry junior also excelled at both sports, scoring over 13,000 runs and taking more than 200 wickets for Derbyshire. Footballers whom he managed would use his love of cricket to their advantage. Derby County's Ian Buxton, who was also a professional cricketer-footballer, recalled: 'Us cricketers got on quite well with Harry. You just had to remember to turn the conversation to how to play off-spinners on a turning wicket.'

Storer the aspiring footballer had trials with Notts County and Millwall before signing for Grimsby Town in 1919. In his early days at Blundell Park he was a goalscoring forward, but by the time Derby signed him for £4,500, in 1921, he had developed into a skilful wing-half. He was good enough to win two England caps in 1924 and went on to make 274 League appearances for the Rams, scoring 63 goals. In 1929 he moved to Burnley but two years later took over as boss at Coventry. There, he combined managing the football club with playing cricket for Derbyshire and in 1936 achieved a remarkable double, steering Coventry to promotion from Division Three (South) and helping Derbyshire win the County Cricket Championship.

After the war he became manager of Birmingham City, taking them to the semi-finals of the FA Cup in his first season and leading them to promotion from Division Two in his third. Just as he was establishing Birmingham in the top flight, Storer resigned in November 1948 to return to Coventry. He remained at Highfield Road until 1953 and, after a spell out of management, took over at Derby in 1955. Derby had dropped down to the Third Division (North) but under Storer's no-nonsense leadership, the club quickly returned to the Second Division.

Harry Storer retired in 1962 and died at his Derby home five years later, six months short of his 70th birthday. But his story doesn't end there for he acted as mentor to two young players hoping to make their way into management one day – Brian Clough and Peter Taylor, the latter having been a goalkeeper under Storer at Coventry. Whenever Derby were playing in the north-east, the pair, then at Middlesbrough, would meet up with Storer and talk football with him until the early hours. Storer despised directors and placed great faith in a player's character and 'bottle'. He would tell Clough: 'When you become a manager and you are leaving for an away game, look around the team coach and count the number of hearts. If you are lucky there will be five. If there aren't, turn the coach round and go back.' Clough never forgot that advice when picking his captains – courageous men like Dave Mackay and Stuart Pearce who led by example. He owed a lot to Harry Storer.

Gordon Strachan
The Mighty Atom

There are few more entertaining managers around today than Gordon Strachan. If conducting a post-match interview with Ian Holloway is the starting point for a surreal journey, putting a microphone under Gordon Strachan's substantial nose can elicit a variety of extreme reactions. He may explode at the most innocuous question, crack a brilliant one-liner and walk off, or regale his audience with an act worthy of the London Palladium. The only guarantee is that he is never dull.

Strachan is harder to read than James Joyce, because he always delivers his wisecracks with a deadpan face. When a hapless reporter asked him for a quick word, Strachan replied instantly: 'Velocity.' When another asked him for his impression of Jermaine Pennant, he snapped back that he did not do impressions. And when yet another scribe searching for team news asked, 'Any changes?' Strachan answered: 'Naw, still five foot six, ginger hair, and a big nose.' Mick Hennigan, who was assistant manager at Leeds when Strachan was a player there, once told him: 'Your tongue can kill a man at 10 paces.'

Strachan used his sharp tongue to good effect when he was managed by Alex Ferguson at both Aberdeen and Manchester United, the player frequently finding himself on the receiving end of one of Fergie's famous verbal lashings known as the 'hairdryer' treatment. Whereas other players cowered in the corner, Strachan stood up to Ferguson – admittedly an unequal contest given the difference in stature – and sometimes even enjoyed the last laugh. In 1981–82 Aberdeen met Romanian side Arges Pitesti in a UEFA Cup tie. Leading 3-0 from the home leg, Aberdeen found themselves 2-0 down at half-time in Romania, causing Ferguson to read the riot act, directing most of his venom at Strachan. As his fury increased, Ferguson took a swipe at a big tea urn without appreciating how heavy it was. As a result he hurt his hand and the pain prompted him to sweep some of the cups of tea on the dressing room table in Strachan's direction, but they missed their target and soaked innocent victims instead. As Ferguson had intended, the row spurred Strachan on and he gave an improved performance in the second half, converting a penalty to help the Dons to a 5-2 aggregate victory. Strachan said: 'When I despatched the ball into the net – a beauty, right into the top left-hand corner – my first reaction was to stick two fingers up at him. It was just as well that I was camouflaged by half a dozen other Aberdeen players and Fergie did not see the gesture.'

Born in Edinburgh in 1957, Strachan supported local team Hibernian as a boy but when a move to Easter Road fell through, he signed for Dundee. After three years at Dens Park, in 1977 he moved to Aberdeen where he developed into a combative right-sided midfield player with an eye for goal. At first, however, he struggled so badly at Pittodrie that his former Dundee team-mate, George Mackie, who had since moved on to Partick Thistle, came up with a novel idea to get the critical Aberdeen crowd behind

Strachan. Before the Aberdeen-Partick fixture, Mackie offered: 'When you get the ball, and I am in a position to tackle you, you feint to take it left and then go right and I will go the other way. You will beat me, no bother.' Alas, when the opportunity arose for Strachan to shine, he got the instructions the wrong way round and the pair ended up colliding.

Under their bright young manager, Alex Ferguson, Aberdeen broke the Old Firm's traditional dominance of Scottish football with two League titles, three Scottish Cups and, in 1983, the European Cup Winners' Cup. But Strachan had grown weary of being beaten with Ferguson's big stick and enjoyed a new lease of life when Ron Atkinson, who believed in treating players as adults, paid £500,000 to take him to Manchester United in 1984. So when Atkinson was sacked and replaced at Old Trafford by Ferguson, Strachan feared the worst and in 1989 he was on his way to Elland Road where, three years later, he helped Leeds lift the League title at Manchester United's expense.

Strachan won a half-century of Scottish caps, contributing five goals, including a strike against West Germany at the 1986 World Cup. By way of celebration, he intended vaulting the advertising hoarding but realising that he was too small to accomplish the feat, he settled for resting his right leg on it, and posing like a mini version of Superman. In 1991 he was named the Football Writers' Player of the Year. Asked for his reaction, he replied: 'It's a tremendous honour. I'm going to have a banana to celebrate.'

Along with porridge and seaweed tablets, bananas formed a staple part of Strachan's diet and enabled him to extend his playing career at the highest level to the age of 40, by which time he had played a total of 635 League games. His final port of call was Coventry, where in 1996 he was appointed player-manager. He told reporters, straight-faced: 'I still eat bananas. And seaweed. I may not be a better player, but I'm a better swimmer.'

He concedes that the pressures of management did sometimes affect him. The morning after a particularly spineless home defeat to Everton he went for a walk to clear his head but was so uptight that the stroll took him 14 miles from home and his wife had to go and fetch him in the car. He was also besieged by agents' videos and in his autobiography he recalled one that was sent to him of a Scandinavian goalkeeper. 'Embarrassingly for him,' wrote Strachan, 'the previous film on the video – of a pornographic nature involving him and a woman we took to be his wife – had not been totally erased. The first five minutes of the tape were infinitely more entertaining than anything we subsequently saw of the keeper.'

When in 2001 Coventry were finally relegated after 34 years of top-flight football (and almost as many escapes), Strachan paid the price but shortly afterwards he took charge at Southampton and immediately turned their fortunes around. As the Saints climbed to fourth place in the Premiership, he announced: 'I'm going home to get myself a Coca-Cola and a packet of crisps, sit in front of the TV and look at the League table on Teletext all night.' There were frequent rows with match officials but he used his wit to sidestep awkward questions. When a reporter asked him about the club's expensive but absent Ecuadorian striker Agustin Delgado, he answered: 'I've got more important things to think about. I've got a yoghurt to finish by today, the expiry date is today. That can be my priority rather than Agustin Delgado.' It was vintage Strachan.

In 2004, a year after taking Southampton to the FA Cup final, where they lost 1-0 to Arsenal, Strachan announced that he was taking a break from management, citing the politician's reason of wanting to spend more time with his family. He stated his management philosophy: 'You can only stay at a place so long and then it's like David Bowie, you have to reinvent yourself.'

In spite of his self-imposed exile from football management, Strachan remained a highly visible personality, appearing as a regular pundit alongside presenter Adrian Chiles on *Match of the Day 2*, where his quirky humour and tactical awareness made the show compulsive viewing. He also appeared as a BBC studio guest for England international matches. Gary Lineker once asked him: 'So, Gordon, if you were English, what formation would you play?'

Quick as a flash, Strachan replied: 'If I was English, I'd top myself!'

In 2005 he returned to management with Celtic, and after a sticky start, led the club to two successive League titles. Naturally he enjoys the banter in Glasgow, where nobody is safe from his acid tongue. 'I've had a lot of fun with Rangers fans,' he says, 'especially taxi drivers. They say things like, "I'd like to wish you good luck but I can't" and I say, "I hope you don't get any fares today."' And with Gordon Strachan you can never be sure whether or not he actually means it.

IN A LEAGUE OF THEIR OWN

Johnny 'Budgie' Byrne
The Cheeky Chappie

Had anyone been told in 1964 that a West Ham United player would score a hat-trick for England in the World Cup final two years later, the automatic assumption would have been that the player in question was Johnny Byrne. 'Budgie', as he was popularly known because of his incessant chattering both on and off the pitch, was the man who made West Ham tick. He scored more than his fair share of goals but he also created them for others with subtle flicks and deliciously weighted through balls, no one benefiting more than Geoff Hurst. Converted from wing-half to striker, Hurst willingly did the donkeywork up front while Byrne, who was less inclined to cover every blade of grass, subtly directed operations from behind. In short, Hurst was a labourer and Byrne a craftsman. Yet when Alf Ramsey reduced his final squad to 22, Byrne missed out. While it may have been true that Byrne's individual flair did not fit easily into Ramsey's rigid tactical framework, there is also a feeling that he was a victim of his own off-field antics.

For 'Budgie' enjoyed nothing more than a laugh and a drink, qualities which were not readily attractive to the England manager. On the eve of England's departure for a May 1964 international in Lisbon, Byrne was one of seven players who went out socialising in London's West End and ended up breaking Ramsey's strict curfew. Unlike some of his fellow miscreants – including Bobby Moore, Bobby Charlton and Jimmy Greaves – Byrne was not yet an established member of the side, but he shrugged off Ramsey's rebuke in the best manner possible by scoring a hat-trick against Portugal, rounded off with a beautifully chipped late winner.

Two weeks later the England party were in Brazil, where Byrne's mischievous streak twice landed him in hot water. First he pushed non-swimmer Jimmy Greaves, fully clothed in his new England suit, into the deep end of a hotel pool and had to dive in to rescue him. Then, while the squad were watching a match between Brazil and Argentina in São Paulo, he endeared himself to the volatile crowd by conducting their chants. Unfortunately, Byrne, who, according to Greaves had 'a sense of humour that was about as subtle as barbed wire', didn't leave it at that and when Argentina scored their third goal, he chose to stand up, face the Brazilian fans, hold up three fingers to indicate the score by which their team was losing, and invite them to join him in a chant of 'Three-Zero'. Immediately, a hail of bricks, stones and rotten fruit descended upon the England group. After being hit in the back with a half-eaten apple, a seething Ramsey ordered the players to run for their lives. Luckily, the final whistle sounded and the Englishmen were able to sprint across the pitch towards safety. Having stirred up the trouble in the first place, Byrne at least had the decency to come up with a bright idea, and shouted: 'Grab yourself a Brazilian player.' Greaves said: 'He then seized goalkeeper Gylmar lovingly by the arm and walked with him off the pitch, knowing full well that no fans would try to harm one of their idols. We all followed Budgie's lead and went off arm-in-arm with bewildered Brazilian players.' Johnny Byrne not only was a riot, he had nearly started one.

He was born in West Horsley, Surrey, in 1939 and was signed up as a youngster by Crystal Palace, for whom he made his debut, against Swindon Town in 1957–58 in the Third Division (South). At the end of that season Palace found themselves in Division Four after the old north and south sections merged to create the Third and Fourth Divisions. Although Byrne showed signs of promise, Palace were unable to find his best position in the forward line and nearly sold him to Brighton for £10,000. He played with a swagger and style that was out of place at that level but it took the arrival of Arthur Rowe as Palace manager in 1960 to bring out the best in him. Rowe, the man responsible for the Tottenham push-and-run side of the early Fifties, encouraged Palace to keep the ball on the ground, a style that suited Byrne perfectly.

In 1960–61 he not only scored 30 goals to help Palace to promotion but also became the first Fourth Division player to be recognised at England Under-23 level. He immediately looked at home alongside the likes of Gordon Banks, George Cohen and, especially, Bobby Moore, a fact that was not lost on Moore's West Ham manager Ron Greenwood. In November 1961 Byrne's stock rose higher still when he became one of the few Third Division footballers to win a full England cap, prompting Greenwood to increase the pressure on Palace to sell their prize asset. He even tried to throw that unknown wing-half Geoff Hurst into the deal as a makeweight, but Palace were not interested. Finally, in March 1962, Greenwood got his man, Byrne moving to Upton Park for £65,000, a record fee between British clubs.

Byrne settled in quickly, using his intelligence to find space and his delicate touch to unlock defences. He was a master of the one-two and, although rather heavily built and lacking electric pace, he could outwit opponents with a clever body swerve. After another inch-perfect pass laid on an England goal for Greaves, Byrne laughed: 'I give 'em to you on a plate, Greavesie. You wouldn't get better service than that at the Savoy.' Greenwood called the deep-lying centre-forward 'England's di Stefano' (in reference to Real Madrid's great Alfredo di Stefano) and Byrne responded by helping West Ham to win the FA Cup in 1964, a season in which he plundered 33 goals. He was voted Hammer of the Year – no mean achievement in a side that included Moore, Hurst and the emerging Martin Peters – but his indiscretions that summer meant that, despite his excellent form, Ramsey placed a question mark against him. Bobby Moore liked a drink just as much as Byrne but was a more committed trainer. With Budgie a night on the town tended to show. On one European trip to Greece with West Ham, when asked whether he would like more champagne, Byrne replied: 'Just one more crate.' He spent the next two days before the match sleeping it off.

He weighed in with 25 League goals in 1964–65 but missed out on West Ham's European Cup Winners' Cup success through injury. He was named in Ramsey's 28-man World Cup squad for 1966, only to be one of the six omitted at the next stage. After a highly respectable eight goals in his 11 England games, his international career was over.

Byrne began to pile on the pounds and now that Hurst was the new goalscoring hero at Upton Park, his influence waned. He started to appear sluggish and, particularly in away games up north, tended to go missing. In 1967 he returned to Palace for £45,000 but his best days were behind him. The following year he joined Fulham for £25,000 but even a switch to midfield failed to recapture his old sparkle and in 1969 he accepted the post of player-coach with South African club Durban City.

Among the players he brought out to South Africa was his former England colleague Johnny Haynes. Naturally, Budgie had a novel approach to management and once asked Haynes if he, Byrne, could criticise him at a team meeting so that the rest of the players, who were in awe of Haynes, would think themselves in good company when Byrne took them to task. Emphasising privately to his old friend beforehand that it was just a pretend dressing down, Byrne duly laid into Haynes in front of a packed dressing room. Never one for taking criticism on the chin, Haynes completely forgot about it being a dummy row and the exercise developed into a full-scale slanging match that nearly ended in blows.

Byrne enjoyed a successful career in South Africa, courageously taking football into the black townships and later becoming involved with the national side. He died in Cape Town in 1999, aged 60. He was remembered as one of the game's most bubbly personalities but ultimately a player who never quite made the most of his undoubted ability. The skill was always there, but sometimes it was reduced to a cameo performance, particularly when the long nights started to take their toll on his body. As his old manager Ron Greenwood put it: 'He was everybody's friend but his own worst enemy.'

Trevor 'Tosh' Chamberlain
The Joker of Fulham

The Fulham team of the late Fifties and early Sixties was packed with colourful characters. There was full-back Jim Langley, with bow legs and a convict's crew-cut; erratic goalkeeper Tony Macedo who used to bounce the ball around his area like one of the Harlem Globetrotters basketball team; the gifted but irascible England star Johnny Haynes;

bearded inside-forward turned manager and TV pundit Jimmy Hill, who was always subjected to terrace cries of 'Give it to the Rabbi'; and last, but by no means least, left-winger 'Tosh' Chamberlain, an eccentric individualist whose talents could best be described as mercurial. That the club chairman at the time was comedian Tommy Trinder was surely no accident, for this bunch would have been just as much at home at the London Palladium as at Craven Cottage.

The relationship between Haynes and Chamberlain held particular fascination. They were like an old married couple who had reached the stage of sleeping in separate rooms and were pondering whether to consult solicitors. They were best pals at school and, indeed, Haynes only joined Fulham because Chamberlain had done so the previous year. And it was partly because of their friendship that Haynes chose to remain a one-club man when many bigger clubs were chasing the signature of the international playmaker, although the fact that Trinder made him Britain's first £100-a-week footballer in 1961 may also have played a small part in his decision.

Haynes and Chamberlain were like chalk and cheese. Haynes was arguably the best passer of a ball in the world at the time but he took the game very seriously and, as an out-and-out perfectionist, became impatient with anyone who did not match his standards. With Fulham, this meant every other member of the team. But it was Chamberlain, as his partner on the left, who bore the brunt of his friend's anger. 'Tosh' was a clown who loved to play to the crowd. He would chat to them while taking corners and was once seen puffing on the remains of his half-time cigarette after the second half had started. He possessed a ferocious shot and once broke a goalkeeper's arm with a penalty, but then again he once broke the ribs of Macedo, his own keeper, with a wild back pass. When he was on song, he was a danger to the opposition goal; when he wasn't he was a danger to the floodlights and any boats that happened to be passing on the Thames. In Haynes's perfect world, Chamberlain was often imperfect, resulting in frequent on-field spats between the two. Michael Parkinson has written that God created Tosh Chamberlain for Johnny Haynes to shout at.

Alan Mullery, later a Fulham and England stalwart, remembers watching the odd couple in action as a schoolboy. 'I was given a ticket to sit on the track round the pitch and watch the first team. There was an empty seat next to me, and with the game going on, the Fulham

No. 11, who I only later learned was called Tosh Chamberlain, came and sat next to me. He said, "I haven't seen the ball for 20 minutes", crossed his legs, grabbed a cigarette from a fella on the terraces and started having a smoke. Next thing, Johnny Haynes hits one of his inch-perfect 60-yard balls to where his winger should have been. Haynesy gave him the biggest rollicking I'd ever heard. So Tosh stands up and takes one last drag, stubs his fag out and shouts back, "When I'm standing out here you don't want to pass it, and when I'm having a fag, you give me a pass!"'

Haynes was very much 'Mr Fulham', ruling the club in all but name, and Chamberlain was one of the few who dared stand up to him. Tosh knew what to expect when he fouled things up, either with a wayward finish or by tripping over his own feet and falling flat on his face, but once he managed to get his retaliation in first. After blazing an astute Haynes pass miles over the bar, Chamberlain turned to see Haynes in his customary hands-on-hips pose, a picture of exasperation and barely concealed anger. This time, Tosh hurled a volley of verbal abuse in Haynes's direction, prompting the referee to rush over and book him. 'You can't do that, ref,' protested Tosh. 'He's on the same bloody side as me!'

Trevor Chamberlain was born in Camden Town in 1933 and won representative honours as a left-back for Islington school sides. Moving to the left-wing, he was capped by England Boys, scoring three goals in four minutes against the Republic of Ireland. In 1948 his club side, White Lion Play Centre, featured in a Cup final at Craven Cottage and he caught the attention of the then Fulham manager Jack Peart. After two years' National Service, he made his League debut in 1954, scoring with his first kick in the first minute against Lincoln City. Described by Michael Parkinson as 'whimsical, a creature of tides and moon', Chamberlain soon met a kindred spirit in new manager Duggie Livingstone, whose team talk before one game was: 'OK, lads, get an early two-goal lead before the opposition realise what a terrible side you are.' Chamberlain went on to score a memorable hat-trick in a 1956 Cup tie against Newcastle (although Fulham lost 5-4) and netted 64 goals in 204 games in the course of his 11 years with the club. He was nobody's fool, although he liked to give the opposite impression.

If he had been felled by a particularly bad tackle and the aggressor had escaped punishment, he would announce his intention to sit the rest of the game out 'until that bleeding ref apologises'. Taking a corner at Leyton Orient, he was so busy concentrating on where he was going to deliver the ball that he missed it completely and kicked the corner flag out of the ground instead. On another occasion Tosh was enjoying one of his good days, skinning the opposition full-back repeatedly. After going past him yet again and scoring a spectacular goal, Chamberlain was trotting back to the halfway line when he heard the full-back mutter: 'If that flash bastard goes past me once more, I'll break his leg!' Thinking on his feet, instead of lining up in his usual left-wing position for the restart, Tosh ran over to the right where a youngster named Mickey Cross was getting a rare outing for Fulham and told him: 'OK, son. I've ruined that full-back. Now you go over and have a go.'

Chamberlain later played for Dover and Gravesend & Northfleet but his heart remains with Fulham and he is still a regular visitor to the Cottage, where he is assured of a warm welcome, especially now that his old pal Johnny Haynes is no longer around to chastise him. Up in soccer heaven, Haynes is probably telling the story of a friendly between Fulham and Sampdoria in Genoa. When Fulham were awarded a free-kick on the edge of the box, Haynes instructed Chamberlain: 'Chip it, Tosh!' Instead, Chamberlain blasted the ball with such ferocity that, according to witnesses, if it had not been for the net, the ball would have ended up in the Mediterranean.

As they went back to the centre circle for the kick-off, Haynes berated Chamberlain: 'I told you to chip it!'

'I did!' said Tosh.

Steve Claridge
Defying the Odds

In a day when highly paid professional footballers are accused of becoming ever more remote from the supporters, Steve Claridge serves as a notable exception. Fans at the 15 different League clubs at which he plied his trade since the mid-1980s were never reduced to peering through huge wrought iron gates for a glimpse of their hero as he drove his BMW or Mercedes into his mansion. Instead, they knew exactly where to find him, and it was usually at the nearest betting office.

While his well publicised gambling addiction – he estimates that he has blown well over £300,000 in the course of his career – may have left a sizeable dent in his wallet, it helped cement his popularity with the fans who saw him as just an ordinary bloke off the street. In fact, his general air was of somebody who had just been dragged off the street, through a couple of hedges, and dumped on a football pitch in somebody else's kit. Looking as though he hadn't slept for several nights, he would stumble on to the pitch, shoulders hunched, socks rolled down, baggy shirt flapping out of his shorts, with that ungainly gait which hinted that every stride might be his last. To use an analogy from his favourite pursuit, if Michael Owen was the human equivalent of a thoroughbred racehorse, Steve Claridge looked more like a donkey from Blackpool beach.

Yet at club after club Claridge was always worth a flutter. As befits the man himself, his goals were not always the prettiest – scruffy scrambles, toe-pokes, close-range headers – but they came along with sufficient regularity to keep everybody but the opposition happy. Furthermore, he always gave 100 per cent, willingly chasing lost causes for the benefit of his more gifted but less enthusiastic team-mates. Although he invariably looked ready to drop after the first minute, he somehow managed to last another 89, often popping up with a late winner. He may not have appeared fit, but he was still playing in the Football League at the age of 40, and not many strikers can say that. Appearances were rarely more deceptive than in the case of Steve Claridge.

Unlikely though it may seem, there were practical reasons for his Worzel Gummidge look. He thought shinpads were cumbersome and didn't like wearing clean socks for a match because they tended to slip around inside his boots. So he used to wear dirty, unwashed socks, carried around in his kit bag from one match to the next. The bag also contained as many as 20 boots, all in various states of filth and disrepair. He had dozens of pairs of boots but could never decide which pair to wear and was known to change boots three times in the course of a match. 'I always felt my touch was better with worn-in boots,' he explained, 'and sometimes I would even wear an odd pair.

I have been known to keep the team waiting as they were ready to run out while I searched for just the right blend.'

Nobody could ever accuse Claridge of being elegant. He used to drive a battered green Escort that was filled with rubbish, and once turned up for pre-season training at Bournemouth in a woolly hat on a baking hot day because he had accidentally hacked off great chunks of his hair while trying to remove a few strands that had become splattered with paint. Neither the Escort nor any other car he has owned seems to have delivered him to his destination on time. Indeed, his lack of punctuality became legendary. He was frequently fined for being late for training, and when he joined Cambridge United, he even managed to be late for his own signing!

On his own admission, he was something of a liability at the wheel of a car. After training at Cambridge, he was eating fish and chips in his car but had left the vehicle in gear, with his foot on the clutch. When his foot slipped, the car ran into the back of a lorry. David Pleat, who was his manager at Luton, recalled that if Claridge had a puncture and the tyre needed to be changed, he would simply leave the car by the side of the road. Before a big game at Millwall, Claridge actually managed to injure himself while getting out of his car in the club car park.

To say he was accident-prone is like saying Peter Crouch is tallish. Hurrying to place a bet, he once drove into a lorry. The crash prevented him putting £1,500 on a horse but as the horse lost, the accident turned out to be a blessing in disguise. In his entertaining autobiography *Tales From the Boot Camps*, Claridge wrote: 'The bill for the damage to his lorry and my car came to £800, so I figured that crash saved me £700. The driver couldn't believe I was so willing to pay and seemed a bit baffled by the smile on my face when I took the money round to his house a few nights later.'

At Aldershot, where he trained on dog-fouled public parks and played with a midfielder, Giorgio Mazzon, who had a disabled sticker on his vehicle, Claridge funded his gambling habit by selling fruit and veg from the back of his own car to the other players. At Cambridge he gambled so much that he had no money left for anywhere to live and had to sleep in a Cortina (on loan from his father) for a couple of nights. He lost £4,500 in one particularly disastrous afternoon and, to round off a miserable day, his car ran out of petrol on the way home. 'It had never occurred to me all day just to save a tenner for petrol,' he lamented. Sometimes he would train with £4,000 in his tracksuit trousers, ready to place a bet as soon as training ended. He was such a good customer that his local bookmaker near Cambridge took pity on him and let him sleep on his sofa. Claridge even ended up working behind the counter. Even when he won, he lost. After winning £16,000 on an accumulator, he contrived to blow the lot on a succession of losing horses before he was able to collect his winnings. 'As my last horse was going down, a Securicor man walked through the door with my £16,000. I can still hear the bookie's words to this helmeted figure chained to a metal case: "It's all right, mate. You can take it back. We won't be needing it any more."'

Claridge never learned the error of his ways. Even towards the end of his career at Millwall, he would ask the club driver to drop him off at the bookies on the way to Blackheath Hospital for injury treatment and again on the way back to pick up his winnings. Yet he insists that his gambling never affected his performance on the pitch, a claim that is borne out by the fact he played in more than 1,000 professional or semi-professional games and always gave value for money.

He was born in Portsmouth in 1966 but failed to break through at his hometown club and signed for Southern League Fareham Town instead. His performances there alerted Bournemouth but after just seven games at Dean Court, he moved on to Weymouth. He returned to League football in 1988 with Aldershot before joining Cambridge United for £75,000 in 1990. There, he had a tempestuous relationship with manager John Beck. The pair once had a fight at half-time after Claridge had been substituted and it was no surprise when he was moved on to Luton Town for £120,000. Five months later, following Beck's departure, Claridge rejoined Cambridge for £190,000.

In January 1994 he moved for £350,000 to Birmingham City, where a return of 35 goals from 88 League games led to a £1.2 million transfer to Leicester City two years later. He became a Leicester folk hero by scoring two crucial goals – the last-minute winner in the 1996 First Division play-off final against Crystal Palace (a characteristic miss-hit) and the only goal of the 1997 League Cup final replay against Middlesbrough, the second giving Claridge his only major trophy.

Following a brief stay at Wolves, he finally made it into Portsmouth's first team, more than 15 years after being rejected at Fratton Park as a youngster. He was twice voted Pompey fans' Player of the Year and in 2000 was appointed player-manager, only to be demoted after 25 games. The following year he joined Millwall on a free transfer, again becoming a firm favourite with the crowd and contributing 29 goals from 91 League starts. After two years at The Den, he tried his luck at management again, this time with Weymouth, and when that ended unsatisfactorily, he returned to playing, first with Brighton, then Brentford and Wycombe. In the summer of 2005 he was appointed manager of Millwall but a boardroom coup ended his reign after just 32 days and before he had ever led the team in a competitive match.

Disillusioned, he tasted further whirlwind spells as a player with Gillingham, Bradford City, Walsall and Bournemouth, with whom, in December 2006, he notched that 1,000th competitive appearance. With nearly 200 League goals to his credit, in 2007 he dropped down to the lower echelons for a final hurrah, winning new fans at outposts such as Worthing and Harrow Borough.

Throughout his career Steve Claridge has defied the odds. For someone who has led such a disorganised lifestyle, he has lasted the distance remarkably well – certainly more successfully than some of the horses he has backed.

Pierluigi Collina
The Eyes Have It

There have always been one or two referees with personality at any given time. Back in the Sixties and Seventies there was the ever-smiling Tommy Dawes; the rotund, high-kicking Roger Kirkpatrick, nicknamed 'Mr Pickwick' because of his mutton-chop whiskers; the terror of Treorchy, Clive 'The Book' Thomas; and more recently that master of the three-card trick, Graham Poll. But none of these was as instantly recognisable as Pierluigi Collina, arguably the most famous and the most accomplished referee in the history of football.

Nature gave Collina a head start over the rest: those manic staring eyes, followed, around the age of 30, by the alopecia he contracted that made all his hair fall out. He has been likened to a character from a horror film but it is worth noting that he has also been voted the world's sexiest referee. Indeed, his looks have been his fortune, leading to appearances in TV commercials, on the covers of video games and even on the catwalks of Rome, where in 2002 he modelled menswear in a fashion show alongside Naomi Campbell and Eva Herzigova. The following year he received an honorary doctorate from the University of Hull but no doubt the accolade that means most to him is the one that has seen him named best referee in the world on five occasions by his fellow officials. David Beckham, Steven Gerrard, Kevin Keegan and Sir Alex Ferguson have all gone on record saying that Collina was the best. Even Paul Ince, who was twice sent off by him, called him a 'fantastic ref'.

So, before his retirement in 2005, what made the financial adviser from Italy so special? Most importantly, players respected him. They knew that he was strict but fair and could not be harassed into changing a decision. One look from those manic eyes was usually enough to deter dissent. Not for nothing was he known as 'The Iron Man'. He said: 'If you have good relations with all the players in a match, including the coaches, it's possible to have a better match. If the players trust and accept a referee and his decisions, I feel that it makes for a better game of football.'

That respect did not occur by chance; Collina achieved it through years of hard work and by thoroughly preparing for each game. He would often watch teams in advance, noting the tactics of individual players so that he could adapt his own game accordingly. 'It's very important to get all the information I can about the teams themselves,' he explained, 'because it's important that a referee knows as much as possible about the way a team plays, and about the way individual players play. It's about tactics. It's completely different refereeing a match where a team plays with three players at the back or four, or with tough midfielders pressing their opponents for the ball, or with two wingers where the play goes out wide. Also if there's a good keeper kicking it long, you have to be well positioned because they can mount a counterattack in a second. Those are characteristics that you have to be aware of. Football has reached a very high standard, and football needs referees to be very well prepared.'

Collina was born in Bologna in 1960 and played as a central defender for a local team, although he admits he wasn't very good.

When he was 17, a school friend, Fausto Capuano, persuaded him to take a referee's course. When one of the referees had trouble with his contact lenses, Collina took his place, immediately earning praise from the older officials. While graduating from university with a degree in economics and completing his military service, he steadily progressed through the referees' ranks, from regional matches to the national league, culminating in Serie A. In 1995, after he had offici-ated at 43 Serie A matches, he was placed on the FIFA list.

He was awarded five matches at the 1996 Olympics, including the final between Nigeria and Argentina, and in 1999 he refereed the dramatic Champions League final between Manchester United and Bayern Munich. After Collina had taken charge of two further German defeats – the 5-1 drubbing by England in 2001 and the 2002 World Cup final defeat to Brazil, the Bayern and Germany goalkeeper Oliver Kahn remarked ruefully: 'Collina is a world-class referee, there's no doubt about that, but he doesn't bring luck, does he?'

Collina's last major tournament was Euro 2004, as he reached the mandatory retirement age of 45 for FIFA referees in 2005. The Italian Football Federation raised its compulsory retirement age to 46 in order to accommodate Collina for another season, but when he signed a major sponsorship deal with Opel (who also sponsored AC Milan), the deal was perceived as a conflict of interest. He was told that he would be unable to referee Serie A games, as a result of which he handed in his resignation, saying: 'People must believe in a referee. If they don't, then we have to go. Without trust we cannot move forward.'

Collina may have been the world's first true celebrity referee, hugely admired by his peers, but he accepted that he was not infallible. 'It's normal to make mistakes,' he said in an interview in 2004, 'but afterwards you have to know or understand *why* you did it on the field, what was missing in your preparation. When you do things well, you have to forget it quickly and look ahead. When you do poorly you also have to forget it, but not as quickly because first you have to understand why you did poorly. That helps you a lot.'

William 'Dixie' Dean
Heading For Glory

Judged by statistics alone, 'Dixie' Dean was an incredible character: 349 goals in 399 League games for Everton; a record 60 goals in one season, despite the fact that he missed three matches; and 18 goals in just 16 appearances for England. But what really elevates Dean to legendary status was that his amazing goalscoring feats were achieved after he had suffered two horrific injuries that would have ended the careers of lesser men. First, while playing for Tranmere Rovers, he was kicked in the groin with such force by the Rochdale centre-half that he lost a testicle. Then, shortly after signing for Everton, he was involved in a motorcycle accident that left him with a broken jaw and a fractured skull. Doctors told him he would never play football again but 15 weeks later he was back doing what he did best – scoring goals for fun.

Dean was an unassuming man with a great sense of humour. He was never booked or sent off and one of the few things in life he hated was his nickname. It was given to him by Tranmere fans due to his dark complexion and curly black hair, which, they thought, was similar to that of African-Americans in the southern United States. Some misguided souls actually thought he was black. Following a game at Tottenham, Dean was walking off the pitch when a home supporter yelled at him: 'We'll get you yet, you black bastard!' A policeman overheard the remark but Dean pushed him aside, saying, 'It's all right, officer, I'll handle this.' With that, Dean waded into the crowd and laid his tormentor out with a punch, prompting the policeman to wink at him and say: 'That was a beauty but I never saw it officially.' Small wonder then that Dean much preferred to be known as William or Bill.

Dean certainly added punch to the Everton attack. He was a constant menace in the penalty area. He had two good feet and because he never needed much backlift, defenders had precious little time to make a tackle. But it was his heading ability that made him a cut above the rest. Although he was a comparatively modest 5 feet 10 inches tall, he could head a ball as hard as many could kick it.

He used to develop his neck muscles by heading an old medicine ball stuffed full of wet paper – something that was hard enough to lift, let alone head. A popular myth at the time was that the steel plates that had been inserted into his head to help mend his skull after the motorcycle accident had contributed to his aerial power, but the plates were soon removed. Dixie Dean had no need of artificial aids. As Bill Shankly once said: 'Those of us privileged to see Dean play, talk of him the way people talk about Beethoven, Shakespeare, or Mozart; he was that good.'

The son of a train driver, William Ralph Dean was born in Birkenhead on 22 January 1907. As a schoolboy he got a job helping the local milkman, and it was lifting heavy milk churns seven days a week that helped build his magnificent physique. He loved playing football and never missed the chance of a kickabout. Once, he was taking his baby sister for a walk when he was invited to join in a game. Using her pram as a goalpost, he and his friends played until dusk, whereupon he set off home and forgot all about the pram. He ran back to find his sister was safe and still asleep.

He left school at 14 to work as an apprentice boilermaker and, although a staunch Evertonian, signed for Tranmere at 16. After scoring 27 goals in 29 League games for Tranmere, he earned his dream move in 1925 when Everton paid £3,000 to secure his services. In his first full season he scored 32 goals but the motorcycle crash in North Wales in June 1926 jeopardised his future. As part of his recuperation, he helped transport corpses to and from the hospital mortuary, perhaps acutely aware that he had come perilously close to joining them. So effective was his recovery that, on his return, he managed 21 goals in 27 matches before really hitting the jackpot the following season. Fortified by his standard pre-match diet of a glass of sherry mixed with two raw eggs, Dean ran riot in 1927–28, passing George Camsell's record of 59 League goals in a season by netting a hat-trick in the final fixture against Arsenal. A third of Dean's 60 goals came from headers and they helped Everton lift the First Division Championship.

As the goals continued to flow, he was so famous that his marriage in 1931 brought traffic in Liverpool to a standstill. Incidentally, he and his wife spent their honeymoon on a tour of Britain's racetracks! He was not one for the limelight but knew that when he ventured out for a quiet midweek drink, he was sure to be besieged by autograph hunters. So before going to the pub, he used to sign his autograph on dozens of slips of paper. He explained: 'I stay in on Mondays and sign all these bits of paper so that when the kids ask for my autograph it doesn't interfere with my drinking!'

His exploits fired Everton to another League Championship in 1932 and FA Cup success the following year. In nine consecutive seasons he scored more than 20 goals and altogether managed 37 hat-tricks in his career. He won his first England cap in 1927 and scored 12 times in his first five internationals – a phenomenal achievement at any level.

By 1937 the physical demands of the game had taken their toll and he was sold to Notts County for £3,000. He played only nine games for the Magpies (scoring three goals) before moving to Ireland, where he helped Sligo Rovers reach the final of the Irish Cup. He eventually retired from playing in 1939 to work in a Birkenhead abattoir. After the war he ran a pub in Chester and later landed a job as a security guard for Littlewoods Pools. In the early 1970s he was rushed to hospital after a duodenal ulcer burst. Although he had been on the danger list, he still found time to joke about his condition. 'They told me I had special blood, Rhesus Negative. They said it was the rarest type. "Never mind that," I said. "Is it the dearest?" I needed 15 pints of the stuff to bring me round.' In 1976 a thrombosis necessitated the amputation of his right leg, leading Dixie to claim that he had been in more theatres than Morecambe and Wise.

He died on 1 March 1980, fittingly at Goodison Park after collapsing while watching the derby match against Liverpool. In 2001 a statue of Dean was erected outside the stadium, bearing the simple inscription: 'Footballer, Gentleman, Evertonian'.

After his earlier illness, messages of support had come from all over the world, some simply addressed to 'Dixie Dean, England'. They found their way to their destination because, even though it was nearly 40 years since his retirement, everybody still knew Dixie Dean. The memory of the man and his achievements will live on forever.

Derek Dougan
The Doog

Throughout his career, controversy followed Derek Dougan with stalker-like zeal. Whether it was as a gangling centre-forward, chairman of the Professional Footballers' Association or chairman and chief executive of Wolves, the outspoken Dougan made friends and foes in equal numbers. His Northern Ireland team-mate Billy Bingham said: 'He was a rebel, sometimes without a cause. He wasn't afraid to give his opinion – on any subject.'

Fans recognised 'The Doog' as one of the game's great characters but some managers, all too aware of his reputation, treated him with caution. After Dougan shaved his head in the early Sixties at a time when such actions were unheard of, even the amiable Joe Mercer, his manager at Aston Villa, lost patience and warned him: 'If you want to be noticed, better do it with the ball.' Bingham admitted: 'Derek had tremendous ability but he was temperamentally unsound, easily upset. He didn't want to be bossed and could make trouble for managers.'

He was not always hugely popular with team-mates either, some of whom found him arrogant. He has been described as an enigma, an intelligent, eloquent man who was nevertheless capable of committing appalling fouls when the red mist descended. Playing for Wolves in 1969, he was suspended for eight matches for swearing at a linesman. Yet he also liked to play the clown. While waiting for a corner to be taken at Queens Park Rangers, he kissed his bald-headed marker, Terry Mancini, on the head, much to the amusement of Mancini and the crowd. And during his time at Leicester, he once ran behind the Filbert Street goal with a Fulham defender following him all the way. It was Dougan's way of showing the crowd how tightly he was being marked.

Born in Belfast in 1938, Dougan worked as an apprentice at the city's famous Harland & Wolff shipyard and played for Distillery, helping them to win the Irish Cup in 1956 before being sold to Portsmouth for £4,000 the following year. While at Fratton Park he won the first of 43 Northern Ireland caps, leading the line creditably at the 1958 World Cup finals despite his tender years. As his 6-foot 3-inch frame began to fill out, he became more of a handful for defenders, combining aerial power with agile footwork. The improvement earned him a £15,000 move to Blackburn Rovers but after playing his part in taking the Lancashire club to the 1960 FA Cup final, he sensationally demanded a transfer on the morning of the Wembley showpiece. He was named in the line-up but gave a lacklustre performance (he was later accused of not trying) and Rovers succumbed 3-0 to Wolves.

He eventually got his transfer, to Aston Villa, in August 1961 but his stay there was not a happy one and his form dipped to the extent that his next move was to Third Division Peterborough United. He remained at London Road for two seasons before Leicester City rescued him for £25,000 in 1965. Rejuvenated, he regained his international place, prompting Wolves manager Ronnie Allen to pay £50,000 for his services in 1967. One of his first matches for the Molineux club saw him kicked by a Millwall fan who had run on to the pitch to remonstrate with him.

The wanderer stayed at Wolves for eight years, scoring 123 goals in 307 appearances and forming deadly partnerships with first Bobby Gould and then John Richards. A League Cup winners' medal in 1974 confirmed Dougan's popularity with the fans, although his temperament did not endear him to Allen's successor, the stern Bill McGarry. Dougan was a typically forthright member of ITV's 1970 World Cup panel and championed players' rights as chairman of the PFA. In 1973 he turned out for an all-Ireland team (billed as Shamrock Rovers XI) against Brazil, scoring one of the goals in a 4-3 defeat. However, the Irish FA had opposed the staging of the game and Dougan, who had also helped organise it, paid the price for his insubordination. He never played for his country again, later claiming that IFA president Harry Cavan had instructed Northern Ireland manager Terry Neill not to pick him.

After two years as player-manager of Kettering Town, he returned to Wolves in 1982 as chairman. He had previously been highly critical of the way in which football clubs were run. 'One wonders what some businesses would be like,' he wrote, 'if they were run on the same haphazard lines as most football clubs are. The amateur director has been kicked out of most industrial boardrooms, but not in football.' He promised to give Wolves back to the fans but the

Bhatti brothers, the Asian businessmen who had bought the ailing club, were unable to instigate a revival and Dougan quickly found that his one-time popularity as a player was no safeguard against supporter unrest. With the leader of Wolverhampton Council complaining that the club had brought the town into disrepute, Dougan was forced out.

In December 2005 Dougan helped carry the coffin of George Best, and the following summer he appeared on the BBC's *Question Time* as a representative of the United Kingdom Independence Party. He maintained his uncompromising stance on whatever topic was up for debate – from 4-4-2 to the European Union – right up until his sudden death in June 2007.

Simon Garner
Smoking Gun

In 14 seasons at Blackburn Rovers, Simon Garner plundered a club record 168 League goals. Yet his career at Ewood Park was threatened from the outset by youth team coach John Pickering, who was distinctly unimpressed by the apprentice's addiction to cigarettes. Accordingly, Pickering recommended to manager Jim Smith that Garner be released. Garner was summoned to Smith's office but instead of kicking him out of the club, Smith advised him not to get caught smoking again…and then offered him a cigar.

Garner never did kick the habit – it is said that he used to have a cigarette at half-time to steady his nerves – but by then his goalscoring exploits were such that he was almost beyond reproach. Tales of his smoking and drinking made Garner a Blackburn folk hero, as did his knack of antagonising local rivals Burnley. When it came to a local derby, Garner invariably delivered. His double strike in a 2-1 win at Ewood Park in 1983 prompted irate Burnley fans to try to burn down the Darwen End stand, seemingly oblivious to the fact that they were in it at the time. His legendary status has also been enhanced by the popular belief that he was responsible for hiring a light aeroplane that flew over Turf Moor during Burnley's failed attempt to escape from Division Four in 1991. With Burnley losing a play-off game to Torquay United and Rovers flying high, the plane buzzed over the Burnley ground at half-time trailing a message that read: 'Staying down 4 ever, luv Rovers, Ha Ha Ha.' The Burnley faithful were not amused.

Like Steve Claridge, Garner never looked a natural athlete but whether it was in a crowded penalty area or at a town bar on a Saturday night, he had that priceless gift for being able to find space. Fans identified with him because his chest seemed to puff out with pride whenever he wore the Blackburn shirt, although he may have been trying to draw breath as a result of his less-than-exacting training regime. He always had time for a laugh and a drink with the supporters and usually judged newly signed team-mates on their ability to smoke or drink rather than play football. Thus he hit it off with Duncan McKenzie who would join Garner puffing away at the back of the team bus.

Nicknamed the 'Lincolnshire Poacher' after his birthplace (he was born in Boston in 1959), he played for Boston United before being snapped up by Blackburn as a 16-year-old. The 1980s may not have been the most illustrious period in Blackburn's history but what highlights there were invariably came courtesy of the stocky striker. Yet manager Howard Kendall nearly sold him to Halifax Town for £40,000, only for Garner to reject the move. Even when he broke the club scoring record in 1989, it was a low-key affair, the celebrations being overshadowed by news of the disaster across the Pennines at Hillsborough.

When a new broom in the shape of Kenny Dalglish, backed by Jack Walker's millions, swept through Ewood Park, Garner was among the dismantled cobwebs. But while Garner may no longer have been an automatic choice, Dalglish made sure the 32-year-old was given one of the three non-playing places on the bench when Blackburn reached the 1992 Second Division play-off final at Wembley. He smoked his way through an entire pack of cigarettes as Rovers reached the newly formed Premiership, and when the team made a triumphant return to Blackburn Town Hall, a slightly inebriated Garner was as happy as any fan. Even though he had played no part in the actual match, the crowd had not forgotten their hero and launched into a chorus of 'There's Only One Simon Garner.'

He never played for the club in the top flight, instead moving to West Bromwich Albion for £30,000...but still wore a Blackburn T-shirt under his West Brom shirt. In 1994 he joined League new-comers Wycombe Wanderers on a free transfer and scored the goal at Wembley that clinched promotion. Two years later his colourful career took an unexpected turn when he was sentenced to nine months in jail for contempt of court following his marriage break-up, although he was released after just four weeks.

He turned out for a handful of non-League sides before hanging up his boots in 2000 to concentrate on his painting and decorating business. He had previously worked as a postman, which was quite appropriate really, because throughout his career, Simon Garner always delivered.

Emlyn Hughes
Crazy Horse

Emlyn Hughes's status as a Kop favourite was earned by virtue of a neck-high rugby tackle he made early in his Liverpool career on flying Newcastle winger Albert Bennett. The illegal lunge on his tormentor also won Hughes the nickname of 'Crazy Horse'. As team-mate Phil Thompson later wrote: '"Crazy Horse" seemed to be apt for a young player who appeared to have boundless energy and a galloping running style with his arms flailing away as he switched from defence to attack.'

Enthusiasm was Hughes's great virtue. Both as a player and in his subsequent career as a team captain on *A Question of Sport*, those boyish features and a smile as wide as the Mersey indicated a man who was truly happy in his line of work. His personality was infectious, making him an ideal choice as captain for both Liverpool and England. The suspicion that like his club manager, Bill Shankly, he was really still a child at heart was reinforced by a ridiculously high-pitched voice. When Hughes became agitated, only dogs could understand him.

The son of a Welsh international Rugby League player, Emlyn Walter Hughes was born in Barrow-in-Furness in 1947. He played rugby at school but soccer held greater appeal and he was signed by Blackpool manager Ron Suart, who promptly converted him from inside-forward to left-half and then left-back. Hughes became established in the 1966–67 season, watched from the terraces by his proud father, who used to extol his son's merits to surrounding fans. After just 28 games for Blackpool, he was snapped up by Shankly for £65,000, a record fee for a full-back. The two men were kindred spirits. Hughes, who was not given to false modesty, liked to relay the story of how Shankly had pranged his car in his haste to drive the player from Blackpool to Lytham St Anne's to be registered with the FA. As a police constable began to take down Shankly's details, the manager asked the officer impatiently: 'Don't you know who's is in this car? This is the future captain of England!'

Shankly's prophecy would eventually be fulfilled as Hughes went on to win 62 England caps, leading his country on 23 occasions. He was quick and he was strong, but in his early years his enthusiasm often bordered on recklessness, as Albert Bennett, among others, would testify. His other failing was that as a left-back he was right-footed, with the result that his charges up the wing would grind to a halt while he stopped to cross the ball with his favoured foot. Consequently, he was more effective when switched to a midfield role, especially as it gave him licence to unleash the sort of ferocious shot that was the trademark of the 48 goals he scored in 665 games for Liverpool. During his 12 years with the club, he won four League titles, the European Cup twice, the UEFA Cup twice and the FA Cup once. A rare setback came in the 1977 FA Cup final, which saw Liverpool lose 2-1 to Manchester United. As he trudged dejectedly up the steps to collect his loser's medal, the Conservative leader, Margaret Thatcher, asked him how he felt. Dispensing with protocol in favour of honest charm, Hughes replied: 'To be honest, love, I'm bloody knackered.' It was probably the first and the last time that anybody called the Iron Lady 'love'.

His time at Anfield was partly soured by a long-running feud with Tommy Smith, whom he had replaced as captain. After Liverpool had beaten Newcastle in the 1974 FA Cup final, several players pushed Smith to the front of the celebrations, ahead of Hughes. Nevertheless, when Bob Paisley succeeded Shankly, Hughes remained as captain.

In 1979, and with his place in the side under threat from young Scottish recruit Alan Hansen, Hughes departed for Wolves for £90,000, and in his first season there led them to victory over Nottingham Forest in the League Cup final. Two years later he was appointed player-manager of Rotherham United but lasted just 20 months before ending his playing career with first Hull City and then Swansea City.

His bubbly personality enabled him to carve out a niche on *A Question of Sport*, where he mistakenly identified a picture of a mud-spattered Princess Anne as jockey John Reid. When HRH subsequently appeared on the show as a member of his team, Hughes again defied protocol by putting his arm around her. Around the same time he did himself few favours by launching repeated vitriolic attacks on England manager Bobby Robson in a national newspaper. As Robson rightly pointed out, what did Emlyn Hughes ever achieve as a manager?

After his TV work dried up, Hughes did the rounds as a popular after-dinner speaker until undergoing surgery for a brain tumour in 2003. He died the following year, aged 57.

Former Liverpool full-back Phil Neal paid tribute to Hughes's outstanding leadership qualities: 'His character rubbed off on us all. I came in as an inexperienced player and he was so effervescent. He used to drive me on a Friday night to meet up with the team bus for an away game and he would convince me we would win 2-0 – just like Shankly would have done. He never dreamed of losing any game.'

John Barnwell, who signed Hughes for Wolves, remembered the player's competitive nature. 'He would make a better cup of tea than anyone, he could play snooker better than anyone, his opinion was always better than yours – that was the character of Emlyn.'

Jimmy Johnstone
Wee Jinky

More elusive than the Scarlet Pimpernel, tackling Jimmy Johnstone was like trying to tackle dust. His ability to twist and turn so that his torso, hips and feet moved in three directions at once baffled the finest full-backs in the world and earned him the nickname 'Jinky'. He could also stop dead in mid-sprint before spinning away at an improbable angle, prompting his Celtic captain Billy McNeill to comment: 'He must have groin muscles of steel.'

The little right-winger's skills were never better demonstrated than in the 1970 European Cup semi-final against Leeds. 'Wee Jinky was out of this world at Elland Road,' recalled Celtic team-mate Tommy Gemmell. 'Terry Cooper, the Leeds left-back, must have nightmares every time somebody mentions Jimmy Johnstone because he gave him a total going over. Norman Hunter was shouting to Cooper, "Kick him!" Cooper turned around and said, "You come out and kick him." Hunter came out and tried to stick it on wee Jimmy. Wee Jimmy just waltzed around him and nutmegged him.'

Cooper was in good company. Johnstone also mesmerised Emlyn Hughes in a 1974 Scotland-England international to the point that Hughes was embarrassed to come off the pitch. Afterwards, Alf Ramsey consoled Hughes by saying: 'You've just played against a world-class player today. He can do that to anybody.' High praise indeed since Ramsey was not exactly renowned for his love of the Scots.

At 5 feet 4 inches tall and weighing just 9½ stone, Johnstone might have looked a pushover but the thatch of ginger hair signified a temper that some opponents sought to exploit, occasionally successfully. The 1967 World Club Championship decider against Racing Club of Buenos Aires in Montevedeo saw Johnstone forced to wash the spittle out of his hair at half-time and sent off in the second half. Seven years later, in a European Cup semi-final, Atletico Madrid players took it in turns to hack him to the ground, but Johnstone always came back for more, rising to his feet to run with the ball straight at his most recent assailant. It is a tribute to his balance and athleticism that, in spite of these repeated attempts by opponents to maim him, he managed to play at the highest level for 12 years without suffering a serious injury.

He honed his remarkable skills around the streets of Viewpark, North Lanarkshire, where he was born in 1944. He attended school at nearby Uddingston on the outskirts of Glasgow and would climb over the railings after school to practise in the deserted playground. He recalled: 'I used to go into the playground and I practised for hours and hours on end, running with the ball, sprinting, twisting and turning. There was a wall about a hundred yards long and as I went up and down I played one-twos off it and then, when I went home, I would put milk bottles down and go in and out of them for another hour or two.'

He was a Celtic fan from a young age and played briefly for one of their youth teams, yet nearly ended up signing for Manchester United. He had a trial with United at 13, but Matt Busby – wrongly as it turned out – thought Celtic had first option on him and honourably chose not to pursue the matter. Alerted by United's interest, Celtic quickly moved in and took him to Parkhead. He made his first-team debut in 1962 and went on to make 515 appearances for the club, scoring 129 goals in the process.

The turning point in Celtic's fortunes came with the appointment of Jock Stein as manager in 1965. Although Johnstone's wayward temperament led to frequent clashes with the manager (Stein's own mother once rebuked him for being 'very hard on that wee fellow'), Jinky was a key member of the 1967 Lisbon Lions, which became the first British team to lift the European Cup. He had already attracted notice with a dazzling display in the second round against Nantes, after which the French press dubbed him the Flying Flea. As for the final against Inter Milan, Johnstone admitted he feared the worst. 'There they were,' he recalled, 'Facchetti, Domenghini, Mazzola, Cappellini: all six-footers wi' Ambre Solaire suntans, Colgate smiles and slick-backed hair. Each and every wan o' them looked like yon film star Cesar Romero. They even smelt beautiful. And there's us lot – midgets. Ah've got nae teeth, Bobby Lennox hasnae any, and old Ronnie Simpson's got the full monty, nae teeth top an' bottom. The Italians are staring doon at us an' we're grinnin' back up at 'em wi' our great gumsy grins. We must have looked like something out o' the circus.'

Yet Celtic prevailed, partly due, Johnstone believed, to the tremendous team spirit that arose from having so many local players in the side. 'Football was the greatest part of our lives,' he said, 'just like the boys from Brazil and Spain. They lived in poverty, like us, and that's where all the great players came from – the street.'

Johnstone's individuality was probably the reason that he won only 23 Scottish caps. When Tommy Docherty took charge he joked: 'On my first day as Scotland manager I had to call off practice after half an hour because nobody could get the ball off wee Jinky.' Johnstone's fun-loving nature also caused concern in some quarters and his fondness for a drink led to the infamous Largs Boat Incident of 1974. Celebrating victory over Wales and with four days before the next game, national team boss Willie Ormond allowed the players a night out in the Ayrshire seaside town of Largs. Stumbling out of a bar at around four in the morning, Johnstone spotted a rowing boat and decided to borrow it. Carried out by the tide, he was already a speck on the horizon when he realised one of the oars had fallen overboard. Two team-mates rowed out to help but their boat sprang a leak and they were forced to head back to dry land. Instead, the coastguard had to be called out to rescue Johnstone, by which time he was standing up in the boat and singing at the top of his voice. On his return to the hotel Johnstone simply remarked: 'Don't know what all the fuss is about – I thought I'd go fishing!' His wife, Agnes, was less impressed. 'Jimmy will be 30 soon,' she told reporters, 'and it's about time he started to act his age.'

Some years later he was a guest when players from Old England and Old Germany replayed the 1966 World Cup final. At the post-match dinner, the 22 participants were seated at a long table, along which a drunken Johnstone proceeded to streak stark naked.

His unreliable temperament was not the sole source of frustration for his various managers. He was terrified of flying, a fact that the astute Stein was able to turn to his advantage before a European Cup tie against Red Star Belgrade. Stein promised Johnstone that he would excuse him from playing in the second leg in Yugoslavia if the winger helped create enough of a lead in the home leg in Glasgow. The psychology worked a treat and Johnstone played out of his skin, scoring twice and creating three of the five goals that made his trip abroad unnecessary.

Johnstone's other great fear was Stein himself. Substituted by the manager during a Celtic game, the winger took off his jersey and threw it in the direction of the dugout. Unfortunately, it landed on Stein's head. Enraged, Stein jumped up and in doing so, cracked his skull on the roof of the dugout, a mishap that led to him chasing Johnstone into the dressing room. Hearing the big man's footsteps behind him, Johnstone panicked and decided to jump into the bath, reasoning that Stein was unlikely to follow him there, but he had forgotten that trainer Bob Rooney used to run a very hot bath after half-time in the expectation that it would have cooled down nicely for the players' use at the final whistle. In mid-leap Johnstone realised he was jumping into a scalding hot bath – but he chose to stay in there rather than face Stein's wrath.

Handed a free transfer by Celtic at the end of the 1974–75 season, Johnstone went on to play for Sheffield United, Dundee, Shelbourne and Elgin City. In 2001 he was diagnosed with motor neurone disease but lived long enough to receive the accolade of being voted Celtic's greatest ever player. He died in March 2006 at the age of 61. At that month's Scottish League Cup final, the entire Celtic squad wore the number seven on both the front and back of their shorts in his honour, and at the end of the match they all put on tops displaying 'JINKY' and number seven. Even many Rangers fans mourned Jimmy Johnstone, who was loved as much for his ready wit as his mazy dribbling. Celtic team-mate Jim Craig told how Johnstone had once pestered him for the ball during a match. Reluctant to pass it to the wee fellow because he knew he was unlikely to receive a return ball, Craig eventually relented. 'When will I get it back?' he shouted, to which Johnstone replied: 'When ah'm finished wi' it, ah suppose.'

Wilf Mannion
Contract Rebel

With his blond hair and youthful looks, Wilf Mannion was sometimes likened to a choirboy. Indeed, the *Manchester Guardian* once wrote of him: 'His style is so graceful and so courtly that he would not be out of place in a lace ruffle and the perruque (a wig).' Yet behind that cherubic appearance lay a steely determination, which led to Mannion becoming embroiled in two major controversies as he sought to improve the lot of the post-war professional footballer.

In 1948 he refused to sign a new contract at Middlesbrough, considering the terms to be 'laughable'. As a result he spent six months out of the game and was forced to work for a building firm in Oldham. Third Division Oldham Athletic saw this as their chance to recruit the services of the England international but were shocked to be quoted a fee of £25,000 by Middlesbrough. They managed to scrape together £15,000 – including £2,000 from a public collection – before admitting defeat. Eventually, Mannion, who had hoped to beef up the League's maximum wage of £10 a week by combining playing for Oldham with selling chicken coops, patched up his differences with 'Boro and helped them in their fight against relegation to the Second Division.

After initially retiring as a player in 1954, Mannion joined Hull City in December of that year but soon found himself in trouble once more following a series of newspaper articles in which he alleged that some players were receiving illegal payments. When he refused to divulge details of these payments, he was suspended by the Football League and never played League football again.

Wilfred James Mannion was born in the South Bank district of Middlesbrough on 16 May 1918, and on leaving school worked as a welder at the local docks while playing football in the evening and at weekends. He signed professional forms for Middlesbrough at 18 and developed into a supremely talented inside-forward, creating goals for others and also weighing in with 110 goals in his 368 appearances for the club, including four in an amazing 9-2 thrashing of Blackpool at Ayresome Park. Despite being only 5 feet 5 inches, he was competitive in the air, using timing to compensate for his lack of height. But it was with the ball at his tiny, dancing feet that he really excelled, weaving mazy patterns at pace and employing outstanding balance and a deceptive body swerve to leave opponents tackling thin air. He was particularly effective in tight situations, where his stocky frame and intricate close control could shake off the closest of marking.

He won the first of his 26 official England caps in 1947 and in the same year starred in Great Britain's 6-1 demolition of the Rest of Europe at Hampden Park. He dismissed the subsequent press accolades, describing himself as 'just a useful cog in a well-oiled machine'. There was little prospect of Mannion getting carried away with his new-found status since he travelled home from Hampden sitting on a cardboard case in the corridor of the third-class section of a train. Small wonder that he was eager to take a stance against footballers' low wages at a time when the clubs were reaping the financial rewards of the post-war boom in gates.

He had the misfortune to be a member of the England team humiliated 1-0 by the United States at the 1950 World Cup, and won his final cap two years later at the age of 53. When Middlesbrough were relegated at the end of the 1953–54 season, Mannion decided to call it a day, only to be tempted out of retirement by Hull for whom his debut attracted 40,000 people – nearly double the Tigers' average attendance. However, the newspaper furore overshadowed his stay on Humberside and following the ban he drifted into player-management in the non-League ranks, turning out for the likes of Poole Town, Kings Lynn and Haverhill Rovers. Nevertheless, his respect within the game remained such that Pele invited him out to Brazil to pass on his skills to youngsters at Pele's football academy.

Having retired from the game in the early Sixties, Mannion was reduced to working on building sites and for the railway. After his death in 2000, Middlesbrough fans lined the streets in tribute as his funeral cortege made its way through the town. Bryan Robson, 'Boro's boss at the time, said: 'Whenever I spoke to him, there was never any remorse about playing when he did. He never showed any jealousy about the money that is in the game at the moment. Great players like him could play any time, anywhere and in any decade.' Wilf Mannion, the 'Golden Boy' of Teesside, is commemorated by a statue at the Riverside Stadium.

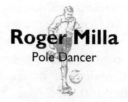

Roger Milla
Pole Dancer

Cameroon's Roger Milla was the grand old man of the 1994 World Cup. At an age when most men's idea of exercise is picking up the remote, the 42-year-old was still wiggling his hips rhythmically around the corner flag in the famous goal celebration that had first delighted the watching millions four years earlier. It was an expression of unconfined joy as Milla broke his own record as the oldest goalscorer in a World Cup tournament. Even for neutrals it was refreshing to see an unsung hero able to do the business on a world stage in the twilight of his career.

He was born Albert Roger Miller in the Cameroon capital of Yaoundé on 20 May 1952 but later changed his surname to a more African spelling. His father's job on the railways meant that the family was frequently on the move but wherever he ended up, the football-crazy youngster found somewhere to play barefoot. He signed for his first club, Éclair de Douala, when he was 13, moving to Léopard de Douala five years later. At the age of 22 the 6-foot-1-inch striker switched to Tonnerre Yaoundé, helping them to win the African Cup Winners' Cup in 1976. In that same year he won the first of his 81 international caps and was named African Footballer of the Year. These achievements earned Milla a move to the French club Valenciennes, but he spent most of his two years there languishing in the reserves. He fared little better at AS Monaco, shuttling between the bench and the treatment room, or with the Corsican club Bastia, but a transfer to Saint Etienne in 1984 helped him rediscover his goal touch. After 22 goals in 31 appearances, he signed for Montpellier, where he spent three prosperous years before retiring from French club football in 1989 with 152 goals to his name.

Far from being the end of Milla's career, it was only just the beginning. He had already appeared in the 1982 World Cup finals – Cameroon's first – and two years later had been top scorer as the Indomitable Lions won the African Cup of Nations. In 1986 he was voted Player of the Tournament in the same competition but shortly afterwards announced his retirement from international football. Testimonials at Douala and Yaoundé drew nearly 100,000 fans, whereupon Milla moved to Réunion Island in the Indian Ocean to play nothing more than local league football for Saint Pierre.

However, his peace was shattered by a phone call from Paul Biya, the President of Cameroon, pleading with him to come out of retirement and help the country in their hour of need at the 1990 World Cup. Unable to refuse such a request, he went to Italia '90 where his electrifying bursts of pace – remarkable for a man of 38 – dribbling skills, composed finishing and unique goal celebrations lit up the tournament. Coming on as a substitute, he scored four times as Cameroon became the first African team in history to reach the last eight of the World Cup. He struck both extra-time goals in the 2-1 victory over Colombia in round two, the second after he had cheekily robbed Colombian keeper René Higuita on one of the latter's frequent excursions from goal. Milla recalled: 'I was looking for a chance to pounce. I'd positioned myself between René Higuita and the last defender waiting for a poor pass, which is exactly what happened. I'd played with Carlos Valderrama at Montpellier and we'd spoken about René's game and I'd seen a few cassettes of Colombia. I knew he liked to play with the ball outside his area and I was ready for him.'

Ultimately, it took two Gary Lineker penalties for England to see off Cameroon in the quarter-finals but only after Milla had been involved in both Cameroon goals. In recognition of his achievements, Milla was again named African Player of the Year – the first man to win the award twice. He said: 'I think the whole world enjoyed seeing a 38-year-old score four goals at the World Cup finals.'

But Milla was not finished yet and four years later he was on World Cup duty again, the oldest player ever to appear in the finals. Although Cameroon were eliminated at the group stage, Milla's historic consolation goal against Russia – followed by the trademark Makossa dance – was one of the highlights of the tournament.

This time he retired for good, and the man who once had a reputation for being difficult and demanding became an ambassador for African football and causes. In 2006 he was named the Best African Player of the Last 50 Years, his popularity enhanced by that dance routine. Yet Milla admits that he had never intended it to be a solo performance. 'The dance was an improvisation,' he says. 'I wanted to involve everyone in the celebration. I wanted the whole team to join in.' Instead, they just stood back and admired the old man's nifty moves.

Len Shackleton
The Clown Prince

Training with the England squad, Len Shackleton listened while manager Walter Winterbottom outlined a routine. 'I want all you five forwards to run down the field, interpassing the ball,' explained Winterbottom, 'until you come to the goal, where there'll be no goalkeeper. Then put the ball into the net.' Shackleton, lying on the ground, looked up and asked sardonically: 'Which side of the net, Mr Winterbottom?' Shackleton loved to be seen as the scourge of authority. In his 1955 autobiography he famously included a chapter entitled 'The Average Director's Knowledge of Football' and left the following page blank. His contempt for those in power goes a long way to explain why he won only five caps. One selector, when asked why Shackleton had been constantly overlooked, replied: 'Because we play at Wembley Stadium, not the London Palladium.'

Therein lies another reason for Shackleton's frequent absence from England squads – his refusal to take the game seriously, a trait that earned him the title 'The Clown Prince of Soccer'. He had a fund of tricks, all performed with the old leather ball, which weighed a ton when wet. During his time at Sunderland, fans used to arrive early at Roker Park just to see Shackleton performing his tricks during the kick-in. One of his favourites was to cut his foot under the ball so sharply that it would spin towards an opponent and then come back to him as if it were on a piece of string. Time and again he would fool defenders by putting backspin on the ball. Thinking he had lost control, they would dive in for a tackle, only to find that the ball wasn't there and had spun back to Shackleton, who, by the time they had recovered, had gone merrily on his way. His artistry was such that he could make the ball come back to him from as much as 15 yards away. Once at Highbury he kicked the ball towards the crowd after the referee had awarded a free-kick. The crowd booed but their jeers turned to cheers when the ball bounced three times towards them, then suddenly changed direction and bounced three times back to Shack!

Another ploy was to play one-twos with the corner flag, and he once complained that Chelsea should fit stronger poles after he broke one with a pass at Stamford Bridge. He would return throw-ins to team-mates with his backside – just to be different – and deliberately bounced corner kicks on to the crossbar, thereby causing chaos in the opposition defence. During his days at Bradford Park Avenue, it was a tactic that brought his team a number of goals. Future England boss Ron Greenwood, who played with Shackleton at Bradford, said: 'There was no one quite like our Len. He was a showman, a crowd-pleaser, a character who was larger than life. Some of the things he did had nothing to do with the winning and losing of a game, but the crowds loved him.'

If bored during a match, Shackleton would sit on the ball or stand with one foot on it pretending to look at his watch. He even made fun of fellow professionals not blessed with his considerable talents. Another contemporary, the great Stanley Matthews, remembered how in a game for Sunderland, Shackleton, having beaten a full-back, put his foot on the ball and pulled the cuff of his shirt sleeve back, implying he was checking his wristwatch and not taking any notice of events on the field. 'As the full-back came roaring in for a second bite of the cherry,' wrote Matthews, 'Len dragged the ball back with the sole of his foot, to the delight of the Roker Park crowd but to the great annoyance of the opposing full-back, who quite rightly felt he had been made a fool of. The full-back in question tackled fresh air, Len slipped away with the ball at his feet and rubbed salt in the wound by arrogantly gesturing with his hands that he was taking a cup from its saucer and sipping tea.'

Another to be mocked in public by Shackleton was Arsenal goalkeeper George Swindin. Utilising his masterly dribbling skills to full effect, Shackleton took the ball right up to the goal-line with the stranded Swindin floundering in the Roker Park mud. He then beckoned Swindin towards him, saying: 'Come on, George, it's not in yet.' He then waited until Swindin made a frantic dive for the ball before coolly rolling it over the line for a goal.

Shackleton was blessed with long feet and toes that he could wrap around the ball. His control was also enhanced by the fact that he wore soft rugby boots, which gave him a better 'feel' for the ball and were so effective that he could almost catch it on his foot. Billy Elliott, a team-mate at both Bradford Park Avenue and Sunderland, enthused: 'He used to bend ball from free-kicks like David Beckham. One of his assets was his pace over the first five yards which took him past his opponent. It was unbelievable. His strength showed when he received the ball at his feet. If you played the ball in front of him, he would just stand with his hands on his hips and he wouldn't go for it, but he was a good man to have when you were leading with a few minutes to go. Then he would take the ball to the corner flag or along the touchline and it would be difficult for the other team to get the ball off him. As regards skill, I don't think there was anyone to touch him, even by present-day standards.'

Shackleton honed these skills with a tennis ball on the cobbled streets of Bradford. He was born in the city on 3 May 1922, his grandfather a talented amateur cricketer and his father a robust amateur footballer. The father was a hard taskmaster, given to little more than grudging praise, telling his son after one five-goal haul: 'Your sister Irene could have back-heeled another three into the net!'

Young Len lacked his father's physique and even at the age of 13 stood only 4 feet 11 inches tall and weighed just over 6 stone. Nevertheless, he was picked to play for England schoolboys and as a promising inside-right came to the attention of Arsenal, who signed him as an apprentice. Already disillusioned on discovering that his first task was to cut the Highbury pitch, he lashed out when manager George Allison put his foot up on a railing and asked the youngster to tie his shoelace. 'Fasten the bloody thing yourself!' snapped Shackleton. So it was no great surprise when Allison released him, claiming that at 5 feet 2 inches Shackleton was too small to make the grade. Allison suggested that Shackleton return to Bradford and become a miner, an engineer or a commercial traveller instead and inadvertently rubbed salt into the wound by showing him the new television set in his office. To young Shackleton it felt as if he was being treated as a provincial yokel condescendingly being shown a marvel of new technology. The Highbury experience instilled in Shackleton the dislike of authority that would manifest itself in later years.

So he returned to Bradford and signed for Park Avenue, going on to score 166 goals for the club in six years of wartime football, combining his sporting career with working down the mines. His cheeky skills blossomed on the pitch, never more so than when he back-heeled a penalty into the net after running almost from the halfway line. The unfortunate goalkeeper was Manchester City's Frank Swift, no mean showman himself. At the end of his long run-up, Shackleton aimed a mighty air kick at the ball, causing Swift to dive in anticipation. But the ball remained on the spot, whereupon Shackleton turned around and back-heeled it into the net with Swift stranded.

Shackleton's goalscoring feats earned him an England call-up in 1946 but he gave away the free-kick that led to Scotland's winner and was not chosen again for another two years. In the meantime, Newcastle had paid Bradford £13,000 for his services and he marked his debut by scoring six times in a 13-0 trouncing of Newport County. Three of his goals came in a two-minute spell and he knocked in the last of the six with his backside. Despite this sensational start, there were soon mutterings of discontent about Shackleton's contribution on Tyneside. Legendary centre-forward Jackie Milburn was neither the first nor the last to accuse Shack of not being a team player. Milburn said: 'He had no interest other than entertaining the crowd. He would rather beat three men than lay on a winning goal.' The story goes that Newcastle manager George Martin told Shackleton before an important game: 'If you get a hat-trick in the first 20 minutes, you can come off.' Shackleton duly obliged and then walked off, leaving the manager livid as there were no substitutes in those days. Newcastle eventually lost 4-3. As relations deteriorated, he frequently fell out with the Newcastle board and finally slapped in a transfer request after being dropped. In 1948 Sunderland offered him a way out, paying a British record transfer fee of £20,500.

Shackleton's bitterness regarding his time at Newcastle remained and he once remarked: 'I'm not biased when it comes to Newcastle – I don't care who beats them!' And even though he had left the club three years earlier, Shackleton tried to persuade the Newcastle players to strike over poor pay before the 1951 FA Cup final. He actually went into their Wembley dressing room in an attempt to stir up discontent, but as Newcastle went on to beat Blackpool 2-0, it appears that his visit was more irritating than unsettling.

Naturally, his dislike of Newcastle endeared him to the Sunderland supporters, although their adoration was not necessarily shared by his new team-mates, particularly burly Welsh inter-national centre-forward Trevor Ford. Shackleton took mischievous pleasure in giving Ford what appeared to be perfect passes, only for the ball to be laden with his favourite backspin, thereby making it nigh on impossible to control. The result was that Shackleton looked an artist while Ford merely looked clumsy. Once, during a friendly match in Holland, Shack waltzed through the entire opposing defence before rolling the ball back to Ford with a cry of, 'Don't say I never give you a pass.'

Eventually, Ford lost patience and told Sunderland manager Billy Murray that he would not play if Shackleton were in the team. However, it would be Ford that was sacrificed, sold to Cardiff City in 1953.

The Welshman later vented his frustrations with Shackleton in print. 'Twenty-one other players on the field,' he wrote, 'were transfixed as Shackleton did tricks with the ball, the like of which I'd never seen before. The crowd loved it. This was the clowning Shack at his best, but where did it get us? Precisely nowhere. The result was that when he did make a move, the opposing defence was in position and the attack broke down. Time and again when I thought Shack was going to slip a goalscoring pass to me he would veer off.'

Shackleton's desire to taunt defenders by beating them more than once was perhaps understandable given the close marking to which he was repeatedly subjected. After receiving the close attention of Fulham's Len Quested throughout the first half, Shackleton produced a piece of string at the start of the second and said to Quested: 'Tie this to the back of my shirt and keep hold of it. That way, you can keep on my back for the whole of the bloody game!'

Shackleton scored 101 goals in 348 games with Sunderland before retiring with an ankle injury in 1957. He feared that he might be blacklisted by directors in the wake of his controversial autobiography but remembered how a member of the Portsmouth board told him how much he had enjoyed the book. 'At first that surprised me,' said Shackleton, 'but then it suddenly dawned on me what was happening. He obviously didn't think of himself as the average director – none of them did. They obviously thought: "Oh, he's not talking about me, it's the other lot."'

On retirement he became a sports journalist and in that capacity was instrumental in helping Brian Clough to land his first two managerial posts, at Hartlepools and Derby. The Clown Prince died on 28 November 2000, leaving behind a host of memories and an uncompromising philosophy that explained why he was more popular with fans than with team-mates, managers or international selectors. 'I used to enjoy the game. If I wanted to make the ball go through somebody's legs, I'd do it. Whether it was the right thing to do for the team or not was just hard luck.'

Charlie Tully
Celtic Jester

If Len Shackleton was the joker in the English pack during the Forties and Fifties, Charlie Tully was his counterpart north of the border. As well as sitting on the ball during play, he would deliberately play one-twos off the backs of referees and the shins of opponents. And like Shackleton, he loved to make fools of defenders. He would point his finger to where he was going to pass the ball before subtly sending it in a totally different direction. Once, while playing for Glasgow Celtic in a friendly against Lazio in Rome, his mazy dribble resulted in two Italian defenders bumping into each other. When they went looking for revenge, Tully armed himself with a corner flag and pretended to fence with them in swashbuckling style.

In fact, corner flags made Tully's reputation, his party piece being the scoring of goals direct from a corner. He achieved the feat for Northern Ireland against England in 1952 but his finest hour came in Celtic's Scottish Cup tie against Falkirk the following year. Taking a corner, he whipped the ball straight into the Falkirk net, only for the referee, presuming that the ball must have been placed outside the arc, to disallow the goal and order him to take it again. Undeterred, Tully simply replaced the ball in the arc, swung the corner over and once again planted it straight into the net. This time there was no dispute.

For all his tricks and unquestionable ability, Tully could also frustrate. His happy-go-lucky approach to games made the inside-forward an inconsistent performer, and his love of the good life also contributed towards his winning only 10 caps for Northern Ireland. He was certainly not short of confidence. Before the aforementioned 1952 international in Belfast, Tully asked England full-back Alf Ramsey: 'Do you enjoy playing for your country, Mr Ramsey?'

'I do, Mr Tully,' replied Ramsey courteously.

'Make the most of it today, then,' replied the irrepressible Irishman, 'it might be the last chance you get!'

It was no empty threat. Tully scored twice (including the goal from the corner) in a 2-2 draw.

Born in Belfast on 11 July 1924, Tully played for Belfast Celtic before crossing the Irish Sea to join Glasgow Celtic in June 1948 for the sizeable fee of £8,000. He had been idolised in Belfast and his arrival in Scotland triggered a frenzied response from Bhoys fans. His debut was an uninspiring, goalless draw at home to Morton, but soon the crowds were flocking to Parkhead to catch a glimpse of the exciting new attraction. The following month a breathtaking performance in a Scottish League Cup tie against Rangers catapulted Tully to the status of cult hero. The brute force of the Rangers defenders proved no match for Tully's dancing feet and he inspired Celtic to a 3-1 victory. Tully Mania swept through the East End of Glasgow. Tully cocktails were sold in bars, Tully ties went on sale in shops and green Tully ice cream was devoured in cafés. He was the most talked about player in Scotland and he loved every minute of it. A joke doing the rounds at the time told how the Pope was visiting Glasgow and Tully was showing him around. People in the crowd turned to each other and said: 'Who's the guy in white with Charlie Tully?'

However, on one occasion the joke was on Tully and his Celtic team-mates. For their first floodlit game – a friendly in Detroit in 1951 – they took to the field with soot under their eyes after an opposing player claimed they needed the 'warpaint' to reduce the glare of the lights. 'It didn't dawn on us that we were being kidded,' said Tully. 'The home team said they didn't put soot on their faces because they were accustomed to playing under the lights.'

Tully scored 47 goals in 319 appearances for Celtic and was rewarded for his service with a free transfer in 1959 so that he could become player-manager of Cork Hibs. He had further spells in management with Bangor and Portadown, and the football world was shocked when he died in his sleep at home in Belfast in 1971, aged 47, and just a few months after playing in a charity match in Edinburgh. During the funeral procession, Belfast's Falls Road was packed with mourners from both sides of the sectarian divide.

Ian Wright
The Fox in the Box

As with Marmite, you either love or hate Ian Wright. To Crystal Palace and Arsenal fans he was a supreme marksman to many others he is a major irritant. An ebullient, super-confident character never short of a word, Wright was the sort of striker against whom defenders could never relax for a nanosecond. He was always harassing, niggling and, waiting to pounce on the slightest error, but sometimes his notoriously short fuse carried him into dangerous territory, and when that delightful smile was replaced by a sinister scowl, his dismal disciplinary record threatened to undo all his good work.

Successive managers tried to iron out the flaws in his temperament and he remembers Arsenal boss George Graham reading him the riot act after a clash with Spurs' David Howells in a North London derby. 'George Graham slaughtered me and told me that I was a disgrace to myself and a disgrace to Arsenal and that he wouldn't put up with another incident like the Howells affair. But he also told me that it was the fire in my belly that made me such an effective player and that I should never lose that, just learn how to control it.'

Wright certainly never lost that fiery edge. There was the much-publicised little-and-large feud with Manchester United's Great Dane, Peter Schmeichel, plus numerous fines and suspensions, but Wright remained largely unrepentant. Following one such fine, he commented: 'When I called Coventry supporters a bunch of wankers, it was the best £15,000 I ever spent.'

Wright's tale is one of persistence and passion. Ian Edward Wright was born in Woolwich in 1963 and even as a schoolboy footballer he hated losing. 'I would go mental if we were losing or things weren't going right for me,' he admitted, 'and it was usually my team-mates who got slaughtered.' As a teenager he served five days in Chelmsford Prison for non-payment of motoring fines but the experience encouraged him to do something positive with his life. However, his dream of becoming a professional footballer appeared a remote one when, rejected by Southend and Brighton, he worked as a labourer and plasterer while playing Sunday League football with Greenwich

Borough. His lucky break came when Palace scout Peter Prentice saw him score four goals in a game and invited him for a trial. Impressing manager Steve Coppell, Wright signed professional forms for the Eagles in August 1985, three months short of his 22nd birthday. He was given a three-month contract paying just £100 a week.

Coppell was immediately struck by Wright's attitude. 'On his first day at Palace,' said Coppell, 'he told me he wanted to play for England, a bold statement for someone who had just walked in off a building site.' Wright acknowledges that he gave the impression of being cocky. 'Steve reckons I was an arrogant little so-and-so who strutted around as if I owned the place, but I was as nervous as a kid starting his first day at school.' He quickly learned the harsh reality of the professional game after nutmegging senior pro Jim Cannon in training and going on to score. Cannon was so furious that he punched the young upstart and pushed him face down in the mud.

Wright soon made his mark at Selhurst Park and, forming a potent partnership with Mark Bright, helped Palace into the top flight in 1989 and to the FA Cup final the following year. In 1991 he won his first England cap and, after 117 goals in 253 starts for Palace, made a £2.5 million move to Arsenal. He scored on his debut against Leicester City in a League Cup tie, following it up with a hat-trick on his League debut against Southampton. The North Bank had a new darling.

Wright went on to be Arsenal's top scorer for six seasons in a row, playing a major part in the club's success under George Graham. In 1997 he broke Cliff Bastin's 50-year-old Arsenal goalscoring record with a hat-trick against Bolton, and by the time he left for West Ham in 1998, he had taken his Arsenal total to 185 goals in 288 appearances. Such statistics should have made him an England regular yet he never really established himself at international level, his 33 caps being spread over seven years and yielding just nine goals. But Wright was more than a goalscorer – he was a born entertainer. He may have got under the skin of opponents but he had a wonderful rapport with the Highbury crowd who loved his flamboyant celebrations and jokes such as using the Arsenal ball boys as pre-match target practice. He would do just about anything for a laugh.

So when his career had wound down with West Ham, Celtic and Burnley, it was perhaps no surprise that he moved into the world of entertainment, presenting his own TV show, starring in commercials for everything from insurance to chicken sauce, and appearing as a regular soccer pundit where his outspoken views have turned presenter Gary Lineker's hair even greyer.

Lest anyone be swayed by his modest England record, consider this: when Thierry Henry (who would eventually break Wright's Arsenal goalscoring record) signed for the club, vice-chairman David Dein showed him a video containing the best of Ian Wright. The message was clear – do it the Wright way and you won't go far wrong.

COLOURFUL
CHAIRMEN

John Cobbold
The Good Life

Unveiling a major sponsorship deal, Ipswich Town chairman John Cobbold told the assembled media: 'It has been suggested that we'll squander the sponsors' money on wine, women and song. That is not true. We don't do a lot of singing here at Portman Road!'

'Mister John', as he was known to all and sundry, was the Old Etonian chairman of Ipswich from the mid-1950s until 1976, when he was succeeded by his equally eccentric brother, 'Mister Patrick'. The Cobbolds were a family of brewers, and as such placed greater importance on the contents of the club's drinks cabinet than its trophy cabinet. Patrick once described a crisis at Ipswich as 'when we run out of white wine in the boardroom'. They were very much enthusiastic amateurs who took victory and defeat in their stride, the only tangible way of telling if the result mattered being in the amount of champagne they consumed: John would drink one bottle of champagne if Ipswich won and two if they lost.

When the club ventured into Europe under manager Bobby Robson in the 1970s, John would return from these trips with numerous bottles of duty free wine. His capacity for alcohol could be problematic and before the chairman ever went out for an evening in a strange European city, Robson had to write Mister John's name on one of the cuffs of his shirt and the hotel name on the other, so that he didn't get lost. He was known to appear decidedly the worse for wear but was such a charming man that everybody overlooked any embarrassment. At one function he stood up to speak but before he had uttered a word, he slid gracefully under the table and had to be carried out of the room. On another occasion John and Patrick had a food fight in the train dining car on the journey back from a match at Middlesbrough in full view of Robson and the players. The fight ended with John tipping a jug of water over Patrick, but it was pretty much par for the course, Robson describing them as 'lovable naughty schoolboys who never grew up'.

Mister John was born in 1927 and the Cobbold family became involved with Ipswich Town in the 1930s, John becoming a director at the age of 21. A bachelor, he lived alone with his stammer and a family of donkeys that would wander into the house on his 2,000-acre Suffolk estate. He wasted no time in laying down the ground rules to the club's managers. Shortly after Alf Ramsey was appointed, John poured a couple of drinks to celebrate and then said: 'This will be the first and last time I ever offer you a drink in this boardroom.' Tossing Ramsey a key to the drinks cabinet, he added: 'From now on, Alf, feel free to come in and help yourself.'

Under the Cobbolds, Ipswich became renowned for their friendly and abundant hospitality. John and his fellow directors used to meet the opposing team and officials in person when they arrived at Ipswich Station and after the match, in the boardroom, made it a rule never to talk about the game they had just watched. 'That's not for us,' said John. 'We know nothing about the game. The point of being here is to say, "Hello, well played, have a drink, and what time's your bus home?" to our guests.' He was always generous in defeat and would say in a manner alien to most current club chairmen: 'Today it wasn't our turn, but we've given the other team the pleasure of winning. That's something. You have to love the game more than the prize. The game is more important than the prize because without the game, there is no prize anyway.'

He never interfered in team affairs and had no interest in any player the manager was signing because he would not have heard of him anyway. When Robson signed Paul Mariner from Plymouth, John thought he was buying a sailor! This blissful ignorance of football matters was illustrated perfectly one afternoon at Leicester. With Ipswich 2-0 down, John patted Robson on the shoulder and said: 'The team's playing frightfully well, Bobby. Have you been doing something special in training?' Robson was puzzled until he realised that Cobbold thought Ipswich were winning. 'Mister John,' he said, 'We're losing 2-0. We're the away side, we've changed to yellow. Leicester are playing in blue.'

Although most managers would welcome a chairman who showed little interest in, or knowledge of, team affairs, it could occasionally prove frustrating. Alf Ramsey's successor, Jackie Milburn, was desperate to halt a losing sequence and used a train journey from London to Ipswich to outline his plans for the future to the chairman. Milburn was heavily hinting that he needed money to dip into the transfer market and, convinced that he had Mister John's full attention, was about to quote him the price for a certain player when Cobbold pointed out of the train window and exclaimed: 'Just look at the size of the bollocks on that bull!'

'He [Cobbold] was a very educated man,' said Bobby Robson, 'with an incredibly posh voice. He could swear like a trooper and get away with it because he had that beautiful, polished accent.' Memorably, he concluded a banquet speech to Ipswich's FA Youth Cup winning side of 1975 by telling the players' parents that he wanted them all to go home that night and have 'a jolly good fuck so the boss can come back here in 18 years' time and have another FA Youth Cup to celebrate!'

Under Mister John, Ipswich stood by their managers at all times, even when results were poor. When one of the players, Tommy Carroll, was in a contract dispute and demanded to see the chairman, John greeted him in his office and said: 'Well, here I am, have a good look at me.' Then, pointing to Robson, he continued: 'There's the manager, over there. He runs the club, so talk to him. Now I'm sodding off.'

Under Mister John, board meetings were deliciously unpredictable. At one, he suddenly stopped fellow director Cecil Robinson in mid-sentence to pick up a phone that hadn't rung.

'Hello?' said John into the receiver.

'The telephone didn't ring, John,' said Robinson.

'I know,' replied John, 'but I never like to leave anything to the last minute.'

His mother, Lady Blanche Cobbold, the club's Honorary President, was quite a character herself. At the 1978 FA Cup final, where Ipswich beat Arsenal, she was asked by FA secretary Ted Croker whether she would like to meet Labour Prime Minister Jim Callaghan. A staunch Tory, Lady Blanche answered brusquely: 'No, actually, I wouldn't. I'd much rather have a gin and tonic.'

Mister John died in 1983, by which time his brother Patrick was in the chair. Once alleged to have taken a monkey to a game at Portman Road, Mister Patrick also regularly took a black retriever to matches and allowed it to drink water from the club's trophies. Once, he was showing VIP guests the club's new glass-fronted executive boxes, which, he said, allowed the occupants to see out but were constructed in such a way that nobody could see in. To prove his point, he aimed a succession of V signs at two policemen who were standing 20 yards away looking at the boxes. When the officers suddenly marched towards the box, Patrick yelled: 'Oh my God! Send for the architect!' Mister John could rest in peace, safe in the knowledge that the club was in good hands.

Bob Lord
The Great Dictator

Bob Lord was the polar opposite of John Cobbold: a gruff, abrasive northerner whose most redeeming personality trait appeared to be that he treated all people the same – he was rude to everyone. He was chairman of Burnley from 1955 almost right up until his death in 1981, but his influence extended far beyond the Lancashire mill town as he became the senior vice-president of the Football League and chairman of the FA Cup committee.

A local butcher by trade, Lord was outwardly about as cuddly as one of his pork carcasses. To call him controversial would be like saying 'Fatty' Foulke was a little on the plump side. He hated journalists, he hated the television companies, he was dismissive of players – 'footballers couldn't run a fish and chip shop,' he once said – and, most surprisingly for someone who claimed to have Burnley FC's best interests at heart, he had no time for the club's supporters. He didn't approve of supporters' clubs and only allowed the London Clarets to be formed in 1976–77 because he thought they were too far away to interfere in the running of what he saw as his club. Marcel Marceau would have had a better dialogue with supporters. One fan remembers a young boy of around seven, wearing a new Burnley scarf and hat, leaning into the team coach at an away game in London and saying politely, 'Happy New Year, Mr Lord.' Ignored, he tried again. Still ignored, he climbed on to the first step of the coach and repeated the friendly greeting. This time there was a reply. 'Get off the bus,' snapped the Burnley chairman.

His ability to upset people was legendary, particularly on the rare occasions that he didn't get his own way. He once stood for President of the Football League, only to lose out to Newcastle United's Lord Westwood. The Burnley chief called the decision a disgrace and said the problem was that Lord came at the wrong end of his name. 'I wasn't born with a silver spoon in my mouth,' he complained.

Indeed he wasn't and could justifiably lay claim to being a self-made man. He began in business with a horse-drawn cart, from which he sold meat, buying out his boss at 19 and then landing a contract to supply the town's schools. Bob the butcher won himself a place on the board of Burnley FC in 1951 at the age of 43 and, after one failed attempt, rose to the position he coveted, that of chairman. One of the first things he did was to change the club rule whereby each chairman held office for just three years before retiring in order to let another board member have his turn. Lord had no intention of stepping aside for anyone; the only 'person' able to depose him was the Grim Reaper and that took 26 years.

Lord was a decisive man. If obstacles were put in his way, he contemptuously shoved them aside. As he set about making Burnley a force to be reckoned with, his bluntness brought the club some unwelcome headlines. He claimed that fewer than 10 per cent of footballers knew the laws of the game and attacked the people of Manchester for being too sentimental in the wake of the Munich air crash. When the criticism of him became too fierce, he blamed the press for misquoting him. He would sometimes spare a couple of words for journalists but the second word was usually 'off'.

Yet for all his dictatorial approach, there is no doubt that Lord loved Burnley Football Club and contributed enormously to the most successful period in the club's history. Although the only time he got close to the players was when he sold them meat from a basket after training, he defied the odds by keeping the small-town club in the First Division and setting in place the structure that would enable them to win the League Championship in 1960.

In some respects he was an unlikely visionary. He realised the necessity of producing home-grown players and oversaw the construction of two new stands, along with lounges and hospitality areas in the stand that still bears his name. He saw television coverage, particularly proposed live matches, as a major threat to attendances (a point borne out 40 years later), although he subsequently undermined his argument by making a crude anti-Semitic remark, declaring: 'We have to stand up against a move to get soccer on the cheap by the Jews who run television.' Despite the outrage caused by his comment, Lord forged ahead and banned TV cameras from the ground for several seasons. He stormed: 'If the BBC don't shift their cameras from Turf Moor, I'll be down there myself and personally burn them. They are on the ground without our consent and I don't care if even Harold Wilson [who was then Prime Minister] has given them permission.'

Lord remained irascible to the last. In 1980, visiting Fulham chairman Ernie Clay – an old adversary – was thrown out of Turf Moor for something he had said at half-time. But cancer was one battle that even Lord could not win. The illness forced him to step down as chairman in the autumn of 1981, and less than two months later he was dead.

Opinion remains divided as to whether Bob Lord was hero or villain. One of his associates used to visit Lord's grave and when asked whether he was paying his respects, replied: 'No, I just wanted to make sure he hadn't got up again.'

And when, at the 2005 Burnley Beer Festival, the Burnley Supporters' Club (which Lord had banned) produced a new ale, they decided to name it after him. A spokesman said: 'We did consider other names, but somehow Bob Lord's Bitter seemed appropriate …especially as he was a teetotaller.'

WILD BOYS

Jim Baxter
England's Tormentor

Moments of glory for the Scottish national side occur less frequently than sightings of the Loch Ness Monster. But there is one date that is forever etched in the heart of those loyal, long-suffering Scottish fans: 15 April 1967. That was the day when the Scots came to Wembley to take on the reigning world champions. Naturally, England were expected to win in a canter but the Scots had other ideas and emerged triumphant 3-2. As it was England's first defeat since lifting the World Cup, the Tartan Army wasted no time in proclaiming Scotland as the new world champions. The man who ran the show that day with a breathtaking combination of skill and arrogance was Jim Baxter, a cultured wing-half blessed with a left foot that could open a tin of salmon.

Not content with outwitting the opposition at every turn that afternoon, 'Slim Jim', as he was known, proceeded to rub salt into English wounds by repeatedly juggling the ball on the left wing in front of 90,000 people in an incredible display of 'keepie uppie'. He was mocking the English players, daring them to take the ball off him. Football historian Bob Crampsey said: 'England had no idea what to do about it and Baxter was not about to solve that problem for them – it was a wonderful moment.' Baxter, who before the game had been betting with his team-mates on how many nutmegs he would make over the 90 minutes, later recalled: 'I enjoyed taking the mickey out of England any day of the week, but that day was special. Alan Ball's voice kept rising another couple of octaves to the point that no one could even make out what he was trying to say!'

Baxter once said of his fellow Scot Charlie Cooke: 'When he sold you a dummy, you had to pay to get back in the ground.' Well, Baxter himself also had the gift of being able to wrong-foot players simply by dropping a shoulder, and he had the confidence to go with it. Before an international against Italy, he boasted to team-mate Billy Bremner: 'If I don't put five or six nutmegs on [Gianni] Rivera today, then I won't have had a decent game!' He succeeded, too, making one of the world's best midfield players of the time look foolish. Baxter appeared to have everything but, like all too many other phenomenal talents, he was prevented from achieving his full potential by a life-style of womanising, gambling and drinking.

James Curran Baxter was born in Hill of Beath, Fife, on 29 September 1939. As a boy he was so skinny that clubs overlooked him and he began his working life down the mines with his father. He eventually signed for the quaintly named Fife junior side Crossgates Primrose for a fee of £2 10s (plus an extra £30, which he gave to his mother so that she could buy a washing machine). In 1957, at the age of 18, he joined Raith Rovers as a part-timer for £200, the Raith boss, Bert Herdman, admitting: 'His fantastic confidence attracted me almost as much as his ability.' At first Baxter continued working down the mines but he soon signed on full-time at Starks Park and earned international recognition for the first time in 1958 when he was selected for Scotland Under-23s against Wales. Baxter remembered the occasion well, particularly the fact that when he signed a couple of autographs, he was aware that the youngsters had no idea who he was. 'That was the day I made up my mind that I was going to be noticed,' he said later. 'I knew that I could play but I had to make sure that everybody else knew as well.'

The first step towards that goal came two years later with a move to his boyhood heroes, Rangers, for a Scottish record fee of £17,500. At Ibrox, every game was high profile and Baxter revelled in it, his sublime skills steering Rangers to trophy after trophy. In his five years there, he won three Championship medals, three Scottish Cup winners' medals and four Scottish League Cup winners' medals, and it was said that his very presence on the pitch was worth a goal start to Rangers. He took particular delight in beating Celtic and although his first Old Firm clash ended in defeat, he was on the losing side only once more in 17 further encounters. After one Cup final victory over the bitter rivals, Baxter led the celebrations by grabbing the match ball and stuffing it up his shirt, the act merely adding to his popularity in the blue half of Glasgow. He had a tremendous rapport with the Rangers fans. 'Almost from the word go,' said Bob

Crampsey, 'he became a cult figure and he achieved almost messianic status. Fans weren't blind to what others might have seen as faults. They knew he liked a drink, that he liked to stay out late and they knew he wasn't a dedicated pounder of the track, but they liked the package. I think, more than anything else, that he was the player they would have liked to have been.' In return, Baxter's philosophy was simple: 'If you're good at something and you're paid to do it, why not give value for money?'

Inevitably, Baxter's brilliance was soon recognised at full international level and in 1961 he won the first of his 34 caps, in a 5-2 defeat of Northern Ireland. Although the 1967 game with England is generally considered to be his finest, Baxter himself believed that his performance in the 1963 defeat of England at Wembley was even better. Scotland played most of the game with 10 men after Eric Caldow broke his leg, but Baxter scored twice to give the Scots a famous 2-1 victory. The second was a penalty and as Caldow was the regular taker, the onus fell on Baxter even though he had never taken a spot-kick before in his life. Showing characteristic composure, he kept his cool to beat Gordon Banks.

But the Ibrox dream started to sour in 1964 when Baxter broke a leg playing in a European Cup tie in Vienna, chopped down for taunting the opposition once too often. On his recovery, he was sold to Sunderland for £72,000, in 1965, but during his 18 months at Roker Park he never quite recaptured the form he had shown at Ibrox. Never the most committed trainer in the world, he was now more often to be seen with a drink in one hand and a glamorous girl on the other. Before a Scotland friendly with Portugal in 1966, Baxter and Charlie Cooke staggered back to the team hotel at four o'clock in the morning to be greeted by irate trainer Walter McRae. The next morning the pair were forced to perform press-ups until they were physically sick in front of their team-mates.

In 1967 Baxter joined Nottingham Forest for £100,000 but he proved an even bigger disappointment on the banks of the Trent, costing Forest more than £2,000 a game. He stayed in Nottingham for 18 unhappy months until, in a bid to recapture past glories, he rejoined Rangers. However, he was a pale imitation of the player he was when he left Ibrox and with the arrival of new manager Willie Waddell, Baxter knew his days were numbered. He played his last game for the club in December 1969 – a 3-2 win over Aberdeen –

bringing to a close a Rangers career that saw him score 24 goals in 254 appearances.

He retired almost immediately at the premature age of 30 and, eager to pursue his favourite hobby, bought a Glasgow pub where he regularly held court on football. Eventually, however, his love of the good life saw his business collapse and his heavy drinking resulted in two life-saving liver transplants in the mid-1990s. Finally, in April 2001, Jim Baxter lost a long battle against pancreatic cancer.

The tributes were led by Eric Caldow, who said of Baxter: 'He loved football – all he could talk about was football – he was just a genius. He was arrogant, but he wanted to win. That left foot of his, nowadays it would be worth £20 million – just for the left leg alone!'

In memory of their finest hour, the Tartan Army flooded a radio station phone poll in an attempt to get the new Wembley Stadium footbridge named after Baxter, just to annoy the English. Baxter would have enjoyed the joke.

Once, towards the end of his life, he was asked whether he would have changed his lifestyle if he had been paid the vast sums of money that footballers earn today. Quick as a flash he replied, 'Definitely. I'd have spent £50,000 a week at the bookies instead of £100.'

George Best
Simply the Best

When he was doing the rounds as an after-dinner speaker, one of George Best's favourite stories concerned the time he went to a casino with Miss World, Mary Stavin, and won £20,000. Afterwards they went back to Best's room at the Holiday Inn, Birmingham, and rang the night porter for champagne. The porter arrived to see the money spread out on the bed. He looked at Stavin, he looked at the money, and asked quietly with a disconsolate shake of the head: 'Tell me, Mr Best – where did it all go wrong?'

The story has been re-told many times and says as much about the self-deprecating humour that endeared Best to so many in spite of his obvious faults as it does of his attitude to life. Best would argue that a career in which he dated a succession of beauty queens, had sex with seven women in one night, and drank copious amounts of champagne was not exactly a failure and instead was something of which most men could only dream. And to an extent he was right, but then no other man possessed the footballing gifts that Best had in his prime: the close control, the balance, the pace, the two-footedness, the courage, the deadly finishing, the flair and invention. So to see them ultimately squandered on a steady diet of birds and booze after just six years at the top was a terrible waste, although Best would point out that those talents were his to waste.

Best's life should have been a fairytale story – the shy Belfast boy who through his astonishing skills with a ball finished up with the world at his feet. But there was to be no happy ending for this Prince Charming – just a decline into alcoholism, bankruptcy, jail, ill health, allegations of wife-beating and an early death.

The son of an iron turner in the Harland & Wolff shipyard, Best honed his skills by practising with a tennis ball on the streets. His big break came in 1961 when he was spotted by veteran Manchester United scout Bob Bishop while playing as a 15-year-old for Cregagh Boys Club in Belfast. His local club Glentoran had previously rejected Best for being 'too small and light', but Glentoran's loss was most definitely to prove United's gain. Certainly Bishop had no doubts and that same day sent a telegram to United manager Matt Busby stating: 'I think I have found a genius.'

Best came over to England for a trial along with his pal Eric McMordie, but within 24 hours the homesick pair had fled back to Belfast. Best was persuaded to return to Manchester, where the club placed him in the care of a maternal and kindly landlady. McMordie, too, eventually made it back to England and went on to enjoy a fruitful career at Middlesbrough. Best conceded that he needed building up before he was ready for the first team. 'The first game I played for United I think they thought I was the ball boy. I must have weighed about eight stone.'

His senior debut came at the age of 17 in September 1963 – on the left wing in a 1-0 victory over West Bromwich Albion at Old Trafford. Albion's full-back that day was Graham Williams, already an established Welsh international, but after being nutmegged early on, Williams was given a complete runaround by the youngster.

When the two men met some years later, Williams asked Best to stand still for a moment so that he could look at his face. 'Why?' asked Best. 'Because all I've ever seen of you,' explained Williams, 'is your arse disappearing down the touchline.'

Best was primarily right-footed at first but after watching Real Madrid's Francisco Gento warming up at Old Trafford, using both feet, he resolved to become two-footed and had mastered the art by the time he was 18. This was obviously a powerful weapon in his armoury as full-backs never knew whether he was going to go down the line or cut inside. All too often they ended up on their backsides as Best turned them inside out with his ability to perform 180-degree turns on the spot. Or he would destroy them with a sudden burst of acceleration. As one observer put it: 'He had feet as deft as a pickpocket's hands.' He was courageous, too, taking on men twice his size, taunting them like a bullfighter and ultimately leaving them in a heap on the ground. Busby said admiringly: 'He had more ways of beating a player than anyone I have ever seen.'

As his body grew stronger, he became more than just a wing wizard and Busby acknowleded that Best was actually the finest tackler at the club. The reaction of Nobby Stiles or Paddy Crerand to that statement is probably unprintable but Best himself admitted: 'I could look after myself.' And he had to, because, with his precocious skills, he quickly became a marked man.

Two weeks after his debut he scored his first goal (against Burnley) and ended the season on six as United finished runners-up to Liverpool. In his second season, 1964–65, his 10 goals helped United capture the League title. In the meantime he had won the first of his 37 caps for Northern Ireland, although another sad aspect of Best's career would be that, because of his nationality, he never had the opportunity to exhibit his skills in a World Cup finals tournament. However, he did light up the international stage on a number of occasions, none more so than in a 1966 European Cup quarter-final against Benfica in Lisbon. Best ran amok that night, scoring twice in United's 5-1 victory, and he went on to torment the same opposition two years later as United memorably lifted the European Cup. He was also named European Footballer of the Year for 1968.

By then, Best had become the first celebrity footballer, receiving over a thousand fan letters a week. Stanley Matthews may have had his fans in the Brylcreem days but they were nearly all boys; Best's fans were almost exclusively girls, many of whom left him in no doubt that they wanted more than just his autograph. With his long hair and good looks, his was a face that adorned thousands of bedroom walls. He appeared on *Top of the Pops* and was dubbed 'El Beatle' by the Portuguese press following the 1966 Benfica match. The George Best Fan Club even had branches in Tokyo and Moscow. He opened two nightclubs in Manchester, owned fashion boutiques in partnership with Manchester City's Mike Summerbee, and appeared in advertising campaigns for everything from oranges to bras. Everybody seemed to want a piece of George Best. In a moment of reflection later in life, he admitted that his looks were partly a curse. 'If I'd been ugly,' he said with characteristic candour, 'you'd never have heard of Pele.'

If only Best had possessed the discipline of Bobby Charlton, he could probably have coped with the fame and adulation. As it was, the two men had little in common, Best once demonstrating his disdain for his illustrious team-mate by throwing eggs at a portrait of Charlton that hung on a pub wall.

Best began drinking, gambling and womanising to excess. Every week the tabloid newspapers had a new story about his antics, whether it was about his latest dalliance with a beauty queen or the time when he reportedly bedded a just-married bride in a hotel bedroom while downstairs in the bar his team-mates plied her husband with drink. Busby tried to talk sense into his prodigy, but Best later admitted that when called into his office for a dressing-down, he would simply look beyond the manager and count the patterns on the wallpaper. Best's extra-curricular activities inevitably began to take their toll, and even by the time that he scored six goals against Northampton Town in a 1970 Cup tie, he was only operating at 75 per cent efficiency.

Best always maintained that he only started drinking because the once great United team was in decline. Busby had retired as manager in 1969, handing over the reins to first Wilf McGuinness and then Frank O'Farrell, neither of whom were strong enough to control the wayward genius. Best said: 'Instead of revolving around me, the team now depended on me and I lacked the maturity to handle it. I began to drink more heavily, and on the field my list of bookings grew longer as my temper grew shorter.'

He was sent off playing for Northern Ireland after throwing mud at the referee, and in January 1971 he turned up late for an FA disciplinary commission meeting because he missed the train. Four days later he refused to travel with the United team to London for a match against Chelsea. Instead, he spent the weekend in the flat of actress Sinead Cusack, with photographers camped outside. He became increasingly unreliable, going missing for days on end and skipping training. He even missed Bobby Charlton's testimonial match, instead preferring to spend the time drinking at a pub a few miles from Old Trafford.

The appointment of Tommy Docherty as manager in 1972 heightened Best's disillusionment. The two men rarely saw eye to eye and matters came to a head when Docherty claimed that Best had turned up drunk with a girl on his arm before a Cup tie at Plymouth and he refused to let him play. Twice Best announced his retirement and twice he changed his mind, but the damage caused by his absences from training were all too visible: he had put on weight and had lost that electric acceleration. Finally, in 1974, he was sacked by United for excessive drinking and persistent failure to attend training sessions and matches. His last competitive game for the club was at Queens Park Rangers on New Year's Day – a match that saw him barracked throughout. He had scored 137 goals in 361 League appearances for United, but at 27 he was on the scrapheap.

He would subsequently joke about his unreliability: 'They say I slept with seven Miss Worlds. I didn't – it was only four. I didn't turn up for the other three.' Then he would add: 'I used to go missing a lot – Miss Canada, Miss United Kingdom, Miss Germany…'

Over the next 10 years, he appeared sporadically for a number of clubs, notably Fulham and Hibernian, without ever looking capable of turning back the clock. At Fulham he was fined and suspended for making an obscene gesture at opposition fans. On a tour of Norway he went out drinking one night before eventually stumbling back to the team hotel. Remembering that he had a plane to catch back to England, he told the concierge that he needed a wake-up call for the morning.

'Certainly, Mr Best,' came the reply. 'What time would you like it for?'

'Seven-thirty on the button,' mumbled Best.

The concierge looked up from his notepad and said witheringly: 'But, Mr Best, it's twenty to eight now!'

He tried his luck in America, where in 1978 he married Angie

Janes in Las Vegas. But he was drunk at the ceremony and had to borrow a ring from the best man because he had forgotten to buy one. The following year he signed for San José Earthquakes, only to miss his first press conference and go on a four-day drinking binge instead. He also had spells with Stockport County, Cork Celtic, Dunstable Town, Bournemouth, Brisbane Lions and Ford Open Prison, the last the result of a drink-driving conviction and an assault on a policeman. Meanwhile, in the ultimate ignominy, his Madame Tussaud's waxwork had been melted down.

In 1978 his mother, Ann, drank herself to death. It was to prove a tragically prophetic omen. Best's alcoholism was there for all to see when he made a slurred, shambling appearance on *Wogan* in 1990. Was this sad figure really the same person who had been idolised throughout the sporting world in the 1960s?

In 2002 he underwent a liver transplant and joked: 'It's typical of me to be finishing a long and distinguished drinking career just as the Government is planning to open pubs 24 hours a day.' But any public sympathy for his plight largely evaporated when he openly carried on drinking. His second wife, Alex, also claimed that he had physically abused her.

Best's health deteriorated rapidly and on 25 November 2005, aged 59, he died from a lung infection and multiple organ failure. His funeral attracted more than 100,000 mourners. The bad times were forgotten and only the good ones remembered; the Best who could destroy the opposition rather than the Best who ended up destroying himself. Fans had never seen his like before and maybe never will again. In Belfast they have a saying: 'Pele good; Maradona better; George Best.'

As for Best, one of his most famous quotes might serve as a suitable epitaph: 'I spent a lot of money on booze, birds and fast cars. The rest I just squandered.'

Eric Cantona

Alive and Kicking

On the eve of Eric Cantona's court appearance following the notorious 1995 'kung fu' attack on Crystal Palace fan Matthew Simmons, Manchester United team-mate Paul Ince stayed with him at a Croydon hotel. Come the morning of the case, Ince put on his best suit in order to create a favourable impression in court and then knocked on the door of Cantona's room. The Frenchman stood there in a jacket and a long-collared white shirt, which was unbuttoned to reveal his chest. 'Eric, you can't go to court like that,' said Ince. 'I am Cantona,' came the reply. 'I can go as I want.'

On the face of it, that was Cantona: the stereotypically arrogant Frenchman, a law unto himself, and also without doubt one of the most complex personalities ever to grace the English game. On the pitch he adopted a decidedly regal air, the ramrod straight back, the upturned collar, the chest stuck out, the unhurried style, almost defying an opponent to have the temerity to tackle him. Yet this elegance would vanish the moment the red mist descended, when he was suddenly reduced to the level of a barroom brawler. In common with most controversial figures, he polarised opinion. To some he would always be '*Le Brat*'; to others, especially United fans, he was 'The King'.

To borrow his most famous quote, trouble seemed to follow Cantona like seagulls follow a trawler. Eric Daniel Pierre Cantona was born in Paris on 24 May 1966 but was raised in Marseille. He started out as a goalkeeper before developing as a forward, a role in which he was greatly encouraged by his father, who advised him to make the ball do the work by passing it rather than running with it. He told Eric: 'There is nothing more simple than football. Look before you receive the ball and then give it and always remember that the ball goes quicker than you can carry it.'

Cantona junior began his career with Auxerre, where he spent two years in the youth team before making his first-team debut in 1983. After a year away on National Service, his outstanding form on his return to Auxerre earned him an international call-up against West

Germany in 1987. Cantona's volatile nature had already been evident at club level. He had punched a team-mate on the nose, fallen out spectacularly with others, and had been involved in a fracas with seven opponents after an Auxerre reserve match, but it was when manager Henri Michel elected to drop him from the national team in September 1988 that the volcano really erupted. In a TV interview, Cantona said eloquently: 'I hope that one day people realise that Henri Michel is the most incompetent manager in world football. I was reading an article by Mickey Rourke, who is a guy I really like, and he referred to the people who awarded the Oscars in Hollywood as shit bags. Well, I think that Henri Michel is not far from being included in that category.' The attack was all the more devastating for its careful, considered nature; it was not a typical post-match rant. However, Cantona's assessment was not that wide of the mark, as Michel was sacked shortly afterwards when France failed to qualify for the 1990 World Cup.

In that same year he was transferred to Olympique Marseille, but within a few months he was in hot water again, banned by his new club for a month for ripping off and throwing away his jersey after being substituted during a friendly with Torpedo Moscow. Struggling to settle at Marseille, he went on loan first to Bordeaux and then Montpellier, where he again underlined his reputation as *l'enfant terrible* by throwing his boots in the face of team-mate Jean-Claude Lemoult, an incident that led to six players demanding Cantona be sacked. However, other members of the Montpellier side, including the influential Laurent Blanc, backed him and Cantona repaid the loyalty by helping Montpellier win the French Cup.

His form persuaded Marseille to take him back but, despite being instrumental in the team's 1991 title triumph, he rarely saw eye-to-eye with chairman Bernard Tapie and coach Raymond Goethals and was transferred to Nimes. In December 1991, while playing for Nimes, he petulantly hurled the ball at the referee. Summoned to a disciplinary hearing by the French Football Federation, he demanded to be treated like any other player in the French League, to which the disciplinary committee chairman, Jacques Riolaci, replied, in reference to Cantona's past misdemeanours: 'You can't be judged like any other player. Behind you there is a trail of the smell of sulphur.' Cantona was banned for a month and responded by walking up to each member of the committee in turn and calling him an idiot, whereupon the ban was increased to two months. Given his 'previous', Cantona might have considered that he escaped lightly, but instead he decided it was the final straw and announced his retirement from football at the age of 25.

Fortunately, the new French national coach, Michel Platini, was a Cantona fan and persuaded him to make a comeback, advising him to kick-start his career in England. He was lined up to sign for Sheffield Wednesday but took umbrage when manager Trevor Francis told him he was only on trial. Cantona did not do auditions (well, not football ones) and walked out after less than a week, only for Howard Wilkinson to snap him up for Leeds United for £1 million. Despite becoming an instant favourite at Elland Road and helping Leeds to the League Championship, Cantona eventually fell out with Wilkinson over non-selection and Leeds decided to recoup their money by selling him to Manchester United for £1.2 million in November 1992.

Those who thought that Alex Ferguson was taking a gamble in signing the tempestuous Frenchman were soon forced to acknowledge that Cantona was the bargain of the decade. He inspired United to their first Championship title in 26 years, followed a year later in 1994 by the Cup and League double. The fans took to him immediately, not only for his goalscoring and creativity on the pitch but for his demeanour off it. Whereas many of his contemporaries locked themselves away behind the large wrought iron gates of their mansions, Cantona opted to live in a modest three-bedroomed semi in Manchester and could regularly be seen in ordinary bars in the city. This endeared him to the fans, along with his willingness to sign countless autographs for youngsters. With his deep interest in philosophy, he was clearly more intelligent than the average footballer and, for all the bad press he attracted from time to time, Ferguson could not speak highly enough of him. Ferguson's loyalty was sorely tested in March 1994 when Cantona was sent off twice in the space of three days, but he continued to stand by the player whose form was such that he was voted PFA Player of the Year and was even recalled to the French national team for the last of his 45 caps.

Then, on the evening of 25 January 1995, it all went horribly wrong. United were drawing 1-1 with Crystal Palace at Selhurst Park when Cantona was sent off following a clash with Palace defender Richard Shaw. As Cantona walked along the touchline towards the dressing room, Palace season-ticket holder Matthew Simmons ran down to the front of the stand and started hurling abuse at him. Cantona reacted furiously, vaulting the barrier rail and launching a two-footed kung fu attack on Simmons' chest, the force of which knocked the stunned supporter to the ground. Simmons retaliated with a flurry of punches before Cantona floored him again with a right-hander. The fight was then stopped by United keeper Peter Schmeichel, who managed to drag the still seething Cantona away. Simmons wasted no time in reporting Cantona to the police but his move backfired when it emerged that he himself was a nasty racist thug with a history of violence. Public opinion was now firmly on Cantona's side, a survey revealing that 40 per cent of British men would rather go on holiday with him than with Claudia Schiffer. When the assault case came to court, Cantona was sentenced to two weeks in jail, reduced on appeal to 120 hours' community service. More damagingly, he was suspended for seven months by the FA.

He never complained about his punishment but simply got on with the job of teaching football to youngsters in Greater Manchester. He returned to the United team in October 1995, and the following May scored the only goal in the Cup final victory over Liverpool. As he walked up Wembley's 39 steps to collect the trophy, he was spat on and verbally abused by Liverpool fans. This time he calmly wiped away the spit and walked on.

In 1997 he announced his retirement from football, having won five League titles in six years. He had scored 64 goals in 144 appearances for United. As for his bad boy reputation, he denied that he had deliberately quietened down since the Selhurst Park episode. 'I often get asked about the change in my temperament since the incident at Crystal Palace. The truth is there hasn't been a big change. People think I've suddenly learnt to feel at ease with myself, but the fact of the matter is that I was never ill at ease in the first place. Everyone has their bad moments.'

Cantona made a brief return to the game as captain of the French National Beach Football team but now devotes most of his energies to his new career as a film actor. He professes to have no interest in appearing in blockbuster movies. 'I don't want to be in *Terminator*,' he says. 'I don't want to go to Hollywood. I like making films that I find interesting and intellectually challenging.'

In 2001 Manchester United fans voted him their Player of the Century, quite an accolade considering he was up against the likes of George Best, Bobby Charlton, Denis Law and Duncan Edwards. Best himself once said of Cantona: 'I'd give all the champagne I've ever drunk to be playing alongside him in a big European match at Old Trafford.' Praise does not come any higher than that.

Chic Charnley
Repeat Offender

There may be football fans south of the border who have never heard of Chic Charnley. Yet with an appetite for aggravation that is positively voracious (including a record-equalling 17 sendings-off in professional British football), the midfielder is a living legend in the bars around Glasgow.

Trouble doesn't just follow Charnley around; it actively stalks him. His first famous scrape alone was enough to assure him of cult status. It occurred while Charnley and his Partick Thistle team-mates were training in Glasgow's Ruchill Park. It was a hazardous enough place at the best of times, with dogs regularly straying on to the pitch to snap at the players' heels, but this time the locals had different weapons with which to terrorise the footballers. Charnley takes up the story: 'We were training one morning and two guys came wandering along with a dog. We stopped to let them pass and it soon became clear they were up to their eyeballs with something. They started shouting abuse at us, so I stupidly said, "Come back at 12.30 and we'll finish this." They returned 10 minutes later with a Samurai sword. One of them started swinging it at the players. So I picked up a cone and swung it at the guy and he just about cut my right hand off. The more I think about it now, the more stupid I think my actions were. Anyway, they then ran for it and Gerry Collins, Gordon Rae and I chased after them. Gordon managed to get hold of the sword, snapped it over his knee and threw it over a fence. They were sorry boys by the time we had finished with them.'

Charnley played for Partick in four separate spells during an eventful 21-year career. A shrewd passer with a reasonable goal-scoring record, he was tipped for greatness early in his career but, despite being an avid Celtic fan, he never achieved his dream move, principally because the big clubs were put off by his terrible disciplinary record. In fact, the nearest he came to realising his dream was when, while playing for Partick, he wiped his nose on one of the Ibrox corner flags – a gesture that infuriated the Rangers support. Charnley reflects: 'But I paid for that when a plastic bottle thrown from the Rangers fans hit me in the face at Firhill.'

James Callaghan Charnley (perhaps his mother had a fondness for Labour politicians) was born in Glasgow in 1963. A good schoolboy prospect, he hardly played any serious football between the ages of 12 and 18 because he was too busy following his beloved Celtic. But when a friend started playing for a local amateur side, Possil Villa, Charnley followed suit and the following year, 1982, he signed a professional contract with St Mirren. However, by his own admission, he would not listen to the coaches and had no respect for the rules of football, and after just one first-team game at Love Street he was shown the door. A short stint at Ayr United ended in similar fashion and Charnley drifted back into the amateur game. There he was spotted by Clydebank chairman Jack Steadman, who, despite Charnley being sent off in both games that he watched, decided to take a chance on the wayward talent.

Charnley thought he had made it. 'I can remember in one game going into the Kilbowie stand at half-time. Andy Roxburgh was the Scotland manager at the time and he came in after me with a cup of tea. I said to him: "Andy, any chance of a cap?" He replied: "Why? Is the sun in your eyes?"'

In 1988 Scotland's most famous pigeon-fancier, John Lambie, who would proceed to sign Charnley on a regular basis throughout his tempestuous career, took him to Hamilton Academicals. A hard taskmaster with an interesting line in discipline, Lambie once hit a player on the jaw with a dead pigeon! He nearly inflicted serious damage on Charnley, too, when in revenge for a prank, he dropped a heavyweight medicine ball on to the player's head. Nevertheless, Charnley concedes that without Lambie he might have ended up in jail. The following year Charnley followed Lambie to Partick, where he produced some of the best football of his career. It was not to last. A move back to St Mirren ended when Charnley spat at an Ayr United player after being sent off and was promptly sacked by the club.

He tried to make a fresh start in Sweden but a year later was back in Scotland, first with Partick again, then with Dumbarton, Dundee and Hibernian. In 1998 he joined Northern Ireland club Portadown, where he equalled Rangers winger Willie Johnston's long-standing British record of 17 red cards by getting himself sent off against Glentoran. Probably Charnley's only regret was that such an historic moment did not take place on Scottish soil.

Although he did guest for Celtic in Mark Hughes's testimonial match at Old Trafford, the big move always eluded him. He acknowledges that his disciplinary record was to blame. 'My problem was that I took it personally. If somebody took me down with a bad tackle, I would target them. Before long, people started to recognise it and used to try and wind me up. I've had 17 red cards, but five or six of them were down to my reputation, and not my actions.'

At least John Lambie remained faithful. The story goes that he fell out with the wife of former Celtic manager Liam Brady at the 1994 World Cup after she labelled Charnley a pub player. Lambie told her: 'Listen, hen, if yer man had 10 pub players like Chic Charnley, then he might still be in a job at Celtic!'

Robin Friday
Royal Icon

When Robin Friday was found dead in his London flat on 22 December 1990, having suffered a heart attack at the age of just 38, his passing barely warranted a mention in the national press. To the majority of fans outside Reading and Cardiff, he was just another lower division footballer with a dodgy haircut and an even worse disciplinary record, little more than a name on the opposition team sheet. But to the few who witnessed his unexpected rise and all too predictable fall, Robin Friday was no ordinary player.

He once walked into a hotel bar on an away trip carrying a swan under his arm; he playfully grabbed Bobby Moore by the testicles while waiting for a corner to be taken; he kissed a policeman on duty at the ground after scoring a winning goal; he pulled down the shorts of an opponent during a match; he danced naked in pubs and clubs; he mooned at passers-by from the team coach; he was jailed for impersonating a police officer and confiscating drugs from people; and he once defecated in Mark Lawrenson's kit bag. Friday did all this and much, much more. Abundantly skilful but with a fragile temperament that was exacerbated by drink and drugs, Friday was every fan's dream and every manager's nightmare.

He did nothing by halves. He was sent off seven times in amateur football before joining Reading, he was married three times, and he was banned from one pub in the town 10 times. He would turn up for training with a mysteriously acquired black eye – that is, when he turned up for training at all. When the Royals' manager Charlie Hurley said he was thinking of giving him a chance in the first team at the weekend, Friday promised: 'Look, boss, I'll go home, I won't drink, I won't fight.' Hurley replied: 'I don't mind you lying, but not three times.'

Friday always considered himself more sinned against than sinning. There was never anything malicious about his off-field scrapes, while his frequent suspensions were the result of the brutal treatment he received from defenders. When opponents kicked him, he would laugh in their face and retaliate later. 'I have a lot of skill and opponents don't like me taking the mickey out of them,' he said. 'They give me a lot of stick. Players go out of their way to kick me. You can only take so much when you're constantly kicked so I give it out as well. People think I'm mad, a lunatic, but I'm a winner.'

The Robin Friday story began on 27 July 1952 in Acton, West London. On leaving school he became a plasterer for a couple of months but finished up in Feltham Borstal for theft. There, he starred in the borstal football team and near the end of his sentence, one of the staff recommended him to Reading, as a result of which he appeared three times for the Royals' youth side. When that didn't work out, he joined Hayes, combining his football with a job as a roofing asphalter. It was while working on a building site that the 20-year-old suffered a horrific accident, impaling himself on a spike. The spike went through his backside into his stomach, narrowly missing a lung. He managed to pull himself off the spike and survived after an emergency operation, but was later told that he had been a fraction of an inch away from death. Already it seemed that Robin Friday's life was destined to be short but eventful.

He soon made an impact at Hayes. The team started one match with only 10 players because Friday was finishing a pint in the local pub, and when he finally took the field 10 minutes after the start he was clearly drunk and spent the game staggering around the pitch. Naturally, the opposition ignored him...until he scored the only goal of the game. However, a more disciplined performance from the young striker in an FA Cup tie against Reading encouraged Charlie Hurley to pay £750 to take Friday to Elm Park in 1974. So eager was he to impress that in his first training session he put three first-team players out of action, as a result of which Hurley had to bring him off and tell him, 'Robin, slow down a minute. Let's talk about what you're doing here before you finish off the rest of the team!'

When his senior call-up arrived, Friday responded with three goals in his first three games. With his socks rolled down (he never wore shinpads), his shirt hanging out and his long hair, he became an instant cult hero with the fans, and before long people were going to Reading just to see him play. Not only did he have outstanding ball skills for a big man, he was also entertainingly unpredictable. He would kiss opposition defenders at corners and once, while waiting for a flag-kick to be taken in a game against Rotherham, he pulled down the shorts of United's Barry Wagstaff, a former team-mate at Reading. And when he scored a last-minute winner against Rochdale, Friday ran up to a policeman on crowd control and kissed him. Friday said afterwards: 'The policeman looked so cold and fed up standing there that I decided to cheer him up a bit.' Friday may even have known the officer personally as his riotous post-match antics saw him spend a number of nights in police cells.

Hurley did his best to keep the fans' favourite under some sort of control but it was never going to be easy shackling someone with tattoos of 'mild' and 'bitter' on his chest. The manager used to sniff Friday's breath for alcohol before a game. 'I told him, "If at all possible, try never to drink two days before a game." But,' added Hurley ruefully, 'I think that might have been asking a lot of him.'

Friday missed the start of the pre-season in 1974–75 because he had been staying in a hippie commune in Cornwall, but when he did eventually show up he was the star performer in friendlies despite the fact he hadn't trained. He was never keen on training at the best of times. Reading coach Maurice Evans said: 'He would play with the ball all day. Give him a ball and he loved it. But make him do some running and he hated it, detested it, thought it was a terrible waste of time.' His preparation for that season was further hindered by an operation to remove tattoos from his fingers. With Robin Friday such considerations were part of the package.

He was certainly his own man. He painted the walls of his flat black because he said there was nothing worse than getting stoned and looking at strange wallpaper patterns. Other players never really knew what to make of him. When Reading travelled back from an away game in the north-east on the same train as West Ham players, Friday was lounging in the buffet car, with his straggly hair, leather coat, black T-shirt and jeans, shouting to a team-mate: 'Get us a fucking drink, will ya?' One of the West Ham players moaned, 'Bloody supporters, they get everywhere', whereupon Reading goalkeeper Steve Death leant over and whispered: 'Actually, that's our centre-forward.'

In 1976 Hurley's patience finally paid off when Friday's goals helped Reading gain promotion from Division Four. Among his contributions was a brilliant individual effort against Tranmere, when Friday hooked a vicious volley over his shoulder into the top corner from outside the box. World Cup referee Clive Thomas was so impressed that he went up to him and said: 'I have to tell you that is the best goal I have ever seen.' Friday merely shrugged. 'Really? You should come down here more often. I do that every week.'

If only Friday had been that reliable. Instead, his prolonged absences from training riled his team-mates to the point that Hurley became powerless to protect him. His form stuttered in the new season and so when Cardiff offered a knockdown £30,000 for his services, Friday was on his way to Wales after 53 goals and numerous assists in 135 games for Reading. Cardiff manager Jimmy Andrews commented that by obtaining Friday so cheaply he felt he was taking advantage of Reading, but was simply warned: 'You'll see.' Andrews quickly found out what they meant when Friday was arrested at Cardiff railway station on the day he arrived, having travelled from Reading with just a platform ticket.

As at Reading, the initial portents were promising. Friday made a spectacular debut for Cardiff in January 1977, giving Fulham's

Bobby Moore the runaround and scoring twice in a 3-0 victory. He went one better against Luton, netting a hat-trick, and as he reeled away after the third he flicked a contemptuous V-sign at hapless Luton keeper Milija Aleksic. But Andrews was not strong enough to control his wayward pupil, whose drink- and drug-fuelled behaviour became increasingly erratic. Staying in a hotel after an away defeat, Cardiff's players were woken in the middle of the night by a noise from downstairs. Upon investigation they found Friday standing on the hotel snooker table in just his underpants, hurling snooker balls around the room.

The crunch came the following October. Following a tussle with Brighton defender Mark Lawrenson, Friday lashed out and was sent off. He made a premature exit from the ground, but not before he had defecated in Lawrenson's kit bag. After that there was no word from Friday for two months, and when he did finally reappear it was to inform Andrews that he was quitting the game and going back to roofing. He had played just 25 games for Cardiff.

Friday was a wasted talent. His Cardiff team-mate Paul Went said: 'He was a big guy but had so much skill he used to terrorise defences when he was going at them. If someone had got hold of him at 16 or 17 and taken him under their wing to try and curb that temper he would have been an England international without doubt. On his day there was no one better, he would just take your breath away.'

Three decades after he left the club, Friday's infamous antics are still the subject of debate in Reading, where he had the honour of being voted the Royals' Player of the Millennium – no mean feat for somebody who was at the club for less than three years, and even then only when he felt like it.

Maurice Evans echoed Went's views and once told Friday: 'If you would just settle down for three or four years, you could play for England.'

Friday simply looked at him and said: 'Yeah, but I've had a far better time than you've ever had in your life.'

Hughie Gallacher
The Hero Who Died of Shame

On the sunny morning of 11 June 1957, two young trainspotters noticed a small man wearing a flat cap standing on a footbridge over the main London to Edinburgh railway line at Gateshead. Appearing troubled, the man paced back and forth for half an hour, muttering to himself and openly weeping. Suddenly he heard the whistle of the northbound express approaching and, pausing only to say 'Sorry' to the two youngsters, stepped off the bridge, clambered down an embankment and walked into the path of the train. His decapitated body was found 100 yards down the line at a point known locally as Dead Man's Crossing. It was that of Hughie Gallacher, once a hero to fans of Airdrieonians, Newcastle United and Scotland but now a man who had decided to take his own life the day before he was due to appear in court on charges of mistreating his son.

The pint-sized forward was one of the Wembley Wizards who thrashed England 5-1 at Wembley in 1928. The following year he scored five times in a 7-3 victory over Northern Ireland in Belfast despite receiving a note at half-time saying that he would be shot unless he eased off in the second period. Gallacher ignored the threat and the next day went visiting friends in the city. As he passed the Queen's Bridge, he was forced to dive for cover when a bullet ricocheted off a nearby wall. He scored 22 goals in just 19 appearances for his country and retired from football having scored 387 goals in 541 Scottish and English League games – an incredible record. Yet his unquestionable ability was sometimes overshadowed by a fiery temperament and a tempestuous private life.

Gallacher was born in Bellshill, North Lanarkshire, on 2 February 1903, a tough industrial community described as having 'far too many pubs for its size'. At school he played in goal before moving to an outfield position where his team-mates included another future Scottish international, Alex James. On leaving school, Gallacher worked for a munitions factory and then, after the First World War, down the mines. Although he was only 5 feet 5 inches tall, he was a tough little character, courtesy of training sessions at a boxing gym in

Hamilton. He employed those boxing skills to deal with defenders who tackled him over-vigorously, with the result that he was regularly sent off.

In 1920 Queen of the South signed the 17-year-old on wages of £6 a week, but off the field his life was already in turmoil. He married young – against his parents' wishes – and the union lasted less than three years, not helped by the death of the couple's baby son, also named Hughie. Gallacher himself nearly died when struck down with double pneumonia, but he managed to pull through. After a year with the Dumfries outfit, Airdrieonians offered him £9 a week and, despite the break-up of his marriage, Gallacher scored 33 goals in 1923–24 and another 32 in 1924–25. His average of approximately a goal a game helped the small Lanarkshire club to three League runners-up positions and a Scottish Cup triumph in four seasons. So when Airdrie accepted a £6,500 offer for Gallacher from Newcastle in 1925, the Scottish club's fans were so angry that they threatened to burn down the wooden stand.

Gallacher became an instant hero on Tyneside. Appointed captain, his goals took Newcastle to the League title in 1927, but storm clouds had again been brewing in his private life. While awaiting his divorce he had caused a scandal by becoming involved with the 17-year-old daughter of the landlord of one of his favourite pubs. The girl's brother took exception to the relationship – particularly on discovering that Gallacher was still technically married – and the resulting brawl ended up with both men in court. Gallacher did eventually marry the girl but only after his divorce had cost him £4,000 and left him broke. Not that anyone would have known it by Gallacher's immaculate attire and free spending in the local pubs. Occasionally, his fondness for drink spilled over on to the pitch. He was accused of being drunk and disorderly during a Newcastle friendly in Hungary but escaped punishment by convincing the gullible authorities that he had been using whisky and water as a mouthwash.

Although Gallacher was immensely popular with the fans, that view was not always shared by his Newcastle team-mates, particularly the less talented members of the team whom he had publicly belittled. Such arrogance landed him in trouble during a match with Huddersfield in 1927. Gallacher had been taking revenge for a series of bad tackles until referee Bert Fogg decided to take his name.

Gallacher replied loftily: 'If you don't know my name, you've no right to be refereeing. What's your name?'

'Fogg,' answered the official.

'I might have guessed,' mocked Gallacher. 'You've been in a fog all afternoon!'

But Gallacher was not finished there and at the end of the game he pushed Mr Fogg into the team bath, an action that earned him a two-month suspension.

In 1930 he moved to Chelsea for £10,000, but trouble followed him south and he was arrested for disorderly conduct after a fight with a gang of Fulham fans outside a café. On another occasion an opposing player found him lying drunk in the street the night before a vital match. Meanwhile, financial problems continued to plague him and when he signed for Derby County in 1934–35, part of the transfer deal involved Derby paying off his sizeable debts. He did not linger long at Derby or at Notts County, Grimsby Town and Gateshead, his playing career ending with the outbreak of the Second World War.

His last years were shrouded in unhappiness. He was already under suspicion of having received illegal payments from Derby when, in 1950, his second wife, Hannah, died of a heart attack. With a family to support and no future in football, he took factory jobs and began drinking more heavily than usual. The alcohol often made him aggressive and in May 1957 his youngest son, Matthew, was removed from his care after Gallacher lost his temper and hurled an ashtray that hit the boy a glancing blow on the head. Unable to face the press coverage of his case, Gallacher took his own life, leaving behind a suicide note that read: 'I'll never forgive myself for having struck Matthew, even if I live to be a hundred.' When news broke of his tragic death, the streets of Newcastle were packed with mourners keen to remember only Gallacher the player, the sturdy little centre-forward who terrorised defences the length and breadth of the land. The headline in the *Newcastle Journal* said it all: 'HUGHIE OF THE MAGIC FEET IS DEAD'.

Garrincha
Wasted Away

He lost his virginity to a goat (no kidding), killed his mother-in-law in a car crash, drunkenly ran over his father, slept with hundreds of women and sired at least 14 children before dying of alcohol poisoning. Oh, and one of his legs was 2½ inches shorter than the other. Welcome to the topsy-turvy life of Garrincha, the dynamic little Brazilian whose dazzling array of skills helped his country win two World Cups.

Manuel Francisco dos Santos was born into poverty in Pau Grande, near Rio de Janeiro, in 1933. He had a number of birth defects: his spine was deformed, his right leg bent inwards and his left leg was markedly shorter and curved outwards. Bizarrely, his deformed knee joints were ideal for hitting shots with the outside of the foot and it was his swerving banana shot that would become his trademark. By then, he had been given the nickname 'Garrincha' (meaning 'Little Bird') on account of his distinctive gait and slim frame. Appropriately, he played on the wing.

Living an almost feral existence, he went to work in the local factory 14 and played for the works team. As word of his amazing dribbling ability spread, the 'boy from the woods' turned professional with Botafogo when he was 19. Already married, he left behind his wife and young family but took a girlfriend with him to Rio. On his first appearance he hit a hat-trick against Bonsucesso and went on to score 232 goals in 581 games in his 13-year stay with Botafogo. He was a nightmare to play against because no defender could tell which way his wonky legs would take him. River Plate full-back Nair was mercilessly tormented during a friendly, the final humiliation being when Garrincha deliberately left the ball behind and sprinted up the line. Having chased shadows all evening, poor Nair dutifully followed Garrincha while the crowd roared with laughter.

Garrincha was notoriously disorganised. He never trained, had no agent and often signed blank contracts. Given a bonus after a World Cup, he handed the cash to his wife, who hid it under the children's mattress. Years later, they remembered the money but discovered only a mass of rotting paper, the bonus having been destroyed by bedwetting.

He had made his international debut in 1955 against Chile, but it was at the 1958 World Cup that the little man's talents really came to the fore. He destroyed the USSR almost single-handedly. At one point, after leaving a defender on the ground, Garrincha put his foot on the ball and offered to help the player to his feet. Having done so, he then dribbled past him again. Time and again on the big stage he would nutmeg a player, run past, wait for him to catch up, and then nutmeg him again.

In the wake of Brazil's triumph, Garrincha put on weight, largely because of his drinking. In May 1959 he went on tour with Botafogo to Sweden and got a local girl pregnant. On his return to Brazil, he drove home to Pau Grande and ran over his father, then drove off without stopping, hotly pursued by an angry mob who, when they caught up with him, found Garrincha to be so drunk that he had no idea what he had done. It has been calculated that in that year alone he made three different women (including his wife) pregnant.

Remarkably, he still had the energy to play football and the 1962 World Cup proved even more profitable for Garrincha. With Pele injured in the second game, Garrincha was switched to centre-forward, responding with two brilliant individual goals in the 3-1 quarter-final victory over England and two more in the semi-final against Chile before blotting his copybook by getting sent off for retaliation. As he left the pitch he was hit by a bottle thrown from the crowd, but following a personal plea to FIFA from the Brazilian President he was given clearance to play in the final and proceeded to collect a second World Cup winners' medal. As the players celebrated, a sultry Brazilian singer named Elza Soares walked in and embraced a naked Garrincha in the shower, thus beginning a stormy affair that lasted for over 15 years.

While the pair lived in Rio, Garrincha's wife and ever-expanding family remained in Pau Grande. The situation turned many Brazilians against him. He and Soares were harassed in Rio and physically attacked when they visited Pau Grande. Meanwhile, injuries and excessive drinking were taking their toll on his career. He limped out of the brutal 1966 World Cup clash against Hungary in what would be the last of his 51 internationals and Brazil's first defeat with him in the team. In the same year he left Botafogo for Corinthians. His star in decline – he was no longer able to secure lucrative contracts – his financial problems heightened when his wife and their eight children decided to reclaim much of his money. Spurned by the leading Brazilian clubs, he tried to offer his services abroad but nobody wanted to employ a drunk. A Saudi Arabian team did show interest but Garrincha refused to play for teetotallers.

In 1969 he crashed his car into a lorry, killing his mother-in-law, and as his personal life disintegrated, he became violent towards Soares, punching her in a drunken rage. Although by now an incurable alcoholic, he was paraded on a Rio carnival float in 1980. Wearing the yellow shirt of Brazil he sat there in a daze, oblivious to all around him, unable even to recognise his old friend Pele. Incontinent, impotent and penniless, Garrincha ended his days sleeping on a towel. He died in 1983 at the age of 49, attached to a drip in the alcoholics ward of a Rio hospital.

Those who never saw the little master play but only knew the shell of a man in his later years were reminded of a popular Brazilian football saying: 'Pele was the best, but Garrincha was better.'

Paul Gascoigne
Daft as a Brush

Paul Gascoigne's life has been a game of two halves, usually followed by several pints. There was the bright, energetic, mischievous youngster with the football world at his feet, and then the sad, alcohol-ridden figure who had allowed so much of his ability to go to waste. As the late Tony Banks remarked, in one of the more astute political observations of the past 20 years, 'God gave him this enormous footballing talent but took his brains out to even things up.'

On the one hand there was the lovable Gascoigne, displaying his impudent skills on the pitch, bursting into tears at the prospect of missing the 1990 World Cup final, and wearing comedy breasts in public. Then there was the loutish Gascoigne, belching into a microphone at Lazio, lashing out at manager Glenn Hoddle's furnishings after being omitted from England's 1998 World Cup squad, getting involved in scuffles and, on his own admission, beating up his wife, Sheryl.

Gazza was a born prankster but unfortunately there was rarely anyone around willing to tell him if he happened to be going too far. Many of his jokes were harmless fun but others hinted at the influence of the alcohol that would eventually dominate his life. Here are some of his finest moments.

Playing for Rangers against Hibs in 1995, he booked referee Dougie Smith. When the official dropped his yellow card, Gazza picked it up, mockingly booked himself and then brandished it at the referee. Smith was not amused and, to jeers from the crowd, promptly booked Gazza for real.

An hour after an England match he met celebrities Danny Baker and Chris Evans in a Hampstead pub while still wearing his full kit, including boots.

Strolling through London with Gary Lineker, Gazza jumped on to a crowded bus and then demanded that he be allowed a go at driving it. Amazingly, the driver agreed.

On another visit to London, Gazza jumped out of his car and persuaded a workman to let him have a turn on his pneumatic drill.

As an apprentice at Newcastle he jumped on the groundsman's tractor, aimed it at the dressing rooms and, jumping off in the nick of time, knocked 25 bricks out of the wall. He was fined £75.

He once walked into the Middlesbrough canteen and ordered lunch despite the fact that he was wearing only his socks.

The organisers of the TV coverage at Italia '90 decided to use footage of each player mouthing his own name to camera. Gazza mouthed 'fucking wanker' and the world's broadcasters had to use it throughout the tournament whenever he played.

The day after Bobby Robson labelled him 'daft as a brush', Gazza turned up for England training with a brush sticking out of his sock.

With his 1988 transfer from Newcastle to Spurs in danger of collapsing, Gazza accepted Tottenham's offer to join the negotiations in London and asked if he could bring a few friends along, too. Spurs paid for Gazza's drunken pals to stay at an exclusive Hertfordshire hotel but when they checked out, club chairman Irving Scholar was ready to read the riot act. However, Gazza defused the situation by telling Scholar: 'Me and the lads would like to thank you for the best three days of our lives.' As Scholar said: 'How could anyone get angry after that?'

Gazza once sniffed a referee's armpit while the official had his arm raised to signal a free-kick.

He crashed Middlesbrough's team bus at the club's training ground, causing £14,000 of damage.

Warming up before a Crystal Palace-Tottenham fixture, Gazza wrestled a Yogi Bear mascot in the goalmouth and then aimed a playful kick at another mascot who was dressed as Postman Pat's cat, Jess. He later found out that it was a woman in the cat costume and that his boots had hurt her. 'Jess' demanded an apology.

Jimmy Greaves summed him up as 'Tyneside's very own renaissance man – a man capable of breaking both leg and wind at the same time.'

Gascoigne's troubled life began in Gateshead, where he was born on 27 May 1967. At school he explained the fact that he had written his signature over and over again in an exam by telling the teacher that he was practising it for when he grew up to be a famous footballer. He certainly had the talent to support the prediction and, following unsuccessful trials at Ipswich Town, Middlesbrough and Southampton, he signed for Newcastle United in 1983. As an apprentice there, one of his duties was to clean Kevin Keegan's boots, a task that excited him so much that he took them home one day to show his mates – but accidentally left them on a bus. Fortunately, Keegan saw the funny side.

Gascoigne made his first-team debut in 1985 and in his three years at St James' Park scored 25 goals from midfield, creating countless more with his surging runs and exquisite passing. But for some the writing was already on the wall. Newcastle team-mate John Bailey said: 'He can be a loony with a fast mouth. He's either going to be one of the greats or finish up at 40, bitter about wasting such talent.'

In 1988 Gascoigne moved to Spurs for a British record fee of £2.3 million. On his return to Tyneside with his new team, he was pelted with Mars Bars (his favourite snack) by fans angry at the sale of their star player. Later that year he made the first of 57 appearances for England, and after a series of outstanding performances at the 1990 World Cup was hailed the most gifted England player of his generation. The impromptu waterworks in the semi-final against

Germany further endeared him to millions and saw him voted BBC Sports Personality of the Year for 1990.

And that was about as good as it got. He came out for the 1991 FA Cup final against Nottingham Forest frighteningly fired up and suffered torn cruciate ligaments after lunging into a reckless tackle on Gary Charles. He was out of the game for more than a year and on his return was sold to Italian club Lazio for £5.5 million. 'Coping with the language shouldn't prove a problem,' he said. 'I can't even speak English yet!' Sadly, he resorted to the international language of belching when asked a question on live TV. The crude reply went out just as the Italian people were sitting down to dinner and created such an unholy row that the matter was even raised in the Italian parliament, where it was seen as an insult to the nation. To another TV interviewer he yelled, 'Fuck off, Norway', prompting England assistant manager Lawrie McMenemy to apologise. 'You'll have to excuse Gazza,' he said. 'He's got a very small vocabulary.' As Gascoigne's behaviour became increasingly boorish, even George Best waded in with condemnation. 'He wears a Number 10 jersey,' said Best. 'I thought it was his position, but it turns out to be his IQ.'

In 1995 he joined Rangers and despite his brilliant individual goal for England against Scotland at Euro '96, his drinking was beginning to spiral dangerously out of control. At half-time during a game for Rangers he had a brandy after arguing with team-mate Ally McCoist. He then went out and scored twice in the second half, leaving manager Walter Smith and his assistant Archie Knox shaking their heads in disbelief. His misguided sense of humour again raised its ugly head when he provoked Celtic supporters by pretending to play the flute, a Protestant symbol in Scotland. Smith lamented: 'People think Gascoigne and I have a father-and-son relationship. Well I've got two sons and I have never felt like hitting them, but I have certainly felt like smacking Gascoigne a couple of times.'

Confronting his demons, in 1998 Gascoigne was admitted to a private clinic to tackle alcohol addiction. He then had spells with Middlesbrough, Everton, Burnley and Boston United, sandwiching a short stint in China. At each fresh outpost there were occasional glimpses of the old Gazza before his lack of fitness kicked in. In a bid to rid himself of everything associated with his undisciplined Gazza image, he announced in 2004 that in future he wanted to be known as G8 because 'it sounds a bit like great, well it does with my Geordie accent'. He also revealed that he wanted to break into management and was granted his wish the following year at Kettering Town. The football world held its breath…but only for 39 days. That was how long Gascoigne lasted before being sacked by chairman Imraan Ladak, who claimed that the manager was 'under the influence of alcohol before, during and after several first-team games and training sessions'. Then, in February 2008, Gascoigne was sectioned under the Mental Health Act after an incident at a Tyneside hotel.

Gascoigne has been refreshingly honest about his battle against alcoholism and depression. He knows that drink has cost him his career and plenty more besides. 'I drank at the wrong times,' he admitted recently. 'I got into trouble and let myself down. Without the drinking I could have been one of the best players in the world.'

Jimmy Greaves
Back From the Brink

Jimmy Greaves doesn't believe it was the pressure of football that drove him to drink. In fact, he says it was quite the opposite – it was retiring from football that made him hit the bottle. 'It was the emptiness of not playing,' he reflects. 'The bottom fell out of my life. I felt an old man at 31.'

Between 1972 and 1977 Greaves was almost constantly drunk. 'I became a walking vegetable. I can remember waking up in my car not knowing where I was. I'd look at my watch and if it was dark I wouldn't know if it was morning or night. It took me a long time to realise that if I didn't stop drinking I would kill myself.' Later, when asked to name the biggest influence on his career, he jokingly replied: 'Vladimir Smirnoff.'

However, his is one alcoholic's story with a happy ending. He has not touched a drop since 1978. He has won back his self-esteem and his beloved wife, Irene.

Greavsie was always fond of a drink, often in the company of his old mate Bobby Moore. In the build-up to the 1966 World Cup, the pair used to sneak off to the pub at night from the England training camp, leaving via Jack Charlton's room, which had access to a drainpipe or a fire escape – that is, until Alf Ramsey found out and threatened them with expulsion. Their most infamous jaunt was with West Ham in 1971, on the night before a third-round FA Cup tie at Blackpool. In the mistaken belief that the match would be postponed due to a frozen pitch, Greaves, Moore, Brian Dear and Clyde Best stayed out late at a Blackpool nightclub. Although Best drank only Coca-Cola, Greaves downed 12 pints of lager and when, to the quartet's horror, the match was given the go-ahead, the hungover Hammers lost 4-0. To add to their woes, a disgruntled fan phoned the club and a national newspaper to report the revelry, as a result of which all four were fined and Greaves and Moore were dropped.

Throughout his playing career Jimmy Greaves often gave the impression of being casual and disinterested. For 89 minutes of a game he might make little or no contribution, but as soon as the slightest sniff of a goalscoring opportunity presented itself, the ball was in the back of the net. He could put away a chance even quicker than he could a pint. His career record of 357 League goals plus another 44 in just 57 England appearances makes him the most clinical finisher this country has seen in the past 50 years.

He was born in East Ham, London, in 1940 and joined Chelsea, scoring 114 goals for their youth team in 1956–57. He made his first-team debut in August 1957 and scored on his debut against Tottenham. It was a habit he never lost. By the time he was 20 he had already netted 100 League goals and from just 133 appearances, so Chelsea fans were none too pleased when an £80,000 fee took him to AC Milan in 1961. 'AC Milan were on another planet to English clubs,' remembers Greaves. 'Whereas at Chelsea I would enjoy an old-fashioned greasy spoon fry-up after training, I was suddenly presented with a bowl of pasta.' Greaves did not take to the Italian food, or to the regimented system that banned sex and alcohol for three days before a match. Despite scoring nine goals in 14 games in Milan, he longed for home and jumped at the chance to join Spurs four months later. Manager Bill Nicholson paid £99,999 for his services because he didn't want to burden Greaves with being the first £100,000 player.

The goals continued to flow as Greaves helped Spurs to two FA Cup successes and, in 1963, the European Cup Winners' Cup. The semi-final of that competition against OFK Belgrade produced a rare black mark in his Spurs' career when he was sent off for retaliation. Afterwards, Tottenham's veteran trainer and kit man, Cecil Poynton, laid into Greaves in no uncertain terms: 'It's your own fault,' he raged, 'you ain't got no business being sent off. You shouldn't have reacted like that. You should feel disgraced with yourself. You're the first Spurs player to be sent off in a game since 1928. You've blemished the good reputation of this fine club.' Greaves felt awful and asked casually: 'Who was the last Spurs player to be sent off then, back in 1928?' 'Me,' replied Poynton.

One of his cheekiest goals was a penalty against Leicester City. Gordon Banks, the Leicester keeper, was drying his hands in the back of the goal when Greaves impishly rolled the ball into the net. The referee awarded a goal, despite being chased back to the centre circle by an irate Banks protesting that he had not been ready.

Greaves was equally prolific at international level. He played at the 1962 World Cup, where a stray dog urinated over his England shirt as he tried to catch the animal during the game against Brazil, and he started the 1966 tournament as first-choice striker. However, his form temporarily deserted him and after two lacklustre performances he was injured against France. Although his replacement, Geoff Hurst, had done well, the fit-again Greaves was confident of being recalled for the final. But Ramsey stood by Hurst, and the events of the final thoroughly vindicated his decision. A shattered Greaves boycotted the victory celebrations.

He made his final England appearance in 1967 and three years later joined West Ham as part of the deal that took Martin Peters to White Hart Lane. Apart from the drinking culture that existed at the club, Greaves did not really enjoy his time at Upton Park and the following year shocked the football world by announcing his retirement. In 1977 he made a comeback with Southern League Barnet and, although many of his matches were played through a haze of vodka, he netted 25 goals from midfield and was voted the club's Player of the Year.

After finally winning his battle with the bottle, genial Jimmy formed a double act with former Liverpool forward Ian St John to present the long-running football show *Saint & Greavsie*. Who would have thought that a former alcoholic would be one of the most popular television personalities of the 1980s? As someone once said, 'It's a funny old game.'

Victor Kasule
Vodka Vic

If you have never heard of Victor Kasule, he is the answer to the pub-quiz question, 'Which Scottish-born footballer of Ugandan descent was once booked for singing a George Benson song to a referee?'

Described as 'an armoured car of a winger with a cannon for a shot', the gifted but hopelessly ill-disciplined Kasule terrorised lower division defences both north and south of the border while also causing sleepless nights for the succession of managers who tried in vain to curb his hedonistic lifestyle. He broke so many club rules in the course of his career that he achieved the distinction of being disciplined by three separate clubs within the space of a few months. He once fell out of a hotel window and even managed to break a toe while acrobatically celebrating a goal. If ever a player needed a round-the-clock guard it was the man dubbed 'Vodka Vic' by Hamilton Academicals fans in recognition of his favourite pastime.

Born in Glasgow in 1965 to a Scottish mother and a Ugandan father, Kasule arrived on the national scene in 1984 with Albion Rovers. As one of the first black players in the Scottish game, he was on the receiving end of plenty of abuse but was more than capable of dishing it back...with interest. His impressive form – 18 goals and countless assists in 132 appearances for Albion – encouraged Meadowbank Thistle to pay a club record £28,000 for him in 1987. He scored seven times in 35 matches for the Edinburgh club and a year later was on the move again, this time to Shrewsbury Town for £35,000.

Kasule's strike that brought victory over Leeds in 1988 was rated one of the most spectacular even seen at Gay Meadow but his goals soon became rarities and he managed just four in his 40 games with the club. Although an immediate hit with the Shrewsbury fans – who even named their fanzine *Double Scotch* in honour of Kasule and his fellow Scots – his recreational exploits were making the wrong sort of headlines. When a drinking session hours before a vital 1989 relegation six-pointer became public knowledge, the *Shrewsbury*

Chronicle printed a poem about Kasule, Alan Irvine and Dougie Bell that ended: 'Irvine, Kasule and Bell. They make the manager's life pure hell.' Irvine was outraged. 'The rest of the stuff didn't bother me,' he said, 'it was being associated with Victor!' It was difficult not to sympathise with Irvine. After all, it was Kasule who allegedly overturned team-mate John McGinlay's new sports car on an urgent trip to the off-licence.

At the start of the following season, Shrewsbury chairman Ken Woodhouse declared that Kasule would never play for the club again and manager Ian McNeill tried to recoup his money by sending him on loan to Darlington for a month. But before the month was out, Darlington had sent him back, their manager Brian Little commenting: 'There's nothing wrong with Victor the footballer, but his activities off the field have proved a disruptive factor.'

Desperate to offload Kasule, McNeill found a buyer in Hamilton Academicals' John Lambie, albeit at a knockdown fee of £15,000, in October 1989. On the day of signing, Kasule drove up to Scotland but forgot the necessary forms. He had no option but to drive back to Shropshire – and in view of his reputation, Accies took the precaution of sending a driver to accompany him just in case he never made it. The Hamilton secretary later confessed: 'I have signed whole teams quicker than I have signed Vic Kasule.' Kasule did make one more return visit to Shrewsbury, but it ended in his arrest after he became involved in a street brawl with a local youth. A distinctly unimpressed Lambie handed Kasule a club record fine of £4,000.

Unsurprisingly, Kasule did not linger long at Hamilton, or at Portadown in Northern Ireland, Finland, Malta (where he faced Benfica in the European Cup) or Bohemians of Dublin. A recurring foot injury then forced him into premature retirement and he was last heard of working in telesales in Glasgow. But he remains revered by pub landlords wherever he played and by the fans of Albion Rovers, who in 2005 voted Victor Kasule their all-time cult hero.

Diego Maradona
Addicted to Fame

Maradona put the 'ego' into Diego. Despite the drug scandals that have repeatedly blackened his name, he sees himself as a national hero in Argentina, a symbol of hope to those raised in poverty. When he talks about the 'Hand of God' goal against England at the 1986 World Cup, the feeling is that he is not necessarily implying any outside involvement. As such a revered figure, he expects preferential treatment, even from God's second-in-command. When Maradona attended an audience at the Vatican, he was furious that Pope John Paul II gave him nothing more than a pat on the back and a smile. Raging that the Pope had shown him insufficient respect, he bitterly attacked John Paul in his autobiography, saying: 'You've got nothing going for you. You were only a goalkeeper.'

Maradona remains angry about a great many things, including his portrayal in the media. Above all, one suspects that he is angry at having been exposed as a drug addict.

Born in 1960, he was raised in the slums of Buenos Aires. As a child he fell into the cesspit outside his home – a prophecy of the sort of mess he would get into as an adult. Spotted by a talent scout, he was recruited for the youth team of Argentinos Juniors and, as a 12-year-old ball boy, he used to fascinate spectators by demonstrating his wizardry with the ball during the half-time intervals of First Division games. He made his first-team debut at 15 and his international bow a year later, but he had a temperament to match his precocious talent, and when left out of Argentina's 1978 World Cup squad, he was so angry that he threatened to quit football altogether. Sheffield United nearly signed the virtual unknown in the early 1980s but the Yorkshire club's board refused to raise their bid and instead he moved to Boca Juniors, where he was given a suspended sentence for punching a young autograph hunter. Then, at the 1982 World Cup, he was sent off for kicking a Brazilian opponent in the testicles.

Maradona's worsening reputation did not deter Barcelona from paying a world record £4.2 million for him immediately following the World Cup. It was in Spain that he first dabbled in cocaine, although ironically he was appearing at the time in an anti-drugs advert on TV. He suffered a torrid time in Spain, left with a broken ankle and torn ligaments due to a horrendous tackle from Andoni Goicoechea, the 'Butcher of Bilbao'. When the two teams met again at the 1984 King's Cup final, Maradona was walking off the pitch at the end of the match when he suddenly flattened one of the victorious Bilbao players, sparking a mass brawl in full view of King Juan Carlos. He was swiftly sold to Napoli for another world record fee of £5 million.

The 1986 World Cup was Maradona's crowning moment, captaining his country to glory and being voted Player of the Tournament. His pace and strength (he was built like a pocket battleship) unhinged the world's finest defences, producing spectacular individual goals against England and Belgium. He was without question the finest player in the world but of course, in England at least, his achievements were overshadowed by the infamous 'Hand of God' goal that he punched over Peter Shilton. He later described the goal as 'like pickpocketing the English', adding, 'I was a bit stupid, because I was celebrating with my left fist outstretched. The referee could have cottoned on to that and suspected something was up. I was waiting for my team-mates to embrace me, and no one came. I told them, "Come hug me, or the referee isn't going to allow it."'

The following year he led Napoli to a first-ever Italian Championship, followed by a second in 1990. Overjoyed that the northern teams' monopoly had been broken and identifying with someone from a poor background, the Neapolitans took him to their hearts, and with Napoli also winning the UEFA Cup in 1989, Maradona wigs became the latest fashion accessory on the streets of the city. Meanwhile, his wedding to Claudia Villafane in 1989 in Buenos Aires Cathedral was a huge social event, attended by over 1,400 guests. Maradona, it seemed, could do no wrong.

But his popularity in Italy took a dive at Italia '90 when Argentina beat the host nation on penalties in the semi-final, a match that took place in Maradona's adopted home of Naples. Consequently, some Italian fans turned against him. Worse was to follow in 1991 when he failed a doping test for cocaine and was banned for 15 months amid lurid press stories of drug-fuelled orgies. He would always deny that taking drugs ever affected his football. 'I wouldn't have achieved everything I achieved in Italy,' he says, 'because cocaine, instead of motivating you, discourages you, it dulls you.'

In disgrace, Maradona tried to resurrect his career with Spanish side Seville but was sacked after only a few months. In February 1994, besieged by reporters and photographers at his home in Argentina, he opened fire with an air rifle, injuring five of them. Unrepentant, he maintained that he was simply protecting his family. That summer his World Cup dream turned sour when he was thrown out of the competition for failing another doping test. Maradona protested his innocence, wailing: 'They've cut my legs off.'

He attempted a comeback with his old club Boca Juniors, but finally retired from football in 1997, having scored more than 300 League goals plus 34 in his 91 appearances for his country.

Since then he has rarely been out of the headlines. As his weight ballooned due to cocaine addiction, fears about his health intensified. He spent spells in clinics, notably in Cuba, where he was heartened to receive a get-well ball from Peruvian footballers. His mind flashed back to a 1986 World Cup qualifier against Peru, a match in which he was ruthlessly man-marked by Claudio Reyna, whose tactics included non-stop verbal intimidation and the occasional punch. 'He followed me everywhere,' recalled Maradona in his autobiography. 'At one point I landed heavily on one leg and had to leave the game for the doctor to have a look at it, and the guy followed me to the edge of the pitch! And now there was his signature on the ball! Aged 40 and in Havana I still couldn't shake him off!'

In 2004 Maradona suffered a heart attack, and in the same year, divorce proceedings revealed that he was the father of a boy born in Italy in 1986. Seemingly having conquered his drug addiction, in March 2007 he was admitted to hospital to be treated for alcohol abuse. On discharge, the new slimline Maradona announced that he had quit drinking and had not taken drugs for more than two years.

The Argentine public have followed the Maradona soap opera through every dramatic twist and turn, and for all his failings many have remained loyal to the chunky little number 10 whose nomination as FIFA's Player of the Century was said to have annoyed Pele considerably. Maradona himself has no doubt that he remains an Argentine icon. 'I belong to every Argentinean who has smiled or cried for me,' he says in characteristically dramatic fashion, 'through the good times and the bad.'

Mick Quinn
The Pieman

With his roly poly figure, roguish dark moustache and mullet hairstyle, Mick Quinn was not exactly the most glamorous individual to step on to a football pitch. But as his career record of 231 League goals – many at the highest level – shows, he was one of the most effective. Fans could call him 'Sumo', chant 'Who ate all the pies?' as much as they liked, but Quinn knew his strengths, famously remarking: 'I'm the Premiership's fastest player over a yard.'

At West Ham, while Quinn was waiting for a corner to be taken, a fan once aimed a chicken and mushroom pie at his head, whereupon Quinn promptly caught the pie and started eating it. Later, when he was working for television and covering a match at his old club Newcastle, the fans spotted him and burst into a chorus of 'Who ate all the pies?' At half-time Quinn, ever game for a laugh and eager to live up to his image, bought 50 pies and handed them to fans on the Gallowgate End.

Quinn faced a constant battle with his weight, not helped by his love of junk food and drink. Friends said he could locate a party from any range. During the playing season he would be weighed every week and he developed a ruse whereby if he had put on a few pounds over the weekend, he would get a team-mate to distract the team physio while he was being weighed and would not stand properly on the scales. When he wasn't eating, drinking or chasing women, Quinn could usually be found in the bookies. He described gambling as his 'daily fix' and could lose up to £2,000 in an afternoon. 'One race wasn't enough,' he said. 'I had to go through the whole card. Saturday was always difficult for me – so many great race meetings, but I had to play in a football match, too.'

Quinn was born in 1962 on Liverpool's tough Cantril Farm estate, an area known locally as 'Little Beirut'. He enjoyed horse racing even as a teenager and has described losing his virginity at a party as 'more of a five-furlong sprint than a three-mile chase.' After failing to make the grade as an apprentice at Derby County, Quinn turned professional with Wigan Athletic, making a goalscoring debut against Halifax Town in April 1980. Shortly afterwards, he came to the attention of Social Security after being reported for claiming unemployment benefit while being employed full-time by Wigan. In his defence, Quinn said that he was earning only £35 a week at the time while his father was struggling to make a living as a taxi driver. He had decided to continue signing on and claiming benefit in order to help his family, but now he quickly withdrew his claim. It would not be his last brush with authority.

In 1982 he joined Stockport County, where an impressive haul of 39 goals in 63 League matches earned him a £52,000 move to Second Division Oldham Athletic. Although he continued to score freely, he missed seven weeks of one season after pulling a hamstring during the club's pre-Christmas pub crawl. He fell over while dancing with team-mate Mark Ward on his shoulders, leaving the team to face the busy Christmas period without its main striker. Manager Joe Royle, fearing a backlash from supporters, issued a press release saying that Quinn had injured himself falling down the stairs at home.

After two years at Boundary Park, Quinn joined Portsmouth for £150,000. The Pompey fans took to him immediately, dubbing him 'The Mighty Quinn' and singing, 'He's fat, he's round, he's worth a million pound, Micky Quinn, Micky Quinn.' That Portsmouth side contained more than its fair share of bruising characters – Mick Tait, Mick Kennedy, Noel Blake (of whom Howard Wilkinson once said, 'Blake's even got muscles in his spit') – so Quinn fitted in perfectly. Even manager Alan Ball was heard to remark: 'I've created a Frankenstein's monster of a team!'

At the end of a typically competitive clash with West Brom, Quinn and team-mate Paul Wood showered and changed and then were immediately thrown out of the ground by waiting police officers. Their crime had been to abuse a linesman during the second half. In 1987 Quinn finished as top scorer during Portsmouth's promotion season despite spending 14 days in jail for driving while disqualified. Having been banned for drink-driving, he was twice caught at the wheel of a car, his explanation being that he had been going to buy medication for his sick girlfriend.

In July 1989 he moved to Newcastle United for a fee of £680,000. Quinn knew instantly that it was the right move for him when he was ushered into Jim Smith's office and found the manager watching horse racing on TV. He scored four goals in his debut against Leeds and finished the season as the Second Division's top scorer with 34, but he then fell out with one of Smith's successors, Kevin Keegan (ironically his boyhood hero), and in 1994 was on the move again, this time to Coventry City. Quinn flourished in the Premiership, to the delight of the Highfield Road fans, who would turn up in comedy mullet wigs and stick-on moustaches with cushions stuffed up their shirts in tribute to their new hero. And whenever he was involved in a fracas on the pitch, they would yell, 'Calm down, calm down', in the manner of Harry Enfield's Scousers. The *Daily Telegraph* wrote of Quinn's appeal: 'In an age when the English game is increasingly giving itself over to the athlete as opposed to the artist, it is reassuring to see a 13½ stone roly poly like Quinn, through sheer wit and sharpness of mind, regularly putting one over defenders with more brawn than brains. Certainly, as goalscorers go, £ for lb there are few better than Coventry's bargain.'

Not every fan adored him, however. When he left Coventry to play in Greece with PAOK Salonika, opposing supporters hurled plastic water bottles full of urine at him.

Quinn retired from football in 1996 and, following the lead of his old Portsmouth team-mate Mick Channon, became a racehorse trainer. Quinn's dream of making a living out of his hobby has not been without its problems and in 2001 he was suspended from training for two and a half years after the RSPCA found that three horses in his care were being neglected. The ban was later reduced to one year on appeal.

Looking back on his football career, Quinn says that he trained hard but also liked to enjoy himself. 'I was born with the gift to score goals. Left foot, right foot, headers. I didn't care if they bounced in off my knob as long as they went in.'

BIBLIOGRAPHY

Atkinson, Ron. *Big Ron: A Different Ball Game* (Andre Deutsch 1998)

Best, George. *Scoring at Half-Time* (Ebury Press, 2003)

Blake, Mike. *Sam Bartram: The Story of a Goalkeeping Legend* (Tempus, 2006)

Blundell, Justin. *Back From the Brink* (Empire, 2006)

Bowles, Stan. *The Autobiography* (Orion, 2004)

Castro, Ruy. *Garrincha: The Triumph and Tragedy of Brazil's Forgotten Footballing Hero* (Yellow Jersey Press, 2004)

Claridge, Steve. *Tales From the Boot Camps* (Gollancz, 1997)

Cosgrove, Stuart. *Hampden Babylon* (Canongate Press, 1991)

Docherty, Tommy. *The Doc: My Story* (Headline, 2006)

Fry, Barry. *Big Fry* (CollinsWillow, 2000)

Gascoigne, Paul. *Gazza; My Story* (Headline, 2005)

Greaves, Jimmy. *Greavsie: The Autobiography* (Time Warner, 2003)

Hamilton, Duncan. *Provided You Don't Kiss Me* (Fourth Estate, 2007)

Jones, Vinnie. *Vinnie: My Life* (Headline, 2001)

Mackay, Dave. *The Real Mackay* (Mainstream, 2004)

Malam, Colin. *The Clown Prince of Soccer? The Len Shackleton Story* (Highdown, 2005)

Maradona, Diego. *El Diego* (Yellow Jersey Press, 2004)

Marsh, Rodney. *Priceless* (Headline, 2001)

McGuigan, Paul and Hewitt, Paolo. *The Greatest Footballer You Never Saw: The Robin Friday Story* (Mainstream, 2006)

McKinstry, Leo. *Jack & Bobby* (CollinsWillow, 2003)

McVay, Dave. *Steak...Diana Ross: Diary of a Football Nobody* (Parrs Wood Press, 2003)

Pearce, Stuart. *Psycho* (Headline, 2000)

Quinn, Mick. *Who Ate All the Pies?* (Virgin, 2004)

Robson, Bobby. *Farewell But Not Goodbye* (Hodder & Stoughton, 2005) *he Mavericks* (Mainstream, 1994)

. *After the Ball* (Coronet, 2003)

ordon. *Strachan: My Life in Football* (Sphere, 2006)

, Phil. *Emlyn Hughes: A Tribute to Crazy Horse* (Stadia,

Ian. *Mr Wright* (CollinsWillow, 1996)